Let's face the Music

Let's face the Music

The Golden Age of Popular Song

BENNY · GREEN

PAVILION
MICHAEL JOSEPH

To Beloved Antoinette

First published in Great Britain in 1989 by
PAVILION BOOKS LIMITED
196 Shaftesbury Avenue, London WC2H 8JL
in association with Michael Joseph Limited
27 Wrights Lane, Kensington, London W8 5TZ

Published in association with Yorkshire Television
Copyright © Benny Green 1989

Designed by Tom Sawyer

A CIP catalogue record for this book is
available from the British Library

ISBN 1-85145-4896

10 9 8 7 6 5 4 3 2 1

Printed and bound in Great Britain by Hazell, Watson & Viney Ltd, Aylesbury

Contents

Introduction

FROM THE AGE OF THIRTEEN UNTIL the night before last, I played the music of the men featured in this book. In dance halls and jazz clubs, on concert stages and in private homes, in the secrecy of practice rooms and even, on summer nights, in the open air. I came to conceive for these men an admiration which was not, as a general rule, shared by many others outside the tight little island of the world of professional music. Everyone knew Crosby, but not one member of the audience in a thousand could tell you who wrote the songs Crosby sang in *Mississippi*. George Gershwin was understood in some vague way to be a celebrity, and so, to a lesser extent, was Cole Porter, but for the most part the words and the music were taken for granted. Alan Lerner once expressed his suspicion that audiences thought that he and Fritz Loewe wrote the tunes and the actors filled in the lyrics for themselves. The injustice of this neglect has been to some extent righted in the last twenty years, when the perspective of passing time has revealed the very best writers of popular song to have been considerable artists.

Of the men whose careers are discussed in this collection, Ira Gershwin and I corresponded for some years before I met him in 1976. Arthur Schwartz and Alan Lerner were both friends of mine with a readiness to educate me in the social history of the songwriting world. For the rest I, like every other writer on this neglected subject, have had to rely on the printed evidence, too often bowdlerized, and the recollections of dozens of other songwriters who remembered my subjects, from Burton Lane and Paul Francis Webster to Sammy Fain and especially Johnny Mercer, the songwriter I knew best of all, and without whose delightful table talk I would never have felt the urge to take up the subject. He convinced me, without realizing it, that people generally remained in the dark about the genesis and parenthood of the great popular songs, which was a curious thing when you consider that millions of people measure their lives by them. Not by wars and watersheds, but by the songs they recall from the time. The truth of Mercer's ideas was wonderfully illustrated while I was collecting material for this book. One of the theatre critics in a national newspaper vouchsafed to his readers the discovery that 'Smoke Gets in Your Eyes' was composed by Cole Porter, which is almost in the class of the noodle who believed that George Eliot was one of the Brontë sisters.

None of the men in this collection is better than all the others, or perhaps even than any of the others. Nor does criticism of individual items imply a rejection of anyone's work. All my men were gifted artists, who put the words, and the music, in the mouths of millions. The last word on comparative judgements was spoken by Alan Lerner, who wisely observed, in an appreciation of his beloved hero Lorenz Hart:

> Was Ira Gershwin 'better' than Cole Porter? Was Hammerstein 'superior' to Larry Hart? It is pointless, because they were all master craftsmen, each with an expression of his own. I am exhilarated by the gaiety, style and surprising passion of Cole, overwhelmed by the wonderfully slangy sentimentality and ingenious versatility of Ira, touched by the disarming simplicity of Berlin, and forever impressed by Oscar Hammerstein's dramatic ability.

I can add nothing to that, except to say that Alan, self-effacing as always, omitted to include himself in that list of thoroughbreds.

Benny Green

CHAPTER ONE

George Gershwin

IN THAT EXOTIC COMPROMISE between Broadway backstage gossip and dialectical immaterialism, *I Thought of Daisy*, Edmund Wilson uses as his touchstone of popular musical taste an imaginary melody called 'Mamie Rose', which recurs at significant points in the action. In the closing sequence of the story the narrator, hearing 'Mamie Rose' for the last time, and coming as close as he ever will to an understanding of its intangible allure in the context of his own life, wonders about its genesis, and particularly how its unidentified composer could have arrived at his definitive melody:

> Where had he got it? – from the sounds of the streets? the taxis creaking to a stop? the interrogatory squeak of a street car? some distant and obscure city-sound in which a plaintive high note, bitten sharp, follows a lower note, strongly clanged and solidly based? Or had he got it from Schoenberg and Stravinsky? Or simply from his own nostalgia, among the dark cells and the raspings of New York, for those orchestras and open squares which his parents had left behind? – or for the cadence, half-chanted and despairing, of the tongue which the father had known, but which the child had forgotten and was never to know again?

In his commentary on Wilson's work, Sherman Paul suggests that perhaps the composer Wilson had in mind was either George Gershwin or Irving Berlin, and certainly Gershwin fills the bill in some, although not all of the qualifications. The Gershwin children had not forgotten 'the tongue which the father had known' because they were all American-born, but in other respects Wilson's analysis of the surprising depth of passion in a song he had at first taken for a cheap jingle fits the case of Gershwin very well. If we ignore the technical solecisms in Wilson's account, and if we brush aside the silly patronizing

GEORGE GERSHWIN

implication that popular composers all have some secret source of inspiration which is not their own, we find many striking parallels between the writer of Wilson's 'Mamie Rose' and the composer who said, in 1926, the very year of much of the action of *I Thought of Daisy*, that 'true music must repeat the thought and aspirations of the people and the time. My people are American. My time is today.' The quotation, whose importance can hardly be exaggerated, has been quoted by most of Gershwin's biographers in their despairing attempts to explain away an American phenomenon.

Few major artists this century – and that is what Gershwin was, as Schoenberg was shrewd enough to realize – can have been martyred with such depressing frequency on the cross of biographical imperception; all the Gershwin chroniclers, being either insuperably unmusical or congenitally unliterary, have been reduced either to poking around among the dirty underwear, or burbling conservatory quackery about unresolved discords and the rhythms of jazz. The problem for all would-be biographers of America's popular composers has been that a reticence on the part of close associates has compounded the breathtaking chaos of the profession's way with its own documentation. There are no collected letters. There are no testimonies from relatives. Songs and sometimes entire scores have vanished without trace. Financial arrangements appertaining to stage productions and song publication remain an impenetrable mystery. The only solid evidence is the music itself, and for the most part this is quite sufficient. But in the unique and very remarkable case of George Gershwin it is maddeningly insufficient, for the interesting reason that unlike his professional rivals, George appears to have seen himself as the representative musician of his generation. In a sense he created himself in his own image, and it would be instructive to know why and how. The detailed descriptions of his working methods, his style of dress, his general opinions, his tendencies to hypochondria, his attractiveness to beautiful women, all these are copious. In addition, he may be glimpsed performing the arthritic movements of the early newsreel cinema, and heard discussing his music over the radio waves of the early 1930s. But beneath the professional surface there remain depths of character still unrevealed. Whether one day revelations will surface, whether when all the principals are long gone aspects of his conduct are made public, or whether the passage of time discloses that he was after all a sphinx without a riddle remains to be seen, but at any rate there can have been few twentieth-century figures so fascinating and yet so insubstantial in the impression they have bequeathed. One of Gershwin's biographers, Robert Payne, reminds us of the testimony of Gordon Craig, that when George was in London, Isadora Duncan would sharpen his pencils for him. How many thousands of other tiny pieces in the mosaic are lost to us? Could Lady Edwina Mountbatten have enlightened us on the subject, she who flits so elegantly through George's life and who rescued 'The Man I Love' from an undeserved obscurity? Perhaps. We can only wait and hope. In the meantime, more than forty years after the event, Isaac Goldberg's *A Study in American Music*, for all its breathless paternalism, remains the clearest picture of the composer at work.

Jablonski and Stewart's *The Gershwin Years*, followed some time later by Jablonski's *Gershwin*, achieve perhaps the most comfortable compromise to date between biographical balance and musical perception, although as neither Jablonski nor Stewart had any practical experience of the process of making music, they committed one or two of those solecisms which put the reader uneasily in mind of the English humorist who observed that when we hear the hall clock strike thirteen, not only are we convinced that the clock is wrong, but begin to ask ourselves if it could ever have been right. Jablonski and Stewart talk of 'harmonics' when they mean harmonies, and refer several times to a pure figment of the lay imagination called a jazz song. There is no more such an entity as a jazz song as there is a source of wood called a furniture tree. Jazz is a term which defines a working method of treating a piece of music, not the piece itself. Jazz is anything played by a jazz musician, so that 'Ain't Misbehavin'' interpreted by Yehudi Menuhin is not jazz, whereas 'To a Wild Rose' performed by Nat Cole most certainly is. Gershwin's musical compositions, like those of all the writers of the so-called Jazz Age, were no more related to jazz than Bill Robinson's taps or Bessie Smith's dresses. That Gershwin's music has always been widely admired by jazz musicians is perfectly true, but the aspect of his work which invites improvisation is not some nebulous built-in jazz quintessence but the ingenuity of the harmonic structures. In this sense only could Gershwin, and all his contemporaries, be defined as writers of jazz, that their best songs invited the cadences of improvisers of all styles and eras. Most of Gershwin's professional rivals, particularly Kern, Porter and Rodgers, proved comically obtuse when confronted by the findings of jazz musicians. Porter would implore orchestrators not to deface his work. Rodgers publicly stated that jazz consisted of 'wrong notes'. As for Kern, it was his estate which once considered going to law in an attempt to stop improvisers using his tunes. In this regard as in many others, Gershwin makes a sharp contrast with his rivals, being perceptive enough when it came to jazz to realize that in selecting his work as an ingredient in the creation of jazz, the improvisers were paying the highest of all compliments by implying that they preferred his harmonic originality to that of anyone else. Apparently without pomposity when it came to his own work, Gershwin seems to have relished the very amendments which so outraged Kern and company:

The emergence of the swing phenomenon interested but did not surprise him, for such eminent performers as Benny Goodman, Gene Krupa, Red Nichols, Jack Teagarden, Jimmy Dorsey, Babe Rusin and Glenn Miller had contributed to the gayety of *Strike Up the Band* and *Girl Crazy* as members of the pit orchestra. The Goodman Trio's recording of 'Lady Be Good' delighted him, and he listened with rapture to Art Tatum, the great blind Negro pianist, especially to his playing of 'Liza' and 'I Got Rhythm'. He was so enthused with Tatum's playing that he had an evening for him at his 72nd Street apartment before leaving for Hollywood. Some time after he arrived in California, Gershwin discovered that Tatum was playing at a local night club, and we went together to hear him. It was a small, dingy, badly-lighted room, an intimate version of the too-intimate Onyx Club. We joined the group of enthusiasts clustered around the piano where the blind virtuoso was in full swing. To George's great joy, Tatum played virtually the equivalent of Beethoven's thirty-two variations on his tune 'Liza'. Then George asked for more.

This account, rendered by Oscar Levant, is especially revealing in that the Goodman Trio version of 'Lady Be Good' takes great liberties with the written harmonies by transposing the composition from the major to the harmonic minor at one point in the recording, thereby effecting a radical alteration to the original Gershwin effect. Kern or Rodgers, faced with the same well-intentioned defacements, would have been reduced to apoplexy, but the innocently egocentric George was only flattered. His piano recordings of the late 1920s soon tell us why. Unlike every one of the great songwriters, George was, in his own way, a brilliant pianist with a reasonable grasp of the principles of the 'Stride' piano style, that method of two-fisted improvisation pioneered by James P. Johnson, Willie the Lion Smith and Thomas 'Fats' Waller, and it is revealing that one of the most accomplished interpreters of Gershwin's art, Fred Astaire, was also a talented amateur pianist with an identical jazz style to George.

Let us return for a moment to the hypothetical 'Mamie Rose'. Wilson refers to a distant homeland and a forgotten native tongue. Gershwin's parents left St Petersburg at the end of the nineteenth century, to become members of that classic minority, the foreign parents of American children, martyrs to the widest generation gulf of modern history, from klobyoshe and lemon tea to handball and highballs. Leo Rosten has told the touching story of how he gave English lessons to his own father ('The President of the United States must be an American citizen unless he was born here'). The steady advance of George's father Morris to his present mythical eminence as a kind of hamishe Malaprop who persisted in referring to 'Fascinating Rhythm' as 'Fashion on the River' has been one of the more charming comic developments in the written history of popular music. ('Of course *Rhapsody in Blue* is important. It lasts fifteen minutes, don't it?') But although the predicament of a parent versed in one culture unable to appreciate the achievement of a genius child born into quite another has its comic overtones, it also indicates the great truth about Gershwin, which is that the prodigious vitality and apparently inexhaustible melodic resource of his art had much to do with the hybrid nature of his environment.

The myth of the poor Jewish East Side boy who conquers Broadway has been pushed so hard over the years that we tend to forget that it was not always quite like that. The history of American popular music has had its academics like Kern as well as its miraculous naturals like Irving Berlin. The significance of Gershwin is that within the compass of a tragically brief but staggeringly prolific life (1898–1937), he reconciled Kern's academicism with Berlin's pragmatism to achieve the perfect balance between the contrived and the unselfconscious. It comes as no surprise to those who have idled away the years exploring the harmonic possibilities of Gershwin's music to learn that Kern and Berlin were his two great heroes, for there is no more rewarding sport in all popular art than to take the extremes of those two patrons and watch how they come to an unpredicted synthesis in Gershwin. Kern, with his pretentions to Heidelberg and his grand strategies of modulation, Berlin with the pride of the autodidact and his refusal to prepare his modulations at all, two poles which meet on the centre ground of Gershwin's superlatively poised compromise in moments like, say, the movement from F major to A minor in 'They All Laughed', a movement to which George was especially partial, for he had already deployed it before in 'Somebody Loves Me' (1924) and 'Looking for a Boy' (1925). The point is worth making because it reminds us that Gershwin's art is neither a product of mean streets and pluggers' booths nor of the conservatoire, but of a rare fusion of the two. It has been the failure to grasp the implications of this exotic clash of cultures which has, over the years, bedevilled Gershwin's reputation and, in his own lifetime, caused him some serious difficulties.

The American propensity to think big has claimed other victims than Gershwin. One thinks of the stupid attempts to transform William Saroyan from a whimsical and most moving annalist of a transplanted immigrant community into the Great American Novelist, and there instantly forms the parallel image of Mr Otto Kahn blandly advising George to suffer a little more in preparation for an epic operatic work. Kahn, a millionaire patron of the arts, enjoyed supporting only those lost causes which seemed sure to forfeit their investment, a policy which went comically wrong in his dealings with Gershwin. In 1924, travelling home to New York from London, George was interested to discover that one of his fellow-passengers was Kahn, and took the opportunity of playing him a half-finished melody destined for the first Broadway show he was to write with his brother as lyricist. Kahn was so impressed by the song that he became convinced it would be death at the box-office. Later, when the new show was short of money, Kahn was approached again and told that the song which had so impressed him was to be included in the score. Kahn instantly invested ten thousand dollars and was doubly astonished to realize a few months later that the difficult song, 'The Man I Love' had been dropped and that the show, *Lady Be Good*, was showing a considerable profit. Kahn then wrote to the producers thanking them for the unique experience of making a profit on a theatrical venture.

In December 1928, on the night of the first performance of *An American in Paris*, George went to a party thrown in his honour, and received two gifts, a silver humidor and a speech from Kahn which so bemused the audience that nobody was quite sure exactly what Kahn was trying to say. After comparing George with Charles Lindbergh, he launched into an exhaustive quotation from Thomas Hardy, the gist of which was that because grief had been good for Hardy, it must surely be good for George too:

> The 'long drip of human tears', my dear George. They have great and strange and beautiful power, those human tears. They fertilize the deepest roots of art, and from them flowers spring of a loveliness and perfume that no other moisture can produce.

At this point, having embarrassed the company, Kahn turned directly to Gershwin and pelted him with a further flight of stuffed owls:

> I believe in you with full faith and admiration, in your personality, in your gifts, in your art, in your future, in your significance in the field of American music. I wish for you an experience – not too prolonged – of that driving storm and stress of the emotions, of that solitary wrestling with your own soul, of that aloofness, for a while, from the actions and distractions of the everyday world, which are the most effective ingredients for the deepening and mellowing and the complete development, energizing and revealment, of an artist's inner being and spiritual powers.

To this broadside of humbuggery George's reaction remains unknown, but what Kahn, in his convoluted way, was attempting to say was that it would be enjoyable, desirable and highly rewarding if George, having purged his soul in the fires of misery, should write an opera. Kahn happened to have the Metropolitan Opera House in his pocket.

Whether or not George had suffered enough, his desire to write something 'important' had been animating him for many years before Kahn introduced Lindbergh into the musical pantheon. As early as 1927, during rehearsals of *Oh, Kay!*, he had resolved to write an opera based on DuBose Heyward's undistinguished and paternalistic novel *Porgy*. For the next eight years, this was the project to which George would return again and again, planning his commissions in such a way that he would find the time to write his magnum opus. It has to be remembered that men like Gershwin, Kern and Porter were not complete fools, and were perfectly well aware that the plots, dialogue and characterization of the shows for which they provided the music were generally of an abysmal standard, and that any self-respecting adult composer must aspire to better things. *Show Boat* had been Kern's gesture, *Kiss Me Kate* was to be Porter's. None of these attempts to break the mould of the Broadway life succeeded as spectacularly as Gershwin's *Porgy and Bess*, although when it first appeared, the inevitable happened. In offering the New York of 1935 an opera, George was delivering himself into the hands of commentators unused to anything as rococo as a melody in a modern opera. Indeed, so bereft of melody was the world inhabited by the opera critics of the 1930s that when confronted by it they were incapable of recognizing it, with results as risible as they were in one sense tragic.

In 1935, when the first public performance of *Porgy and Bess* took place, the immediate upshot was a cultural confusion spectacular even by the standards of the operatic world of the period, comical to posterity, unfortunate for the performers, costly for those who had invested in its finances, and something of a disappointment for its composer, who never lived long enough to enjoy the eventual vindication of the work, although perhaps we need not feel too badly on that account. Gershwin, buttressed by an impregnable and wholly justified self-esteem when it came to his own work, appears to have known perfectly well that the ultimate survival of the opera was a foregone conclusion. Unlike a great many composers whose premature death has sadly anticipated belated acceptance of their work, Gershwin is utterly lacking in that pathos which comes from unjustifiable rejection. On the contrary, the ghost of the confident Gershwin smile, wreathed in cirrus clouds of cigar smoke, seems to preside over every performance of *Porgy and Bess* just as the Cheshire Cat's did over Wonderland. Gershwin could afford to smile, because he knew the value of what he was bequeathing to us.

The critics, however, did not know. Their disarray on the morning after the premiere of *Porgy and Bess* may reasonably be described as prodigious. Virgil Thompson described what he had half-heard as 'crooked opera and halfway folklore', while Olin Downes in the *New York Times* grumbled that 'the style is at one moment of opera and another of operetta or sheer Broadway entertainment', no doubt leaving opera-lovers dismayed at his implication that opera can never be entertaining. Of course every creative artist worth his salt is obliged from time to time to endure this kind of twaddle, and Gershwin, having paid his tormentors a tribute that none of them deserved, by answering their complaints in an article in the *New York Times*, got on with his next score. Later the critics, shamelessly conducting their own education in public, recanted. Thompson, noting which way the artistic winds were blowing, decided on reflection that the crooked opera was in fact 'a beautiful piece of music whose melodic invention is abundant and pretty distinguished', while Mr Downes, by now mysteriously reconciled to hybrid strains in the work, made the profound discovery that 'Gershwin has taken a substantial step, and advanced the cause of native opera'.

But the critical stricture which really gave the game away was one by a Mr Gilman of the *Herald Tribune*, who wrote, apparently with a perfectly straight face, that the tunes in Gershwin's opera were too *good*. Bringing the mighty engines of his musical judgement to bear on the problem of *Porgy and Bess*, Mr Gilman came to the conclusion that although Gershwin had incorporated into his score some song hits 'which will doubtless enhance his fame and popularity', it had been mistaken of the composer to do so, for, so far as these song hits were concerned, 'they mar the work. They are its cardinal weakness. They are the blemish on its musical integrity.' Happy world, in which the thematic balance of an operatic score might so easily be adjusted by a mere telephone call to the offices of the *Herald Tribune*. Fortunately for posterity, Gershwin omitted to ask Gilman's advice before finalizing his score, and no more was ever heard on the subject from that perceptive gentleman – which is a great pity, for it was Gilman who, for all his carping foolishness, had touched on the heart of the matter. In retrospect we can sympathize with a critic whose sensibilities have become so benumbed by constant exposure to legitimate opera devoid of melody that the sudden confrontation with a hybrid opera bubbling over with it should prove too rich a dish for his enfeebled musical digestion to cope with. Gilman's predicament, which may be taken as representative of classical criticism in general, is enough to make a cat laugh. Having learned to live with musicians who possessed every attribute of the great composer except the ability to write a good tune, the Gilmans of this world had actually been conditioned to the point where the presence in a musical-dramatic work of a good tune actually disqualified it from inclusion in the operatic category altogether. The false syllogism of the Gilman school of criticism ran as follows: 'X is a much venerated operatic work of the modern school. X has no discernible melodies. Therefore no much venerated operatic work of the modern school must possess any discernible melodies.' It was as though the British Admiralty, having noticed how well Lord Nelson was doing with one eye, were to cashier every officer with two.

Gershwin, however, had been raised in the toughest of all schools, where you either came up with a good tune or you went out and found a job. That is the vital fact about his background which renders him distinct from every other operatic composer who ever had to endure the carping of fatheads. When you were selling a song like 'Swanee' there was no tenor's rich vibrato and throbbing jugular to help the demonstration along, no lush orchestral effects to prop up the structure and mask the deficiencies, no pretentious wedding of babyish plot and infantile characterization to excuse a hackneyed harmonic pattern. Most significant of all, your singer was performing in *English*, so there was not even the mysticism of an incomprehensible foreign language to cow the listener into humble respect. All you had was your tune, and it had better be a good one. These ethics of the song-plugger's booth are as remote from the world of European opera as the Isles of the Hesperides, but that is not to say that Tin Pan Alley writers remained in blanket ignorance of the world of so-called classical achievement. Gershwin as a child had been sandbagged by Rubinstein's *Melody in F*, just as Harry Warren as a juvenile had been stunned into reverence by the arias of Puccini. It was Gershwin, however, who became the first, and also the last, gifted popular songwriter to aspire to the classical form without paying the price of his own melodic vitality.

Now it so happened that at the time of the composition of *Porgy and Bess* the American public at large had little interest in or understanding of conventional classical opera. Sensing the fundamental absurdity of a heroine complaining that she is dying of a wasting disease when it is plain to see she is thirty-five pounds overweight, and bravely refusing to be browbeaten into an enthusiasm it did not feel by the orotundities of operatic Italian, America stayed away in its millions. There was, of course, the occasional exception to opera's lack of verisimilitude; when Enrico Caruso appeared at the Metropolitan Opera House in *Tosca* in 1906, the *New York World* reported next morning:

> So great was the realism in the torture scene that a man in one of the orchestra stalls fainted. The auditorium was in darkness and the affair caused some commotion. When the usher started to drag the man out someone attempted to help him, but in his excitement he grabbed the usher's leg and threw him. Finally the victim of his emotions became conscious and peace was restored.

As for the German variety of operatic inscrutability, in this regard the American public was as one with the Englishman in the Wodehouse story who, stumbling into a darkened room where a stolen prize pig has been secreted, runs out screaming, 'There's a man in there. And he's speaking German.' In fact, so resolutely was the popular face turned away from opera that its more outrageous absurdities became a target for the philistines. In 1936, the very year in which *Porgy and Bess* was fighting for its artistic life, the continent rocked with laughter when Otis

B. Driftwood, alias Groucho Marx, discovering that a great operatic tenor might receive as much as a thousand dollars a night, replies incredulously, 'A thousand dollars a night? Just to sing? Why, for seventy-five cents you can get a record of "Minnie the Moocher". For a buck and a quarter you can get Minnie.' The essence of the joke is that Gershwin belonged in the same huckstering world as Driftwood, and yet was now attempting to cross over.

The attempt was to cause him considerable professional heartburn. He was the most famous and the most respected popular songwriter in the world, but this eminence, which should have been an asset, only proved a handicap. When George approached the opera singer Todd Duncan with the idea of offering him the role of Porgy, Duncan was too steeped in the operatic tradition to take the overture seriously: 'I just wasn't very interested. I was teaching in university in Washington, and I though of George Gershwin as being Tin Pan Alley and something beneath me.' Duncan soon changed his tune and very soon became one of George's most passionate idolaters, but his initial reaction typifies the general contempt with which the operatic world looked down on the fleshpots of the songwriting business. What elevates Duncan's priggishness to low farce is the fact that the contempt was mutual, a joke which was to render George's plight so palpably ridiculous that a review of the prevailing musical climate may be required to explain it.

In 1935, the year that *Porgy and Bess* was first performed, the RKO producer Pandro S. Berman was persisting in a misguided attempt to make a popular movie star out of the coloratura soprano Lily Pons. His production, *I Dream Too Much*, with songs by Kern and Dorothy Fields, proved a box-office catastrophe, because, as Berman later quite rightly observed:

> I don't think the bulk of the American public ever listens to opera. Opera has never made any money on the stage, it's always been supported by the community. The songs aren't popular and the people who do them are not attractive enough for the most part.

Berman is being wise forty years after the event, and it seems incredible that he, a man of such sharp commercial acumen, should have required the costly lesson of *I Dream Too Much* to realize the foolhardiness of his ploy. Miss Pons was by no means the first operatic star to sink without trace in Hollywood, nor would she be the last. Grace Moore and Gladys Swarthout were to follow. It is almost too perfectly symbolic of Hollywood to be true that the only bankable operatic film stars of the period should have been those two bogus practitioners Jeanette Macdonald and Nelson Eddy. And yet although his career as a producer was, financially speaking, a triumphal processional, Berman never quite relinquished his operatic dream, retaining possession for ever after of a leatherbound copy of the shooting script of *I Dream Too Much*, which he would insist on showing to dismayed visitors come to ask questions about Fred Astaire and Ginger Rogers. *I Dream Too Much* was that freak, a Berman loser, and he would disclose the evidence with the air of a man reprising a mystery still unsolved.

It was the formulation of another false syllogism which was to plague Gershwin in the last two years of his career. If, as even Berman had come to acknowledge, opera was a dead cinematic duck, then it followed that as George had aligned himself in the operatic camp by perpetrating *Porgy and Bess*, George too must be a dead cinematic duck. The major Hollywood studios, seeing an opportunity of getting Gershwin scores cut-price in the wake of the commercial failure of *Porgy and Bess*, pretended to be concerned that George had lost the knack of writing hits. He was, in fact, that pariah dog of the industry, a highbrow, and the moguls moved in to take advantage. Berman cajoled George and Ira into accepting less money than they thought fair for writing the songs for *Shall We Dance* by wiring them: 'I think you are letting a few thousand dollars keep you from having a lot of fun' – this from Berman who so jealously guarded his own arrangement with RKO to take ten per cent of the gross of the Fred-and-Ginger pictures. The other mogul to wonder aloud if the writing of an opera had not ruined Gershwin's prospects at the box-office was the largest dwarf in the industry, Samuel Goldwyn, whose idea of musical criticism and of musical etiquette was to ask George why he didn't write hits like Irving Berlin. Later, when posterity was able to examine the upshot of Goldwyn's deal with the Gershwins, it would have been excused for asking the producer why he never made films like Eisenstein. The only apt aspect of the film was its title, *The Goldwyn Follies*; it was a farrago so inept that it took a generation for 'Our Love Is Here To Stay' to emerge from the wreckage. Berman's two Gershwin productions were better, but *A Damsel in Distress* bore so many executive scars that it might almost have been a Goldwyn picture. Its history is interesting only in the way it reveals what genuinely gifted men and women were obliged to endure from the likes of Berman and Goldwyn.

A Damsel in Distress was originally a comic novel published in 1919 by that dedicated friend of the Gershwins, P. G. Wodehouse. The plot concerning a musical comedy composer called George, born in Brooklyn, who comes to London to supervise the local production of one of his Broadway hits, paralleled George's own situation so exactly that he induced Berman to buy the rights. The story of what followed is taken up by Wodehouse in a series of letters to his college friend, Bill Townend. In November 1936, Wodehouse, in Hollywood for the second of his two disastrous stints there, met Astaire, who mentioned the prospect of starring in *A Damsel in Distress*. By March 1937, Wodehouse tells Townend he is within two weeks of starting work on the scenario. By late June he is attempting to clean up the mess which Berman has already made of it:

> I am sweating away at *A Damsel in Distress*. with musical score by George Gershwin. When they bought it, they gave it to one of the RKO writers to adapt, and he turned out a script all about crooks – no resemblance to the novel. Then it struck them that it might be a good thing to stick to the story, so they chucked away the other script and called me in. I think it is going to make a good picture. But what uncongenial work picture-writing is. Somebody's got to do it, I suppose, but this is the last time they'll get me.

Even as this letter was on its way to England, Gershwin was already embarked on the last despairing odyssey of his life, searching for a doctor who could tell him the cause of attacks of vertigo and blinding headaches. By the time Wodehouse had completed his chore, in mid-August, Gershwin was already dead, from the effects of an operation to remove a cystic tumour from the right temporal lobe. Wodehouse surprisingly makes no reference to the tragedy in his letters to Townend, holding his hand on Berman's production for more than forty years. In 1978 a new paperback edition of the novel appeared in print, with a typically amusing preface by the author. After opening with the claim that everything had happened to the book that can happen short of being done on ice, Wodehouse reminds the reader that in 1928 he and Ian Hay had adapted it for the London stage quite successfully. He then describes how Gershwin used his influence to have the story done as a musical picture.

> . . . and it was handed over to the hired assassins who at that time were such a feature of Dottyville-on-the-Pacific. The result was a Mess. . . . Friends have often commented on the dark circles beneath my eyes and my tendency to leap like a Mexican jumping bean at sudden noises, and I find those phenomena easy to explain. It is only fifty years or so since I was involved in the shooting of *A Damsel in Distress*.
>
> 'The Manglers', as the official term was, proved worthy of the trust placed in them by the studio. The first thing they did was to eliminate the story and substitute for it one more suitable to retarded adults and children with water on the brain. They then turned their attention to the hero. There was not much they could do here, but they did their best by engaging Fred Astaire and giving him nobody to dance with, so that he had nine solo numbers. To a jaundiced eye it seemed that there was not a moment when he was not on the screen by himself, singing and dancing his heart out, with nobody to lend him a helping hand.

Wodehouse is here being too gallant. It was not that Berman gave Astaire nobody to dance with. He did something much more damaging. He gave him Joan Fontaine to dance with. As Miss Fontaine, on her own admission, could neither sing nor dance, her presence in the picture is baffling. Miss Fontaine, never a lady lacking in candour, later claimed that the picture put back her career by four years, which is giving her all the best of it. But the most remarkable thing of all about *Shall We Dance* and *A Damsel in Distress* is that for all the ignoble haggling by Front Office, for all the harassment by the moguls and the fits of lunacy from the Casting department, and in spite of his rapidly deteriorating physical condition, George Gershwin, roundly accused by the industry of having evolved into a highbrow incapable any longer of hitting the melodic spot, wrote two of the outstanding scores of the decade, scores which none of his contemporaries could ever have approached. For *Shall We Dance*, he produced 'I've Got Beginner's Luck', 'Let's Call the Whole Thing Off', 'Shall We Dance', 'Slap That Bass', 'They All Laughed' and 'They Can't Take That Away From Me' in addition to a brilliant little contrivance called 'Walking the Dog', scored for what Jablonski defines as 'a salon orchestra' with the intention of lampooning the huge orchestral armies with which the major studios insisted on blanketing their productions. For *A Damsel in Distress*, George produced 'A Foggy Day', 'I Can't Be Bothered Now', 'Nice Work If You Can Get It', 'Put Me to the Test', 'Stiff Upper Lip', 'Things Are Looking Up', and an ingenious pastiche of English eighteenth-century madrigals, 'The Jolly Tar and the Milkmaid'. For *The Goldwyn Follies*, the Gershwin songs introduced posthumously included 'Our Love Is Here to Stay', 'Love Walked In' and 'I Was Doing All Right'. The recital of this astonishing catalogue serves little purpose except to reduce to nonsense once and for all the suspicion among the powers of the West Coast that Gershwin was showing signs of losing his touch.

In the years since his death, Gershwin's reputation has grown far beyond anything he experienced in his own short lifetime. In the concert hall as well as in the saloon bar and the night club his music is a constant presence. His melodies pervade the very air we breathe, and perhaps that was predictable. While he was alive, George's giantesque personality, his constant newsworthiness, his boyish revelling in the fact of his own extraordinary celebrity, all of it dutifully transcribed by the small army of Boswells who danced attendance: all these factors distracted from the work he produced. He and it always seemed indivisible. After all, a quip, a profile, a romance, are easier to grasp than the deployment of the augmented chords in 'Who Cares?', or the way, in bars 25-28 of 'That Certain Feeling', he so nonchalantly planks down the credentials of his genius with a sudden unpredictable flight of melodic fancy, the amazing grace of the descending counter-melody of 'The Man I Love', the riot of diminished chords which form the basis of that lampoon of the military, 'Strike Up the Band', the sublime pastiche of 'By Strauss'. George may not have written many greater songs than those achieved by Porter, Kern, Berlin and company, but he wrote more great songs than any of them. An outstanding popular composer is not a man who writes a great song, but one who goes on writing them, and that George did. The most gifted of his rivals succeeded in writing music which defined themselves. It was George's unique triumph to have defined something larger than himself, something of which he knew himself to be a part, and which, subconsciously or not, he strove to describe and express in his music. The perspective bestowed by passing time reveals that Gershwin so precisely mirrored his own world that there is a very real sense in which today his music has *become* that world. How many hundreds of sound tracks, striving after the metropolitan essence, are obliged to ape his mannerisms, echo his intervals, impersonate his orchestral effects? Long after his death, the filmmaker-musician Woody Allen produced a film called *Manhattan* which reveals, through the introductory sequence of the New York skyline juxtaposed with the main theme of *Rhapsody in Blue* how completely, how faithfully, George had captured in his music the essence of his own Big City experience.

It was a grandiloquent ambition, perhaps better suited to the banalities of some old B-picture featuring a would-be musician who dreams of writing his conshoito, but the evidence suggests that George nurtured it from the beginning. The idle browser through the biographies and the volumes of memorabilia cannot fail to be struck by a curious factor in the assessment of Gershwin's sense of purpose, a small group of photographs showing him in the presence of what could be defined as musical posterity. These photographs are quite different in essence from the numberless glimpses of George conducting the orchestra, George squiring a ladylove, George boarding an aeroplane, George playing golf, George in evening dress attending a first night. In no setting does George look more pregnant with his own possibilities, more representative of the New World, more proud to be what he is, than when he finds himself in the company of eminent musicians. There is an odd but unmistakable sense of the young man gathering himself for the moment, of being perfectly well aware of the nature of the miracle that has brought him here, and taking with touching seriousness the onerous responsibilities of the legate from the East Side in the courts of learning. And in all these moments, while George is having the time of his life, bursting with pride at the adjacency of his heroes, beaming with pleasure at his own conception of himself, his partners in this comic quadrille, all seem to be very slightly bewildered by what is happening: Franz Lehar seems world-weary; Oscar Straus, caparison-ned in a calamitous fur coat, looks like a man resolved to reduce himself to absurdity and succeeding gloriously; Koussevitsky is distinctly apprehensive and Ravel too timorous to look animated. Meanwhile George is on top of the world, arranging himself carefully for these trysts with posterity, smiling affably either at us or at the objects of his hero-worship. Above all there is a strange sense of a young adventurer showing the way for his own culture, his own generation, aware that already he has come further than any of his own contemporaries thought possible.

Only one of George's biographers ever expressed this representative status of George in the context of the music of his own time, and George would surely have savoured the irony that this lone perceiver of his significance was not a musician at all, but his own beloved brother and lyric-writing partner, Ira:

> From Gershwin emanated a new American music not written with the ruthlessness of one who strives to demolish established rules, but based on a new native gusto and wit and awareness. His was a modernity that reflected the civilization we live in as excitingly as the headline in today's newspaper.

America was, of course, more fortunate than it deserved in getting a George Gershwin, someone capable of synthesizing the European tradition with indigenous American styles. *Porgy and Bess* and the concert works are to American music what *Huckleberry Finn* and *Life On the Mississippi* are to American literature, an announcement of the emergence of the native school. Ira's claim may sound a shade over-ambitious – until we remind ourselves that the Tchaikovskiesque main theme of the *Rhapsody* is the best-known concert theme in all twentieth-century music, that 'The Man I Love' is not only a fragment of exquisite beauty but also a formal masterpiece in miniature, that 'Of Thee I Sing' is the only work even remotely to approach the spirit and the technical skill of the pasquinades of Gilbert and Sullivan, and that when we pause for a moment and allow the cumulative effect of the Gershwin oeuvre to wash over the sensibilities, a confused but deeply endearing vision starts to form, of identical twins and bogus butlers and penitent ex-cons, of heiresses posing as waitresses and waitresses posing as heiresses, of Fred and Ginger romancing in time to the music, of Pa Gershwin, proud of the line in 'Embraceable You', 'come to poppa, come to poppa do', of 'I Got Rhythm' and 'Summertime', and that definitive male invocation of the Twenties, 'Oh, sweet and lovely, lady be good to me'. It is indeed a truism of musical history that, as George once said, 'My people are American. My time is today.'

And that, as we follow the story of an extraordinary life narrated in the biographies, and read what happened to them all after 11 July 1937, we digest the starkest of all the stark truths about George Gershwin. He had hardly begun.

CHAPTER TWO

Jerome Kern

When Jerome Kern died in 1945, almost nobody outside the tight little island of the popular music profession yet had any inkling of what he and his contemporaries represented. There existed no effective bibliography of songwriting, no reliable biographical source material. Nor had that benison of the zealous investigator, the tape recorder, been invented. The sound of Kern's voice in his last years echoes faintly from the recordings of a concert announcement or two, but for the most part any sense of his corporeal presence is lost to us. It is quite true that George Gershwin, who died eight years before Kern, is far better preserved. But George the composer was also George the extrovert conductor, the delighted spectator at the dazzling processional of his own life. His voice cuts through the static of emergent radio, he is glimpsed smiling at the newsreel cameras, he is even heard on long-playing album compilations, pretending to be angry at the failure of the comedians Bobby Clark and Paul MacCullough to arrive promptly for rehearsals of *Strike Up the Band*. More important, George attracted a troupe of Boswells, from the scholarly Isaac Goldberg to the anecdotal Oscar Levant, who recorded his table-talk, his family relationships, his tastes in food, clothes, women, and, in the case of his long-surviving brother Ira, his working methods. No such body of acolytes attached themselves to Kern, who appears to have been a difficult professional partner, a dedicated family man, and a personality utterly without George's two great social assets, the magnetism to inspire unqualified loyalty and the technical command to charm the world simply by sitting at the piano. The comedian Bert Lahr remembered hearing Kern play at Billy Rose's house: 'It was embarrassing. You couldn't believe that the melodies which are part of Americana came from the same fingers.' The contrast is underlined by the recollection of another songwriter, Harry Ruby, who always went in awe of George's piano-playing: 'It was far and

JEROME KERN

beyond better than the piano-playing of any of us. As I look back upon it I can say it was a completely different musical world from ours, and we did not completely understand it at the time, though we all reacted to it instinctively. I am also sure we were all jealous of him too.' The point is well made, but what Lahr may not have realized is that it was Gershwin and not Kern who was the odd man out. Almost all the great writers of the age prove on investigation to have been performers of comic ineptitude; it is doubtful, for instance, if Kern was any worse a pianist than, say, Cole Porter or Harry Warren. So where is the seeker after Kern's essence to turn? The one competently compiled biography is meticulously researched, exemplary in its detail, virtually unreadable as a dramatic narrative, and often misguided in its musical judgements.

There is, naturally, a body of anecdotage forming a partial portrait. Kern being asked by David Selznick to play him a few tunes and sweeping out in the highest dudgeon he could muster, saying as he went, 'I don't give samples.' Kern sitting in the deserted stalls during auditions for one of his shows and interrupting a young soprano sporting some eccentric diction: 'She's in danger of rolling off the stage on her R's.' Kern, having been confronted by a dreadful Oscar Hammerstein libretto for *Very Warm For May* and fashioned out of it the masterwork 'All the Things You Are', regarding the subtlety of the famous enharmonic change in the 24th bar and reflecting that 'this one would be too difficult for them' – meaning that the song's structure overstepped the bounds of commercial propriety and was doomed never to make any money. The latter anecdote casts an ambiguous light on Kern, who may well not have taken his own doubts too seriously. A man of acute intelligence and ruthless acquisitive ambition, it sounds most unlike him to have expended so much creative energy on a song whose money-making potential he doubted. By the time 'All the Things You Are' was published, Kern had long since become rich and famous as the composer of precisely the type of ballad typified by 'All the Things You Are'. The time for self-doubt in the face of his own abstruse progressions would have been seven years earlier, when a distinct change in the degree of sophistication of Kern's writing became apparent. The possibility that in expressing doubts about the viability of his own work Kern was merely playing the game of self-dramatization is substantiated by the evidence of the English songwriter Vivian Ellis:

> I once met Jerome Kern, when my publishers were complaining how uncommercial I was. He said, 'Go on being uncommercial – there's a lot of money in it.'

A wily bird who knew precisely what he was about, he almost certainly realized what his own role in the evolution of American song had been;

that so astute a man, with so questing an intelligence, should have been unaware of the historical process of which he had constituted so spectacular a part, seems impossible to accept. For the moment we step back from the anecdotage and the amusing stories, we realize that it was through Kern that the American musical theatre finally flung aside its Hapsburgian trappings and moved on towards the unconscious goal of an indigenous style. If it finally found that style in George Gershwin, it was Kern who contributed by building the causeway from Vienna across which George and his generation so blithely skipped. Gershwin acknowledged the debt most generously by recalling that when, at the age of nineteen, he had abandoned his career as a songplugger, it had been because of Kern's music:

> Something was taking me away from Remick's. As I look back, it's very clear that I wanted to be closer to production music – the kind Jerome Kern was writing. Kern was the first composer who made me conscious that most popular music was of inferior quality and that musical-comedy music was made of better material.

The heroine of the story is George's Aunt Kate, for it was while attending her wedding in 1917 that George heard the band playing 'You're Here and I'm Here' and 'They Didn't Believe Me', and realized how exciting Kern's talent was. It makes a pretty anecdote, but there is something slightly fishy about it. The songs Gershwin mentions were both featured in 1914 productions. 'They Didn't Believe Me' in particular attracted great attention and was proposed years later by Arthur Schwartz as 'the first great colloquial American song'. That a musician as percipient as Gershwin should have taken three years to grasp its import is out of the question, yet the story has survived the scrutiny of all his biographers. More to the point, by the time he achieved the deftness of touch of 'You're Here and I'm Here', Kern had already moved out of the first phase and was into his second, fully embarked on his musical odyssey west.

The key fact about Kern's career is that it was born into a European world. Popular music in the theatre was dominated both by the Viennese school, which won its most glorious victory in the early years of the new century with the antics of the *Merry Widow*, and by London, which had moved on from the pasquinades of Gilbert and Sullivan to the less substantial operettas and musical romances marketed by George Edwardes. For an aspiring American writer to succeed, Europe was the place, and in 1903 Kern arrived in London in search of a reputation. His experiences over the next few years comprise a bewildering mosaic of shows, interpolated songs, vanished manuscripts, small successes and local addresses, extinct restaurants and defunct gentlemen's clubs, all of whose details seem hopelessly lost to the modern world. But an example of what zealous, intelligent research can achieve has been provided by Andrew Lamb, who succeeded in retracing Kern's steps through Edwardian London, codifying all the songs he wrote there and all the shows into which they were interpolated and by whom, and even in piecing together a sketch of the social life Kern enjoyed in London, down to his occupancy with a friend of a flat in Jermyn Street. This friend turned out rather conveniently to be the son of Max Hollander, chairman of the Palace Theatre Company, where, by a not so remarkable coincidence, Kern's first published song, 'How D'Ya Like to Spoon With Me?', was performed. Lamb's explorations have been so assiduous that one wonders what startling results might emerge were he to approach Kern's life as a whole. As an example of Lamb's careful methods, he discovered that Kern, his co-tenant and two other male friends took a box at the Palace Theatre on 12 February 1906, from where they could watch a performer called Millie Legarde perform Kern's first song:

> Hollander tells us that, on the first night of Millie Legarde's performance of 'How D'Ya Like to Spoon With Me?', the four friends were all in a stage box, and he recalls that 'the overtures from the singer were rather embarrassing'. The full significance of this information may begin to dawn if we recall the account of the song's first-night reception that was published in *The Era*. Was it, perhaps, one of Kern and Hollander's party who, in the words of *The Era*, 'appreciated Miss Legarde's invitation and gallantly assured her of the conquest she had made?' Remarkably, the matter can be resolved beyond serious doubt. *The Era*'s vivid account is fascinatingly complemented by a photograph that appeared in the pictorial weekly *The Sketch*, showing Miss Legarde singing 'How D'Ya Like to Spoon With Me?' and beckoning across the orchestra to four young men in evening dress in a stage box. Although the photograph has been given renewed currency in recent times by being reproduced by Mander and Mitchenson in the original edition of their *British Music Hall*, neither they nor anyone else seems to have given much attention to the identity of the four young men. Yet the young man second from the left is quite clearly identifiable as Jerome Kern.

And there, in the text of Lamb's *Jerome Kern in Edwardian London*, is the photographic proof of his theory. It may well be that when subjected to the same keen eye, the rest of Kern's social life reveals him in more amplitude than the conventional works of reference. In the meantime, posterity has to make what it can of a more oblique approach to the enigmatic Kern, by glimpsing him at second-hand through the recollections of his collaborators. In the matter of his lyric-writing partners, Kern was especially well served, once at the very start of his career and once again towards its end. In the spring of 1906, working as a salaried employee for the actor-manager Seymour Hicks, Kern was introduced to a young man whose education at Dulwich College had brought out a natural talent for the composition of light verse, whether in Latin, classical Greek or modern English. In the predictable course of events this diffident young man, Pelham Grenville Wodehouse, would just have emerged from three years of social polishing at Oxford or Cambridge, but the niggardly pension on which his father, a retired colonial magistrate, was obliged to survive, meant the sacrifice of a university degree to the harsher realities of life in Fleet Street. The young versifier was fortunate enough to drop into a journalistic niche which precisely matched his talents. *The Globe* was a London evening paper already ancient by the time Wodehouse arrived at its offices:

> It was 105 years old and was printed on – so help me – pink paper. It carried on its front pages a humorous column entitled 'By the Way'. There was quite a bit of prestige attached to doing it. The column itself was an extraordinary affair. You would quote something from the morning paper and then you'd make some little comment on it. It was always the same type of joke.

What made Wodehouse peculiarly suited to his duties was the convention by which much of the 'By the Way' column comprised rhymed couplets, many of them not so very far removed from the style of comic songwriting then in vogue.

The circumstances of the first meeting between Kern and Wodehouse are confused by the fact that each witness contradicts the other. Kern recalled that he played some tunes to Wodehouse, with Hicks looking on, that Wodehouse took them away and soon returned with the completed lyric. More convincing is Wodehouse's scenario, in which Kern appears as the great musical comedy wiseacre, the very fount of theatrical wisdom, a man schooled in the ways of both backstage and front-office fraternities. Kern is at the Aldwych Theatre sitting in his shirtsleeves playing poker with a bunch of actors:

> When I finally managed to free him from the card table and was able to talk to him, I became impressed. Here, I thought, was a young man supremely confident of himself – the kind of person who inspires people to seek him out when a job must be done.

This mingled awe and admiration for Kern remained with Wodehouse for the duration of their partnership, the dual benefits to Wodehouse being that he found the whole business greatly amusing and that, so long as you had Kern as your ally, even the most nefarious impresarios would think twice before committing some professional misdemeanour at your expense. Recalling his collaborations with Kern between 1917 and 1924, Wodehouse chuckled at Kern's abrasive style:

> Wonderful chap to have with you. I mean, no manager could boss you while Jerry was around. Charles Dillingham was about the biggest manager going in those days, and Jerry went to a rehearsal and heard his number played, and he said, 'Is that the way you're going to play my number?', and they said, 'Yes', and he just went and picked up all the music sheets and walked out. Yet he would have given his eye-teeth to get a song into a Dillingham show.

Although the time was to come when the two men parted, not altogether amicably, Wodehouse never lost his deep affection for Kern, saying that 'his well of melody was inexhaustible, and he loved work. You could not give him too much of it.' Wodehouse continues:

> It was this habit of always working and seldom sleeping that eventually undermined his health. He hated to go to bed. His idea of a quiet home evening was to sit at the piano composing till about five in the morning. Often in the Princess Theatre days my telephone would ring in the small hours.
>
> 'Plum? Jerry.'
>
> 'Good heavens, Jerry, do you know what time it is?'
>
> 'Quite early, isn't it? Are you in bed?'
>
> 'I was.'
>
> 'Oh, well. I've just got that first act duet we were worrying about. Get a pencil and paper.'
>
> His telephone was on the piano, and he would play me the melody and I would take down a dummy and totter back to bed. Jerry probably stayed up and worked on the second act trio.
>
> I remember spending the weekend at his house in Bronxville once, and around midnight I happened to mention that I had taken a bungalow at Bellport, Long Island, for the summer.
>
> 'Let's go and look at it,' said Jerry.
>
> 'Tomorrow, you mean?'
>
> 'No, now,' said Jerry, and he insisted in driving off there and then in his car.
>
> Bronxville is about forty miles one side of New York and Bellport about eighty on the other side. We got there at three in the morning, inspected the bungalow and drove back, Jerry at the wheel, sound asleep most of the time. I had to keep nudging him, and he would wake up and say, 'Oh, did I doze off? Sorry.' It was not one of the rides I look back to as among my most enjoyable.
>
> We did ten shows together and I was devoted to him. I saw him very little after the road tour of *Sitting Pretty* in 1924, and I am told

that he got very solemn and serious towards the end of his life. But in the Princess days he was one of the most cheerful and amusing men I have ever met, and an angel to work with, which many composers aren't.

Apart from disclosing aspects of Kern's personality not to be found elsewhere, Wodehouse makes one very revealing remark in that reminiscence, published in old age, long after Kern's death. His impression that his ex-partner grew into someone 'very solemn and serious' in his last period is a definition of Kern's third and final period as a songwriter translated into personal terms. In another essay recalling his days on Broadway, Wodehouse makes the identical observation. He is thinking back to the larky successes at the Princess Theatre with Kern and Guy Bolton, and talks of the 'Kern melodies of his early youthful days that were so gay and carefree compared with his modern style'. The inference seems to be that with the devious harmonic stratagems of works like 'The Song Is You' and 'Smoke Gets in Your Eyes' went a certain gravity of demeanour which Kern evidently felt fitting in a writer of such professorial weight. Equally clearly, what Wodehouse means by melodies which were gay and carefree are pieces like 'You Never Knew About Me', 'Shadow of the Moon' and 'Go Little Boat'. And it is true that the Princess Theatre scores possessed a unique quality which influenced a whole generation of native American lyricists; Ira Gershwin, Cole Porter, Howard Dietz, Johnny Mercer, Alan Lerner and Oscar Hammerstein are among those who have testified to the revelatory nature of what Wodehouse was doing with Kern's melodies. The case was well put by Lerner, who, in saluting the Princess Theatre team as the 'inaugurators of the American musical', has this to say of Wodehouse:

> The books were light and amusing and the music in the popular voice range, and Wodehouse wrote lyrics that were appropriate to both; clever, graceful and wittily rhymed. Picking up the light verse tradition of W. S. Gilbert, he became the pathfinder for Larry Hart, Cole Porter, Ira Gershwin and everyone else who followed.

It was a happy accident indeed, for just as Kern was stripping away the fustian of the Lehar school, so Wodehouse was democratizing the popular song lyric, replacing the inane euphemisms of Ruritania with those of the young man-about-town with Drone Club connections.

Two songs from this early Kern period which have outlived the incidence of their own birth are those damp twins 'Till the Clouds Roll By' and 'Look For the Silver Lining', twins in the sense that the two structures are so closely related that the shrewd orchestrator can, and once or twice has, used one as a counterpoint for the other. Both are apparently naïve compositions whose emotional effect is liable to nonplus the most sophisticated musicians. Among those who have expressed baffled admiration for 'Till the Clouds Roll By' is André Previn, who, after playing a single chorus at the piano, will shake his head and wonder how Kern did it. Perhaps by a little surreptitious borrowing. More than one artist, striving to find some way of defining the serenity of the two rain-songs, has slipped into ecclesiastical terminology in search of the right phrase. Alec Wilder, in admitting that the 'extreme simplicity of "Look For the Silver Lining" is deceptive, for it is somehow magnetic as well', talks of its evocation of 'a great tried-and-true folk song or hymn tune'. Dorothy Dickson, Kern's favourite among the leading ladies of his earlier years, talked of the 'hymn-like quality' of the rain-songs. Both Wilder and Miss Dickson may have been shrewder than they knew. 'Till the Clouds Roll By' contains unmistakable echoes of a Bohemian hymn tune which Kern remembered hearing his nurse sing to him in his infancy. Sigmund Spaeth, the great American tune detective, the man who could find traces of most classical masters in most popular songs, was gracious enough to define the Bohemian echoes in 'Till the Clouds Roll By' as 'unconscious', but it may well be that there were occasions when Kern succumbed to the temptation to dip into his vast bag of thematic recollections and pass off some fragment as his own. In his London days, when he was striving so desperately to acquire the prestigious gloss of an authentic European that he actually posed as one, according to Wodehouse, his ideal popular composer was the Lancashire music hall writer Leslie Stuart. By the time Kern arrived in London, Stuart, buoyant on the success of deathless pieces like 'Lily of Laguna' and 'Soldiers of the Queen', had turned to the West End stage and the composition of a series of frothy operettas with titles like *The Silver Slipper* and *The Belle of Mayfair*. In the years of Kern's residence in Edwardian London, there was always one Stuart operetta or another in performance, and, judging from Kern's admiration for Stuart's work, he must have seen them all. In 1909, a Stuart show called *Havana* opened in New York, where Kern was working for Charles Frohman. Among the young ladies featured in *Havana* was one Edith Kelly, with whom Kern promptly fell in love. Before long, realizing that Miss Kelly aspired rather higher than a mere jobbing musician, Kern backed off and scuttled back to London, having very nearly embroiled himself in an attachment to one of Stuart's ladies described by Kern's biographer as 'a hard-eyed, sensuous-mouthed beauty'. Nearly seventy years later, when the Princess show *Very Good, Eddie* was revived, scholars of the London Edwardian musical theatre were fascinated to hear one of Stuart's lush ballad themes sailing blithely by.

By the mid-1920s Wodehouse was already committed to his strategic withdrawal from the musical theatre as the ramparts of Blandings Castle began to preoccupy him. His place in Kern's professional life was filled by writers of a very different style. Indeed, no more profound contrast could be imagined to the inspired comic levity of Wodehouse than the solemn poesy of Oscar Hammerstein and Otto Harbach. Hammerstein, born into one of America's most powerful theatrical dynasties, was temperamentally inclined to sentimentality in his versifying, and although he enjoyed far greater commercial success and critical acclaim than Wodehouse the lyricist had ever known, his lyrics, although technically well-turned, were often inclined to the kind of emotional sloppiness which was at last to deliquesce into *The Sound of Music*, a story which Wodehouse, Porter, Hart and the rest of them could never have treated without reducing to a slapstick comedy. At his best Hammerstein was capable of deeply affecting verses, as in 'The Folks Who Live on the Hill' and 'Don't Ever Leave Me', but even in the 1920s there was something about the folksiness of his style which seemed slightly out of joint with the times. Many of his librettos were catastrophes on an epic scale, and need only to be played with a straight face to inspire sublime laughter. This was especially true of his collaborations with Sigmund Romberg, who, being an authentic mittel-European who had once worked as a stage-hand on a Viennese production of the maniacal *The Count of Luxemburg* and never quite regained his composure again, developed a stony indifference to plot, dialogue and lyrics which encouraged Hammerstein to indulge in some of the worst excesses of lame storytelling ever seen in the modern theatre. It is doubtful if anything more crass than *The Desert Song* has ever been perpetrated on a professional stage, a show whose integration hangs on the supposition that a heroine can be so huge a ninny as to be capable of being swept up in the arms of her own fiancé while utterly convinced he is someone else. Because of the enormous prestige attaching to his later partnership with Richard Rodgers, and especially for his work on *Oklahoma!*, Hammerstein has often been credited with having rescued the Broadway musical from banality; one glance at the plot, dialogue and characterization of *The Desert Song* tells us that all he rescued it from was himself. And yet, evidently unabashed by the imbecilities of the Red Shadow, Hammerstein, asked on one occasion why he trod such swampy narrative paths, casually dismissed Porter, Rodgers and Hart and the Gershwins by claiming that 'a story which takes place in a New York penthouse doesn't interest me'. Hammerstein was perfectly entitled to air his prejudices, but it is hard to see how his cardboard heroes, camel-borne across six-pennorth of sand, were any improvement on the identical twins and bogus cops which were stock devices in the days of *The Desert Song*.

Otto Harbach, whose work on Kern's musicals is often so thickly intertwined with Hammerstein's that it is not always clear who wrote what, had none of Hammerstein's advantages in being born into the theatre, but seemed on the contrary to be the very last man to find himself up to the arms in operetta. His modulation from profession to profession constitutes a steady decline from literacy to lunacy, with the profits increasing with each downward turn of the gradient. Born in 1873, he worked his way through Knox College in Illinois by delivering newspapers. In 1895 he won an inter-state prize for oratory and soon after was appointed professor of English at a college in Washington. Having taken a master's degree and collected a doctorate, he seemed committed to the academic life, until his eyesight began to deteriorate, at which he left the teaching profession and went into journalism. By 1902 he had drifted into the theatre, and six years later met up with one of the oddest fish in the Broadway annals, a Bohemian immigrant called Karl Hoschna, who arrived in the United States in 1896 and became the oboe soloist in Victor Herbert's Orchestra. At this stage, with his future seemingly assured, Hoschna suddenly reverted to the comic archetype of the European instrumental virtuoso slightly unbalanced by his own expertise. In 1898, in his twenty-second year, Hoschna sent the following letter to the publishing house of Witmarks, in New York:

Dear Sirs,

I am a native of Kuschwarda, Bohemia, where I was born of musical parentage, August 16th, 1877, and when I entered the Vienna Conservatory, I was assigned to master the oboe in order to gain a scholarship. After winning a Grand Prize at the university and serving as a bandmaster in the Austrian Army, I came to the United States in 1896 and for the past two years I have been oboe soloist with Victor Herbert's orchestra. I now find that the vibration of the oboe's double-reed is affecting my mind and in order to keep my sanity, I must abandon playing that instrument. Consequently I would welcome any position however humble on your staff at any salary you care to pay.

The demented Hoschna was taken on as a copyist and orchestrator, and ten years later suddenly became a successful songwriter. He was paid one hundred dollars to provide the complete score of a farce called *Three Twins*, being married off for the enterprise to the aspiring lyricist Harbach, who by now had marginally increased his earning capacity still further by sliding a few degrees more down the cultural scale and becoming an advertising copywriter. This odd couple, the irrational oboeist and the professor of English, now pooled their considerable cultural resources and came up with that pearl of erudition, 'Cuddle Up a Little Closer', in which Harbach, straining desperately for that bane of the lyricist's life, the triple rhyme, and having worked himself into a corner with 'rosy' and 'cosy', committed the misdemeanour of 'toesy'. Two years later the team had another success with a song which was picked up by Marie Lloyd, 'Every Little Movement Has a Meaning of Its Own', after which Hoschna went on to write interminable operettas, none of which is remembered today, and Harbach drifted through the Broadway musical theatre to such effect that in time he became president of the American Society of Composers, Authors and Publishers. More to the point, Harbach became involved in Kern's career. In 1925 the impresario Charles Dillingham commissioned Kern to write a musical in double-quick time. Having endured a box office disaster with his vehicle for the sought-after Marilyn Miller, *Peter Pan*, Dillingham needed a replacement, which was now provided by Kern, working for the first time with Harbach and his young protégé, Oscar Hammerstein. This musical, *Sunny*, is still celebrated, although not for the plot or the dialogue, neither of which ingredients seemed worthy of the attentions of grown men. But before Harbach and Hammerstein are accused of professional asininity, it is worth reflecting on the construction methods deployed in the Broadway theatre of the period. First, and of vital importance, was an impresario with access to a theatre. Second came the contractual possession of a star name. Third was a supporting cast of artists familiar to the ticket-buyers. Fourth was enough backers to provide the capital for costumes, scenery and rehearsals. Last, and certainly least, in the order of precedence, came the writers, which meant that Kern, Harbach and Hammerstein, like almost every writing team on Broadway, found themselves constricted before they put a word or a note on to paper. Dillingham had virtually thrust them into a straitjacket from the moment they agreed to write the show, as Hammerstein explained:

> It was one of those tailor-made affairs in which we contrived to fit a collection of important theatrical talents. Our job was to tell a story with a cast that had been assembled as if for a revue. Dillingham, the producer, had signed Cliff Edwards, who sang songs and played the ukelele and was known as Ukelele Ike. His contract required that he do his speciality between ten o'clock and ten-fifteen. So we had to construct our story in such a way that Edwards could come out and perform during that time and still not interfere with the continuity. In addition to Marilyn Miller, the star, there was Jack Donahue, a famous dancing comedian; and there were Clifton Webb and Mary Hay, who were a leading dance team of the time; Joseph Cawthorn, a star comedian; Esther Howard, another; Paul Frawley, the leading juvenile. In addition to the orchestra in the pit we also had to take care of George Olsen's dance band on the stage.

With some complacency Hammerstein adds, 'Well, we put it all together and it was a hit.' Some idea of what the writers for Broadway were up against is illustrated by the events at the first unveiling of the libretto for the leading lady. After Hammerstein had acted out the dialogue, recited lyrics and summarized the denouement, Miss Miller said, 'When do I do my tap speciality?' *Sunny* went on the road only half-written; the second act was not forthcoming until the last run-through before the first performance, a deliberate tactic based on the theory of George M. Cohan, who believed it was prudent to delay writing your second act until you had seen how capable your players were at performing the first. *Sunny* went on to run for over five hundred performances, all that audiences really cared about being the persona of Miss Miller and the tunefulness of the songs, which included 'Who?' and 'D'Ya Love Me'.

Hammerstein's relationship with Kern seems to have been very much one of master and pupil. Kern's tendency to bully inferiors often obtruded into the partnership, even though Hammerstein never lost his reverence and affection for the older man. Max Gordon, a producer destined to sprout white hairs during the 1931 production *The Cat and the Fiddle*, described, half-admiringly, the pains of working with Kern:

> He was a terror. When he said at our initial meeting that he was a devil on details, he was not exaggerating. He gave me early samples of this demoniacal drive, particularly in his composing. He would sit at the piano with his music manuscript pad on a writing-desk attached to the keyboard. This saved him the trouble of leaning forward to make his notations on the music stand itself. He wrote his notes in pen and ink. When he completed enough bars, he played them to get an idea of what he had written. More often than not both palms came crashing down on the hapless keys. But when he wrote something that pleased him, he rubbed his hair in great agitation and excitement. He often said that composing resembled fishing: 'You get a nibble but you don't know if it's a minnow or a marlin till you reel it in. You write twenty tunes to get two good ones, and the wastepaper basket yearns for the music.'

Gordon was appreciative of Kern's obsessive regard for the tiniest detail, but found the man's blatant disregard for the finer feelings of his partners almost impossible to live with, corroborating Wodehouse's recollection that Kern seemed never to go to bed:

> He was tireless in his drive for perfection. It seemed that he hardly needed any sleep at all. No detail escaped him. The slightest misplacement of the tiniest prop was enough to send him screaming down an aisle shouting invective left and right.

Gordon describes Kern as 'maddeningly irritating, constantly countering almost any suggestion with an impertinent "Why?", and say it loudly in an annoying manner', that he suffered from 'an almost neurotic need to be right', that 'our clashes were frequent and intense':

> The complexity of this genius — for he was indeed that, as the music library he left behind testifies — was revealed also by his pixieishness. For all his urbanity and sophistication, which over-awed even his poor timid wife Eva, he was, when the mood was upon him, a latterday Peter Pan, a man with a child's heart, who refused to grow up. He was never more gleeful than when one of his gags succeeded. He was beside himself with laughter. Tears streamed down his face. Ten minutes later he could become moody and miserable. He was completely unpredictable. No one knew from one moment to the next what to expect from him. He was not easy to live with.

It was Gordon who all unwittingly presided over Kern's emergence into his third and final period, as the grandiloquent master of harmonic subterfuge whose signature was to be found in the sumptuous ballads constructed in such a way that changes of key were part of their melodic and harmonic pattern. In *The Cat and the Fiddle*, the blithe and witty song, 'She Didn't Say Yes', is based in the key of C but enjoys a brief passade in A major; another piece, 'Try to Forget', begins and ends in F major after lingering in A minor. These modulatory devices were of course not entirely new to Kern's work, but from now on they were to become a dominant feature of all his writing, a mannerism which other musicians soon learned to look for. In his next show, *Music in the Air*, this fetish for modulation led Kern to the composition of one of the great masterpieces of the genre, 'The Song Is You', which is pitched in C major, but then, in an extraordinary middle section, slips into E major, to F sharp minor and then, astonishingly, into B major, which means that when the main theme returns in the home key the effect is the uplifting one of the entire composition rising a semitone. With great percipience, Hammerstein matched this rising repetition with one of his own, so that the revelatory moment in the melody is matched by the reiteration of the phrase 'Why can't I let you know'. That this hyper-sophisticated sort of writing passed muster in the Broadway of 1932 may seem surprising, but the truth was, and always will be, that the general public, knowing nothing either of the terminology of music or of the devious ruses by which Kern worked his magic, either accepts or rejects a tune on its merits. It took to Kern without thinking twice about it, swallowing his abstractions hook, line and sinker.

Yet it seems that the super-confident Kern suffered misgivings about one of the most popular ballads of the twentieth century. In 1926, working on the score of a musical for Ziegfeld, he had written down a fragment for tap-dancing, to be performed while the scenery was being changed. The device proved unnecessary, and six years later, asked by NBC to write a march theme for a series of radio musicals which proved to be stillborn, he amended the fragment. A year later, writing the songs for the musical *Roberta*, Kern slowed the tempo and insisted on personally auditioning every actress who applied for the role of the character who would have to sing it. The ravishing Ukrainian Tamara Drasin was at last selected, and asked by Kern and Harbach to perform the song. After she had done so, neither Kern nor Harbach said anything to her. Nervously she asked what she had done wrong, to which Kern replied, 'Oh, you were all right. We were just wondering about the song.' Considering that the song in question was 'Smoke Gets in Your Eyes', it seems extraordinary that so shrewd a bird as Kern should have remained unsure. Shortly before his death in 1963 Harbach recalled an explosive incident during the genesis of *Roberta*. Kern had been insisting that the slow tempo did not suit the melody, and it was not till Harbach begged him to play it through once very slowly that Kern relented. But Harbach also remembered that he learned never to remind Kern of the incident, because it reduced Kern to violent rage. Today the world never thinks twice about the languid pace of 'Smoke Gets in Your Eyes', and does not give a fig for the possibility that Kern may have borrowed the idea of the unprepared modulation of the song's middle section from a moment in Holst's *The Planets*. Whether or not Kern was closely enough acquainted with Holst to plagiarize his effects, it remains reassuringly true that millions of unschooled singers in the bath have been able to negotiate the melodrama of Kern's leap in 'Smoke Gets in Your Eyes' from the tonality of E flat to that of B major, achieving the required levitation by deploying, not for the last time, the device of the enharmonic change, by which a note retains its pitch but changes its name.

The crushing irony is that in finally exfloriating into the magnificence of his maturity Kern was regressing so far as plot, dialogue and characterization were concerned. Indeed, the shows in which he displayed pieces like 'Smoke Gets in Your Eyes', 'The Song Is You', and that verseless pearl 'Yesterdays', seem in danger of slipping back into the Hapsburgian morass from which Kern had done so much to drag the American musical of his time. The moment *Music in the Air* discloses its own plot, the heart sinks. We are deep in the mire of Trudi-loves-Rudi-and-Mitzi-loves-Fritzi in lederhosen, against a backdrop of cardboard Bavarian mountains. *The Cat and the Fiddle* had been only a marginal improvement, complete with a Rumanian composer as its hero and an American lady singer of sweet ballads as the object of his desire. It was all a far cry from the days when Kern, happily collaborating with Wodehouse, could share derisory jokes about the imports from Europe pouring on to the stages of Broadway, where they would deliquesce, leaving stagnant pools of sentimentality under which the performers invariably sank, gurgling inanities as they went, concerning the virtues of the Countess of Piphenpouf, busily passing herself off as a milkmaid, and her dashing swain, the goatherd Klaus, who is really the Duc de Chambourcy, heir to a thousand clichés. Kern could so easily have frittered away the rest of his life composing the musical accompaniment to the lederhosen brigade, had it not been for a series of events beyond even his control, events which cast him in an unaccustomed role, the astute speculator caught napping.

In 1926 Arnold Bennett began contributing to the London *Evening Standard* an essay fanfared by Lord Beaverbrook as 'a weekly causerie of current literary events, discussed with the candour and pungency that mark all his published work'. Three years later Bennett's column was still flourishing, and in the issue of the newspaper dated 14 February 1929 there was published under his name an essay entitled 'The Power Behind Big Book Prices', which opened with the following reference:

> The Jerome Kern sale of books and manuscripts, recently concluded in New York, presented one of the most remarkable phenomena in all the exciting history of book auctions. Nearly every item showed a rise in value, and many showed a tremendous rise. While prices of shares on the New York Stock Exchange were shooting aloft in a manner to startle the entire world of speculators, the prices of books and manuscripts were outsoaring them, and some rose so high that it seems as if, being out of sight, they could never come down again.
>
> An eighty-page manuscript of Charles Lamb's was sold for £9,600 which had been purchased only a short while ago for the odd £600. (In matter this manuscript was by no means of the first interest.) Even the breathless ascension of Margarine Union shares on the London Stock Exchange is a dull trifle compared with this.
>
> A number of other items provided thrills for the bibliomaniac; but the dispassionate and sane observer was probably less moved thereby, because the items were signed with fashionable names, and to follow the fashion, especially in America, is always very expensive. For which reason, the bidding-up of a mere four-page letter of Edgar Allan Poe's to £3,900 must certainly be accounted the supreme event of this mighty auction. For Poe is still not a fashion in America, and a letter written by Nero after fiddling over incandescent Rome, could hardly have fetched more than the Poe epistle.

And so closed one of the more bizarre chapters in any songwriter's life. It seems likely that Kern first acquired his lust for old books by great men when drifting through Edwardian London. By the time he had won his reputation as a great songwriter, his addiction was so great that, according to one witness, 'he could not pass a bookstore'. Described as 'a prudent buyer', Kern seems hardly ever to have read the books and manuscripts he collected, but instead took a magpie pleasure in their possession. By 1928 he had amassed 1,482 items of literary antiquity whose cost to him over the years amounted to something around $700,000 dollars. His decision to sell them came as a surprise to those who thought they knew him well:

> Now, in the closing months of 1928, when Wall Street still portended sky-high profits, some instinct told him to cash in not only his books but also his stocks at their inflated value. With no apparent regret or sentiment, Kern consigned to his friend Mitchell Kennerley the 1,482 choice literary items he had so intensively sought out.

Kennerley decided to do what he could to turn the auction into a circus, and began alerting the bibliophiles of two continents. He then designed and produced a fulsome two-volume hardbound catalogue of the items for sale, and settled down to review the list of possible bidders, reaching the conclusion that the two most promising were a Dr Rosenbach and a Mr Wells. Without informing either of these genteel bandits of his actions, Kennerley took out an insurance policy for $250,000 with Lloyd's of London against the hazard of death or illness precluding their presence at the ten sessions into which the auction was divided. To all these antics Kern remained indifferent, preferring to detach himself from the event and to write music instead. But on the January eve of the first session, he went to the back room of the Anderson Gallery for a farewell stroll among his books, all neatly stacked and awaiting the auctioneer's hammer. Kennerley was surprised to see him, for he knew how adamant Kern was about having nothing to do with the sale, and asked him how much he would take for the entire consignment. Kern sucked on his pipe and thought about it for a moment before answering, 'I'd take six-fifty or seven hundred thousand.'

The following night Kern sent Kennerley a telegram: 'My God, what's going on?' What was going on was a mad fever for Kern's collection, with the bidding for each item starting at the point where Kennerley and Kern had expected it to end. After a desperate skirmish with Dr Rosenbach, Wells had forked out $68,000 for Shelley's signed copy of *Queen Mab*. Other items included:

Pickwick Papers in the original parts	$28,000
Tom Jones, uncut, in the original binding	$29,000
Manuscript of Lamb's contributions to *Hone's*	
Table Book	$48,000
One page of the manuscript of Dr Johnson's dictionary	$11,000

A four-page letter by Poe quoting Mrs Browning on 'The Raven'	$19,500
Pope's manuscript of the first three books of *Essay on Man*	$29,000
A large-paper copy of *Gulliver's Travels*, first edition	$17,000
Rubaiyat of Omar Khayyam, first edition	$8,000
Hardy's manuscript of part of *A Pair of Blue Eyes*	$34,000

By the time the auction was over, the proceeds had climbed to $1,729,462, leaving Kern not simply richer but also much freer, for the possession of the books had begun to be a burden to him, making it impossible to leave the house unguarded. Now that he had the cash in exchange, he could rid himself of the sense of oppression which the company of Dickens, Poe, Hardy and company had brought down upon him. On the morning after the sale, Kern went shopping in Madison Avenue and purchased some books.

At the time of the auction all the interest focused on the money; a few months later people contemplated the wreckage of Wall Street and wondered by what devious means Kern had been astute enough to sense the coming crash and to sell his collection at inflationary prices while there was still time. But the astuteness was mythical. Most of the proceeds of the book auction had been invested in bank shares soon to prove worthless. The revelatory nature of the book sale lies not in the profits but in the items. It is rare enough for a man to spend vast sums on ancient manuscripts, almost unheard of when the purchaser is someone whose life has been spent melodizing inanities like *Sunny* and *Sally*. Nor was Kern by any means alone in his interests and cultural awareness. Porter and Gershwin were among Kern's professional rivals who were perfectly candid about the anomalies of their predicament, chained to a profession with little interest in anything approaching an adult thought. All three men yearned for the chance to work just for once on a project not totally idiotic, and all three eventually had their chance. For Kern, the loss of financial independence pushed him on to the last phase of his career, west to the fleshpots of Hollywood, an industry whose ethics he despised and whose captains he derided. But the move was more fortunate than he realized, because at a stroke it released him from the Austro-Hungarian stewpot into which he had been tumbling, and flung him forward into the contemporary world by endowing him with a new working partner whose wit and deftness as a versifier must have sent his mind spinning back to the days with Wodehouse.

Like her predecessor at Kern's court, Oscar Hammerstein, Dorothy Fields was born into the Broadway theatre. Her father was the dialect comedian Lew Fields, a star of vaudeville who had dwindled into a producer by the time Miss Fields was growing up. His two sons, Herbert and Joseph, were among the most successful librettists in the musical theatre, but Fields did what he could to dissuade his third child from maintaining the family tradition, saying 'Ladies don't write lyrics', to which Dorothy replied, 'I'm not a lady, I'm your daughter', and went on to become one of the outstanding lyricists of her generation. Her style was as far removed from Hammerstein's as it is possible to imagine, being urban rather than rustic, urbane rather than naïve. Her lines were lean and witty; she was fond of laughing at the embryonic Dorothy Fields who had submitted to the first song publishers willing to entertain her ambition a lyric about college life which included the couplet:

>Every pedagogue
>Goes to bed agog . . .

By the time that Pandro Berman, a producer at RKO, teamed her up with Kern to write for Astaire and Rogers, she was acknowledged as one of the ablest versifiers in the profession. More to the point, she was quite free of the faintest taint of the Hapsburgians. If there were any influences to be detected in her work, they were to be located due west of Vienna; one of her first hits, 'On the Sunny Side of the Street', borrowed its striking title from an early James Joyce short story. She was the perfect choice for the stylish tinsel world already created by Fred and Ginger in *The Gay Divorcee*, *Top Hat* and *Follow the Fleet*, and was to have a dramatic effect on Kern's writing. That it was an effect for the better was quickly acknowledged by Kern, who soon became a close friend and admirer. Although she was to achieve consistent success, Miss Fields at the end of her life looked back to her 1936 chore with Kern, *Swingtime*, as the peak of her achievement. In a sense it could be said to have been the peak of Kern's also, if only because faced with a challenge he found uncongenial, of writing themes which swung and which held terpsichorean promise, he met the challenge with magnificent aplomb, although not without a struggle. It was the combined force of Astaire and Fields which pushed Kern into something approaching rhythmic animation during the writing of the songs for *Swingtime*. They both recall visiting Kern at his home and chivvying him into composing something Fred could dance to. Kern complained that he couldn't deliver that sort of music, but after Astaire had spent several afternoons literally dancing all over Kern's home, leaping over the furniture, drumming on the walls, singing as he went, Kern managed to piece together some rhythmic songs. The piece which gave him especial trouble was the tune to which Astaire might achieve his ambition of dancing a tribute to the great dancer Bill Robinson. According to Miss Fields, 'Kern couldn't get the feel of Bojangles, but at last, with a little help from his friends, he came up with "Bojangles of Harlem".' Another aspect of the Fields influence may be seen in one of the rare examples in Kern's later life of a rhythmically buoyant piece, 'A Fine Romance'. It is no doubt more than coincidence that the writing of this song took place in reverse order, with the lyrics written first and given to Kern to melodize, instead of the usual procedure whereby Kern would hand down a new melody to his lyricist with the air of a prince bestowing largesse. It is also revealing that having set the words of 'A Fine Romance', Kern should have played a charming musical trick on himself by writing another, even more distinguished song whose harmonies ran parallel for a while with those of the earlier song. The final fade-out, featuring the lovers singing a duet, still surprises students of the art in the way that Ginger's version of 'The Way You Look Tonight' runs as a counter-melody to Fred's 'A Fine Romance'. 'The Way You Look Tonight' won the 1936 Oscar in the face of fierce competition from 'I've Got You Under My Skin' and 'Pennies From Heaven', although one of the most dazzling songs of the year, also written for Astaire and Rogers, Irving Berlin's 'Let's Face the Music and Dance' never even received a nomination. An apocryphal story still circulates half a century after the event, to the effect that when Kern won the award for 'The Way You Look Tonight', he pretended to be aggrieved at the neglect of 'A Fine Romance'.

Kern was to write with several other gifted lyricists during a brilliant Hollywood career, including E. Y. Harburg and Leo Robin, but the two outstanding new partners of the last years both discovered the acquisitive, aggressive side of Kern's nature. In 1942 he partnered Johnny Mercer in composing a score for Astaire and Rita Hayworth in *You Were Never Lovelier*, and it is Mercer who gives a glimpse of Kern in the last few years of his life. Mercer was the younger man by a generation, and was keenly aware that in entering into a collaboration with so prestigious a figure he was in effect stepping into history. He had heard of the peaks of asperity to which Kern could rise, but never experienced them. Instead he was delighted to realize that Kern had taken a liking to him; seeking for a reason, Mercer suggested that 'maybe it was because I could make him laugh'. Maybe also it was because Mercer could give him memorable lyrics. Mercer's view of Kern is identical to all the others; what makes it significant is the fact that though prematurely ageing and already suffering from the pernicious anaemia that had killed his father, Kern was still greedy for knowledge, forever striving to learn facts for their own sake:

Kern couldn't stand mediocrity. He was a superior person. He had a quick mind and he knew everything about the theatre, besides the tunes. He knew all about the book, he knew all about the actors' salaries, he knew what the box-office was doing, he knew what the weather was like. He was quite a bright fellow, and he had lots of hobbies too, like he liked to bet the races, he collected first editions, silver, paintings, and I think it filled his time. He was a man who had a lot going for him, and it was like Edison, there just weren't enough hours in the day for him. So when he would get through writing, he occupied himself with these other things.

In fact the partnership worked so well that it seems surprising that it occurred to nobody to sustain it. *You Were Never Lovelier* was the last as well as the first Kern-Mercer collaboration, but for the rest of his life Mercer spoke with warmth and admiration of Kern, remembering how the older man had eased the path of the younger:

> We hit it off right away. I was in such awe of him, I think he must have sensed that. He was very kind to me, treated me more like a son than a collaborator. And when he thought I had a great lyric he said, 'Eva, Eva, come down here', and he kissed me on the cheek and he said, 'Eva, I want you to hear this lyric.' Well, of course I was thrilled that he liked it that much, you know. 'I'm Old Fashioned', that one was.

And yet Kern, for all his affectionate tendencies and his artistic generosity, could not curb the old aggression. One of the more remarkable exhibits in the museum of musical comedy is a copy of the sheet music of 'Dearly Beloved', which says, simply, 'By Jerome Kern'. The same tendency to sharp practice was experienced two years later by Kern's old friend Ira Gershwin, who was persuaded by another songwriter, Arthur Schwartz, to collaborate with Kern in a picture starring Gene Kelly and Rita Hayworth called *Cover Girl*. Schwartz had, much to his own astonishment, been recruited as a producer by Harry Cohn of Columbia, and instantly fulfilled a longstanding ambition by bringing his two heroes together. The film is still remembered for the last great song of Kern's life, 'Long Ago and Far Away', but even with a partner as distinguished as Ira, Kern had to assert his primacy. He did this by telling Ira that as he, Kern, was the senior partner, it would be understood that he, Kern, would split the royalties with him 60–40. Ira, the most generous of men, never bothered to argue the point, but the incident casts a harsh light on Kern's unbending arrogance. Schwartz recalls that in the film's early stages, he would ask Kern to play him the songs, at which Kern would fish out something rejected from an earlier project. Schwartz, who was almost as old a hand at this game as Kern, was never duped by these stratagems, but would let his face reflect his disapproval. Kern would stop playing, scribble the initials ADL at the top of the manuscript and turn to something else. When the production was complete, Schwartz asked Kern the meaning of the initials, and Kern, laughing, replied, 'Arthur Doesn't Like'.

It is striking how in *Cover Girl* Kern returned to the scenes of his youth. The story involves a heroine who also portrays her own grandmother, which meant that some of the action takes place around the turn of the century in the London music hall. The title song represents a beguiling recession into·Edwardian operetta, a perfect evocation of the days when the young Kern, living in Jermyn Street, was saturating himself in the musical romances of the day. He must also have recalled his experience of the music hall, because when at one stage of the story the grandmotherly Rita Hayworth is seen singing her big song, it turns out to be an old Vesta Victoria classic called 'Poor John', written by the renowned partnership of Henry Pether and Fred Leigh. It may or may not have been accidental that when the film was released, no indication was given in the credits that anyone apart from Kern and Gershwin had written the songs, so that a new generation of popular song fanciers left the cinema under the impression that Kern had achieved the remarkable pastiche of a bygone style which was in fact the genuine article, written for Miss Victoria in 1906, during Kern's London interlude. But sharp practice aside, there is no question that the two old masters, Kern and Gershwin, did themselves full justice. The star of the picture, Gene Kelly, later paid the two writers what must have been the most lavish tribute even they ever enjoyed when he described his awe in the face of their seemingly effortless technique:

> They could do anything. If the song didn't work, you'd have a new song next day. They could go up to the hotel room and fix it. They were geniuses in their way, and they're not really given enough credit. You hear a popular ballad and you start to weep, and you find yourself saying, 'Just a minute. This isn't Brahms or Beethoven, you know.'

Kern is said to have regarded 'Long Ago and Far Away' as one of his most inspired melodies, but it is another song, one whose prospects worried him, which has since come to stand for all his great ballads. In 1939 he had returned for the last time to Broadway and conspired with Hammerstein to create *Very Warm For May*. The libretto showed a Hammerstein unrepentant after the lunacies of *The Desert Song*, and the show folded in a few weeks, never to be seen again. But within the rickety structure of the plot Kern had somehow found room for 'All the Things You Are', a composition so daring in its harmonic escapades that it could be said hardly to have a central tonality at all, so freely does it shift from key to key. Its best-known feature is the enharmonic change at the end of the middle section, when the G sharp, sustained over two bars, becomes A flat as it emerges into the final section of the song. This is what led Kern to think the song would be 'too difficult for them', but once again the general public, trusting to its ear without giving a thought to technique or terminology, responded so enthusiastically that it has become one of the great standard pieces of the American theatre.

Kern never quite reconciled himself to the Hollywood life, and must have been hankering for the theatre of his youth when in November 1944 he and Eva returned to New York to meet Hammerstein. The project was a revival of Kern's abiding masterpiece, *Show Boat*, at which point we arrive at the most astounding of all the episodes in Kern's life. The history books record that *Show Boat* is a musical written by Jerome Kern and Oscar Hammerstein in 1926, produced by Florenz Ziegfeld a year later. None of these facts is true. The work of no fewer than five lyricists and three composers may be found in the score, and, so far from having contributed his share of the work in 1926, Kern spent his entire professional life writing *Show Boat* and never lived to complete his work. There is, indeed, no such specific musical work called *Show Boat*, in the sense that no definitive version exists. The *Show Boat* which opened on Broadway in 1927 is not quite the *Show Boat* which was revived five years later; 'Life on the Wicked Stage' and 'Till Good Luck Comes My Way' have disappeared. By the time Universal Studios screened the show in 1936, the hero, Ravenal, has a new number, 'I Have the Room Above Her', while Old Joe, portrayed by Paul Robeson, has acquired a new property of his own, a duet with Queenie entitled 'Ah Still Suits Me'. In the 1946 revival, the duet between Frank and Ellie, 'I Might Fall Back on You', has been dropped, and Ravenal has forfeited 'Till Good Luck Comes My Way'. And there is a new balled for the heroine to introduce in the closing scene, 'Nobody Else But Me'. MGM's 1951 production was such a travesty as to be almost unrecognizable as the show which had opened in 1927. The 1971 London production omitted 'Life on the Wicked Stage', turned away from 'Ah Still Suits Me', and switched 'Nobody Else But Me' from the heroine to her friend.

The truth appears to be that Kern wrote so much music for *Show Boat* that to include all of it in a single production would be to elongate the evening beyond the bounds of propriety. Anyone contemplating production of the work is obliged to make a selective version, and experience suggests that no matter how carefully the selection is made, there will be admirers of the original ready to rise up in protest against the blasphemy of leaving out this or the impertinence of putting in that. Of no other musical work in the popular canon could it be said that the score consists of a stockpot of songs from which producers may choose their items. What is much more remarkable than any of this is Kern's obsessional preoccupation with the work. So far from having completed it in 1926, we know that he continued to refine the score by adding songs and dropping others. Twice in London productions the early piece 'How D'Ya Like to Spoon With Me?' has been included. On both sides of the Atlantic, 'Nobody Else But Me' has been included. This means that *Show Boat* incorporates the first and last published works of Kern's life. The lyricist for 'How D'Ya Like to Spoon With Me?' was Edward Laska. Kern also resorted to the heretical device in his score of incorporating work by other popular composers; 'Goodbye, My Lady Love' had been written by Joe Howard in 1904, and 'After the Ball', the great sensation of 1892, was the work of an ex-pawnbroker called Charles Harris, a hack so simple-minded that he believed the doggerel of his words to constitute great art. Hammerstein, Laska, Howard, Harris, four lyricists in one production. But it is the fifth who brings a sort of symmetry to the eclecticism of *Show Boat*.

At some time in the Edwardian era Kern had written a melody and then tucked it away in the file, against the day when it might be useful. It had no lyric and no title. At the end of 1917, the Princess Theatre team, having scored such a great success with *Oh, Boy!*, began work on a successor to be called *Oh, Lady, Lady!*. Kern then remembered the wordless melody and handed it to Wodehouse, who returned it to him next day with a set of words, under the title 'Bill'. During the out-of-town run it was decided that the song was too slow for the first act, and it was discarded. Long after the Kern-Wodehouse partnership was over, Kern found himself embroiled in the score of *Show Boat*, struggling to write something suitable for Julie to sing in Act Two when she is auditioning in a night club for work as a singer. The situation is virtually the only one in the show which does not have to be integrated into the story; Julie could have chosen anything to sing at an audition. Yet it might be a good idea if somehow this casual song were to have oblique reference to the lost love of Julie's life, a man called Steve. Kern remembered the Wodehouse lyric and decided to let Julie sing about Bill when the audience would know she was thinking about Steve. Kern now had to get his ex-partner's permission, which was instantly forthcoming. Wodehouse later recalled:

> Years after *Oh, Lady, Lady!*, Jerry came to me in Hollywood. I can see him now, coming up my garden, and he asked me if he could use 'Bill' for *Show Boat*, and I said yes, of course he could, and it was a great hit.

But not immediately. The song attracted almost no critical attention at the 1927 opening, and it was only very gradually as the years went by that it overtook all the other songs in the score, including at last even 'Ole Man River', establishing Wodehouse as the fifth and most incongruous of the lyricists credited in *Show Boat*.

Kern never lived to see the 1946 revival. En route to an antique shop on the morning of 5 November 1945, he collapsed in Park Avenue. A policeman called for an ambulance, which soon arrived and drove the

dying man to a hospital. Much has been made of the irony that because
he carried no means of identification, nobody at the hospital knew who
he was. But the failure to recognize him is hardly surprising. Kern was
no film star, no night-clubbing notoriety, and, to the patrolman who saw
him drop to the pavement, must have seemed like just one more old
man pushing his luck too far. Kern's ASCAP membership card was in
his pocket, a clue too abstruse for the medical staff to decipher; when
Oscar Hammerstein arrived at the hospital it was to find Kern lying
unconscious in the ward reserved for derelicts. He was removed to
another hospital, but the cerebral haemorrhage which felled him had
been so severe that he lapsed into a coma and died on 11 November.
President Truman inspired much bitter mirth when, in paying tribute to
Kern, he said that 'his melodies will live in our voices and warm our
hearts for many years to come, for they are the kind of simple, honest
songs that belong to no time or fashion'. In claiming that Kern's music,
which cries out Edwardian romanticism and Hollywood chic, belonged
to no time or fashion, the President was merely resorting to the statutory
twaddle of his profession. 'The Song Is You' simple? 'All the Things
You Are' simple? And yet Truman, with his Missouri bar-room piano
style, may have been thinking of those songs like 'Till the Clouds Roll
By', 'Look for the Silver Lining', 'Don't Ever Leave Me' and 'Why Was I
Born?', whose unembellished structures defy the musicologist to
explain to us why they have the power to move us so.

Kern was one of those fortunate men whose good luck became so
intertwined with his acumen that it is impossible to say where one
ended and the other began. As a young nobody in Edwardian London he
happens to befriend the son of the theatrical impresario. Luck or
cunning? He happens to bump into Wodehouse on the very night in his
career when he realizes that to succeed he needs the stimulus of a witty
writer. Luck or cunning? He sells off his priceless book collection in the
nick of time before the bottom falls out of the American economy. Luck
or cunning? Whatever the truth, before his career had got under way, he
had already been the beneficiary of more good fortune than any man has
a right to expect. In the spring of 1915 the impresario Charles Frohman,
one of Kern's staunchest admirers, decided to sail to London on theatre
business and invited Kern to accompany him. Kern accepted, and the
agreed departure date was 1 May. The sailing time was noon, and
Frohman, being all too familiar with Kern's chaotic sleep patterns,
made a point of reminding him to be sure to rise in time for the voyage.
On the morning of 1 May, Kern's alarm clock failed to do its job, and
the boat sailed without him. Frohman started out for London alone but
never arrived there. The ship was the S.S. *Lusitania*.

COLE PORTER

CHAPTER THREE

Cole Porter

THE SOCIAL COMPOSITION OF American songwriting in the golden age makes educational reading. The vast majority of the successful practitioners represented what might loosely be termed the proletariat, belonging to those minority groups which were, to varying degrees, either under-privileged or dispossessed. There were the Irish-Americans, of whom the brashest, richest and most intransigent was George M. Cohan, and the most talented probably Walter Donaldson. There were the few blacks who contrived somehow to penetrate the ramparts of a white society, usually through their gifts as performers, Thomas 'Fats' Waller, Eubie Blake, James P. Johnson, Sheldon Brooks, Duke Ellington. The largest group, and the most influential, was the Russian-Jewish corpus which fled the demented wrath of the Romanovs, and which not only produced the Gershwins, Irving Berlin, Harold Arlen, Arthur Schwartz, Howard Dietz, E. Y. Harburg and dozens of others, but was also responsible for many of the great instrumentalists and comics of the period. In a separate category were those Europeans who had remained long enough in the old world to receive the fruits of academic education, although not always a musical one. It is one of the whimsies of the Austro-Hungarian empire that quite often its composers had been prepared for life by a thorough education in the principles of engineering, an anomaly which has inspired the reflection regarding the Hapsburgians that while their bridges collapsed their middle eights stood firm. Writers like Friml, Herbert and Romberg were, in the stylistic sense, only part-American, writers who brought to Broadway and Tin Pan Alley the sentimental pleasures of the Beidermeier school. There were other exceptions to the immigrant rule. Away from the great industrial centres of the East there grew up a rustic school exemplified by Hoagy Carmichael and Johnny Mercer. And the case of Oscar Hammerstein, born into a powerful theatrical dynasty, falls into no category but its own.

Most of these writers, and all the immigrants, clutched at the straw of songwriting because it was, apart from Sport and the Stage, the only road open to them. Many succeeded because the thought of failure was too terrible to contemplate. America coined a graphic expression to define this condition; the phrase 'hungry fighter' is an oblique reference to a profession so brutalized that only those trembling on the rim of destitution would ever think of embracing it. And while placing a song was not so bruising an experience as boxing eight rounds, the analogy would seem appropriate enough to Frederick Loewe, who did both for money. Nor did songwriting offer much more financial security than prizefighting. Until the principle of royalty payments for public performance had been taken to the Supreme Court, and there virtually written into the Constitution by Oliver Wendell Holmes, songwriters had no legal existence at all. When the American Society of Composers, Authors and Publishers at last came into being, Victor Herbert was nearly sixty years old, Jerome Kern thirty, Irving Berlin twenty-seven. While too much has been made of the cinematic cliché of the poor immigrant from the East Side who claws his way to triumph by performing his great conshoito at Carnegie Hall, it is certainly true that the successful melodists and versifiers of the period needed to profit from their work in order to exist. And because they constituted an eager, pragmatic, money-conscious band, they were regarded by what used laughingly to be defined as polite society as being beyond the pale. A gentleman might compose the occasional air, or scribble the odd set of verses, but should this trifling happen to brand him with the indignity of financial reward, it was prudent to conceal the fact behind a cloak of pseudonymity. To this day the writers of the sentimental ballad 'The Honeysuckle and the Bee', eulogized by spirits as disparate as Sir John Squire and Charlie Chaplin, are listed as Albert Fitz and William Penn. The true writer was one Sol Bloom, who for twelve years served as Chairman of the Foreign Relations Committee of the House of Representatives, and only after his death was the nature of his scarlet and highly profitable sin disclosed. General Charles Gates Dawes, who, by serving as Vice President to Calvin Coolidge, achieved the bizarre distinction of placing himself in the shadow of a shadow, is listed in the reference books as author of *A Journal of the Great War*, *Notes as Vice President* and *A Journal of Reparations*, but not as the composer of 'It's All in the Game', a harmless little waltz which inflicted incalculably less damage on humanity than did the Coolidge administration. That Bloom and Dawes, by publicizing their uselessness at the expense of a few pretty musical measures, got their moral imperatives mixed up, is confirmed by the case of James J. Walker, twice felonious mayor of New York. Walker, who once made a speech explaining his fiscal policy to the audience at a Gershwin musical first night, was often derided by his political rivals for the tear-jerking absurdity of his lyrics to the great bar-room ballad of the 1905 season, 'Will You Love Me in December as You Do in May?', yet it seems likely that the writing of those words was almost the only entirely legal act of Walker's amazing life. It is after all better to be a saloon poet than a saloon politician, and yet proof of Walker's moral obloquy was more than once taken to be his career as a songwriter. Tin Pan Alley was simply not an acceptable place of work for a respectable young man. There were one or two exceptions. Among the more fortunate exceptions was Alan Lerner's father, who enjoyed a prosperous mercantile career. So, somewhat less grandly, did the parents of Richard Rodgers and Jerome Kern. But the wealth of the Porters was of a different order altogether.

America has another colourful phrase to define the Porters of its society. 'Old Money' is a quaint euphemism for having a rich grandparent. In Cole Porter's case the moneybags was his maternal grandfather J. O. Cole, a philistine shopkeeper who drifted into the brewery business, into cold-storage, into sawmills, into timber and finally into the possession of land whose value rose with the fortunes of the nation. J. O., who knew and cared even less about the fine arts than did the entrepreneurs with whom his grandson was to associate, did all he could to turn Cole into a lawyer, using the family fortune as a bludgeon. In Anglo-American life the Law seems to have played the same role in the lives of popular musicians that engineering did for the Hapsburgs. Arthur Schwartz instantly comes to mind as a gifted songwriter obliged to fritter away much valuable energy on a mastery of jurisprudence. But none of the lawyers-turned-songwriters ever registered half as vividly as W. S. Gilbert, who, in a Liverpool courtroom of the 1850s, scaled heights of professional rejection unknown even to the most eminent leaders of the profession when he found himself the target of an old boot flung at him by his own client, a hardened female pickpocket who, evidently knowing more of the arts of advocacy than her counsel, decided to conduct the case in her own style instead of Gilbert's. The boot narrowly missed Gilbert's head but scored a direct hit on one of the gentlemen of the press, an accident which Gilbert was inclined to take as an explanation for the occasional hostile review of his work. That Gilbert must have been the most inept songwriting lawyer of the nineteenth century seems likely. That Cole Porter was the worst of the century which followed is quite certain. Porter never even reached the stage where clients abused him, and his brief brush with jurisprudence at Harvard Law School was a fiasco mitigated only by his extra-curricular musical activities. Porter had moved to Harvard at the insistence of J.O., who had become anxious at the extent to which Porter's career at Yale seemed to consist in its entirety of writing college shows. Here was the first dilemma of Porter's life: how to reconcile his own determination to write songs with his equally strong desire to get his hands on J.O.'s money.

The resolution of his problem came in 1916 with the New York production of Porter's first professional show, *See America First*. J.O. finally acknowledged the hopelessness of the struggle and set up a substantial trust fund for his grandson based on land and property holdings. Three years later Porter married a rich divorcee called Linda Lee Thomas, whose escape from an uxorious libertine of a husband brought with it the consolation of a large fortune, which she now began to lavish on her young husband. But if the outfacing of J.O.'s interfering nature had been for Porter the great impediment to bliss of the 1910s, the disposition of his great wealth became the nightmare of the 1920s. Now that he had his independence at last, what was he to do with it? The accounts of his gallivanting around the fleshpots of the world in the decade following his marriage make by far the most depressing and even distressing reading to be found in the biographies of his musical generation, a profligate frittering away of priceless creative energy. His life seemed to be an interminable succession of aimless parties peopled by dullards to celebrate only themselves, a drunken sailing about on boats, dashing around on trains, travelling to this palazzo and moving on to the next, perpetrating witless practical jokes, and always the consumption of wealth in a manner so feverish as to suggest desperation, the calculated reduction of existence to a tipsy caucus race mitigated only by the composition of songs for the amusement of resolutely non-musical friends. Most revealing of all was the persistent orchestrating of the facts of his life by Porter in the hope of sketching in the lineaments of a self-portrait more commensurate with his own conception of himself than the truth would allow. Porter, the insatiable seeker after gossip and chit-chat, had the knack of manipulating rumours about himself with great skill. Posthumous biographies disclose that he did not, as he always insisted, fight with the French Army in the Great War, did not enlist in the Foreign Legion, did not retreat to the playgrounds of Europe simply because of the commercial failure of *See America First*. None of this would matter in the slightest were it not for the fact that among those truths which he either distorted or concealed were two of prime importance: the origins of some of his most famous songs, and the nature of his sexual tendencies. During his own lifetime Porter was careful to mislead musicologists and biographers regarding the sources of his inspiration. A dedicated, restless sightseer, he often sketched in exotic backdrops to the genesis of his music. The most notorious of these bogus scenarios concerns his best-known composition of all, 'Night and Day', which, according to the official text, arose out of Porter's exposure to the wailing of Moroccan music. A few years after he wrote the song, Porter fell into the trap of self-contradiction which ensnares most congenital liars when he told an interviewer from the *New York World Telegram*:

I wrote the piece for a spot in *Gay Divorce*. I wasn't trying to plumb any depths or interpret mass psychology of the times. . . . I was living down at the Ritz-Carlton when the song was put together. I put the tune on paper, I remember, on a Saturday, and wrote the lyric the next day while lying on a beach in Newport.

It may well be that the Moroccan edition is the correct one and the Newport Beach scenario a barefaced lie. But the point is that they cannot both be true. One or the other, not both. Worse confusion attends the history of 'Begin the Beguine', which was supposed to have been inspired by the sight of some natives executing a war-dance on an island in the Dutch East Indies. In a letter to a friend written in 1944 Porter claimed to have discovered the beguine in Paris in 1933. Another letter dated 1945 claims that though the opening four bars of the song came from the East Indies, the title came from Paris. Why Porter should have bothered to weave these laborious tissues of moonshine around his work is unknown, except that his lust for publicity may have too often tempted him. Much more revealing are his sins of omission regarding the sources of his music. In 1943, composing songs for a wretched backstage musical at Columbia Studios, Porter enjoyed great success with 'You'd Be So Nice To Come Home To'. No inspirational anecdote attaches to this most engaging melody, even though its main theme has been lifted bodily from Pablo Sarasate's *Zigeunerweisen*, Opus 20, first published in 1878. Sarasate was Sherlock Holmes's favourite violinist and it seems that in his unwillingness to confess a genuine instance of theme-lifting, Porter forwent the chance to weave an amusing tale of Sherlockian intrigue and deduction.

That in disseminating so much twaddle about himself and his work Porter was merely blurring the crystalline grace of his best work only makes his behaviour the more irritating. The true points of importance about 'Night and Day' concern, not the monotony of Moroccan religious chanting, but the unorthodox deployment of a 48-bar duration in place of the conventional 32; the masterly compression of the vocal range to suit Fred Astaire's vocal style, the witty variations on the theme of night following day in the lyric; the daring perversity of the structure of the song's verse, with its one note repeated 33 times over an eight-bar span, followed by a note a semitone higher played 29 consecutive times. Yet even here Porter cannot resist the temptation to indulge in a little poetic licence, apparently in the hope of flattering one of his rich, influential society friends. He later claimed that the opening words of the verse were suggested by an overheard remark by Mrs Vincent Astor about a leaky faucet: 'That drip, drip, drip is driving me mad.' These little scenarios might be more convincing if just for once they featured a hero or heroine who happened to be poor.

Apologists for Porter might remind us that his experience of the poor was hardly extensive enough to accommodate the subtle art of anecdote. Yet this appears to be another false assumption about Porter's life. His extensive homosexual tastes brought him into regular contact with the proletariat. His marriage to a divorcee disenchanted with sex but devoted to Porter's art could not have been a more fortunate arrangement, but the issue of his homosexuality has no significance unless it could be shown to have influenced that art, or at any rate to have shaped a few of its embellishments. Certainly there is a kind of detached elegance about Porter's masterpieces which might indicate tendencies to what the Victorians called Decadence, especially in the ballads of aching romantic yearning, which seem here and there to verge on the brink of a world-weary intensity too desperate to be contained by the melodic theme. But technical expertise controlling a rich vein of musical beauty ensured that his art held together. In any case, speculation about his private life seems unrewarding in a career so crammed with more significant issues. It is true that the parodic version of 'You're the Top' rhymes the breasts of Venus with King Kong's penis, and 'a bridal suite in use' with 'self-abuse', but the joke was strictly for private consumption.

In the constrained moral climate of the theatre in his lifetime Porter was rarely able to do much more than hint at that underside of life with which he was familiar enough. Nor did he exhibit any moral scruples when compromise was demanded of him. When his beautifully crafted song about a prostitute, 'Love For Sale', was presented in the 1930 production *The New Yorkers*, howls of outraged virtue, followed by proscription by assorted radio agencies, caused the hasty adaptation of the offending scene so that the fallen woman could be black instead of white, a concession which instantly placated Mrs Grundy and apparently troubled Porter not at all. Perhaps the only occasion on which a suitably suggestive libretto came Porter's way was when in 1933 C. B. Cochran invited him to provide the songs for the musical adaptation of one of the silliest novels of its day. James Laver's *Nymph Errant* was a feebly lascivious episodic tale of a well-bred young English virgin who leaves her Swiss finishing school intent on being deflowered at the earliest possible opportunity and who becomes embroiled in a succession of fantastical sexual exploits involving Turkish voluptuaries, an amorous sheik, a Russian anarchist, a Riviera lecher, a nudist camp and the stage of the Folies de Paris. And yet, constrained by this farrago, Porter achieved one of his finest scores, using a medical dictionary to construct that pearl among catalogue songs, 'The Physician', and exhorting his audience to fling its corporate bonnet over the windmill and wallow in nameless unspecified delights in 'Experiment'. And yet, in this climate of simulated daring, of spurious passion, of cowardly blackouts at every crisis point, there may be found one of the most explicit invitations to love in the popular catalogue, a stylish erotic hymn called 'You're Too Far Away', with its closing sentiment:

> Till we're so close together that we
> Can't tell any longer what's you and what's me,
> I'll still maintain you're too far away.

Sometimes there were ironies attaching to Porter's most successful songs on which he made no comment and of which he may even have remained unaware. One of the items on which he lavished his most imaginative powers of anecdotage was the marathon melodrama 'Begin the Beguine', an epic which ran to a freakish 105 bars dispensing hothouse passion with every note. The whole *raison d'être* of this song is its voluptuous rhythmic base, which throbs interminably and cries out for the cleansing brush of the parodist, which in the fullness of time it received, as we shall see. Both in the placement of the notes and the sentiments of the words the song insists on the irresistible allure of the beguine rhythm, one of those nondescript microscopic variations on the conventional patterns of Latin-American music which have erupted to upset the commercial balance from time to time over the years, from the tango in 1912 to the bossa nova two generations later. Porter composed 'Begin the Beguine' for a 1935 musical suggested by British celebrations of 25 years of rule by King George V and Queen Mary. Even as the Silver Jubilee pageantry was proceeding in Britain, somewhere in the South Seas, Porter, accompanied by Moss Hart, was concocting the musical *Jubilee*, whose central joke was the essentially bourgeois tendencies of the king and queen in the story. By far the best song in the score was 'Just One of Those Things', which was soon accepted as a standard item, while 'Begin the Beguine', after a brief salute from the reviewers, lapsed back into obscurity, where it might well have remained but for a breathtaking fluke involving a fledgeling bandleader of the period called Artie Shaw. Being a late starter in the Big Band stakes of the later 1930s, Shaw, an autodidact with decided views about everything including popular music, found himself faced by the challenge of leading his orchestra into its first set of recordings. It is much to Shaw's credit that he decided to adopt the policy of confining himself, not to the dross of the current hit parade, but to the stockpot of standard songs to which contemporary writers like Porter had so generously contributed. His first choice was a notorious yodelling exercise contrived by Rudolf Friml and Oscar Hammerstein called 'Indian Love Call', which had first been heard echoing across the trackless cardboard wastes of the Rockies in the 1924 hit show *Rose Marie*, and had never stopped echoing since. Shaw was perceptive enough to notice that once divested of its imbecilic lyric, 'Indian Love

Call' fell into that comforting harmonic simplicity which can be so conducive to exciting improvisation. But 'Indian Love Call', all-pervading though it might be, could not pervade over on to the other side of the record, and Shaw was faced with a choice of items for what that nefarious conspiracy the record industry was happy to define as the B-side. When the Shaw band recorded 'Indian Love Call', the reaction was euphoric:

> Everybody around the RCA Victor studio thought we had a hit record. As it turned out, the RCA Victor people were quite wrong. 'Indian Love Call' had an enormous sale, but that wasn't because it was a hit. It just happened to be on the other side of a rather nice little tune of Cole Porter's, a tune that had died a fast death after a brief appearance on Broadway in a flop musical show called *Jubilee*. I had just happened to like it, so I insisted on recording it at this first session, in spite of the recording manager, who thought it a complete waste of time and only let me make it after I had argued that it would at least make a nice quiet contrast to 'Indian Love Call'.
>
> When this 'quiet contrast' turned out to be what sold the record in the first place, what made it into a big hit record in the second place, and finally into one of the biggest single instrumental hit records ever made by any American dance band – well, naturally everybody was surprised.
>
> I was as surprised as anybody else. For, although I had liked the tune, I certainly hadn't thought of it as a hit possibility. Who would have picked a tune to be a hit after the public had already heard it in a show and apparently been perfectly willing never to hear it again? How could anybody in his right mind figure to make a hit record out of a dead tune with a crazy title like 'Begin the Beguine'?

This famous recording, which transformed Shaw, not altogether to his liking, from a young hopeful clarinettist into a brand image, also had the effect of making 'Begin the Beguine' one of the century's most famous songs, although at what cost neither Porter nor Shaw, nor indeed anyone, ever acknowledged. It seems that what was required to make the song appealing to a wide audience was the dismantling of its rhythmic structure, the very inspiration for its creation. Shaw's version of 'Begin the Beguine', the only one which ever had any impact, is a conventional fox-trot, from which the latin elements have been excised in the cause of big band swing. In 1944 Porter wrote a song called 'Let's End the Beguine', performed by Beatrice Lillie in *Seven Lively Arts*. But the self-parody is feeble, and pales before another demolition of the period, from the revue *Sigh No More*, in which Noël Coward told the story of 'Nina from Argentina', a young lady with a violent disgust for everything South American, including Porter's song:

> She declined to begin the Beguine,
> Though they besought her to.
> And in language profane and obscene
> She cursed the man who taught her to.
> She cursed Cole Porter too.

There is no record of Porter ever having taken offence at this, and in any case he had already fired the first shots in the mock-war between the two men. In *Jubilee* the character Eric Dare, a fashionable English playwright, is a facetious sketch of Coward. A more pointed lampoon had appeared in the Kaufman and Hart farce *The Man Who Came to Dinner*, in which Coward is once again used as the model for an English dramatist, Beverly Carlton, who no sooner makes his entrance than he sings his latest song, 'What Am I To Do', composed by Porter at Kaufman's request:

> What am I to say
> To warnings of sorrow,
> When morning's tomorrow
> Greets the dew?
> Will I see the cosmic Ritz
> Shattered and scattered to bits?
> What not am I to do?

Porter published the squib under the name of Noël Porter, and Coward is said to have been much amused. The two men had a great deal in common, both as versifiers and as personalities, and to a limited degree could be said to be mirror-images, Porter representing the chic of America between the wars, and Coward the same qualities of Britain in that age. Each possessed complete mastery of the most demanding of all aspects of the songwriting art, the ability to put words to his own melodies, and each took pleasure in casting himself as the detached urbane darling of society commenting waspishly on its foibles. But there the parallels end. Porter's satire, such as it was, never cut very deep because he retained a snobby affection for the company he kept. Coward was the genuine article, a commentator perfectly capable of telling the story of his own nation in his own lifetime, even though the comment often went unnoticed behind the inspired persiflage of his rhymes.

Porter's only close working partnership with an Englishman was not with Coward but with P. G. Wodehouse, who had a hand in the 1934 success *Anything Goes*. The story of that show makes a better narrative than the sequence of events adopted by the librettists, who total no fewer than four. The original writers were Wodehouse and his old running mate Guy Bolton, but when their script, involving high jinks on an ocean liner, was pre-empted by the real-life tragedy of the *Morro Castle*, which sank off the New Jersey coast with the loss of more than a hundred lives, the producers, unable to locate Wodehouse and Bolton, turned to Howard Lindsay and Russell Crouse to rewrite the show. Wodehouse has recorded one glimpse of the collaborators at work:

I have many pleasant memories of the days when the show was being readied for production, but none I like to recall better than the episode of the drunk at Le Touquet. That was where we collaborators finally got together. At the outset we were rather a scattered bunch. I had a villa at Le Touquet on the Normandy coast of France. Guy was living in Sussex, England, and Cole Porter, as far as I can remember, was in Heidelberg. It was Howard Lindsay, who was to direct the show, who suggested that it would be a good thing if we saw something of each other and had a conference or two, and he finally got us assembled at Le Touquet, which seemed a good central meeting place.

The first thing Guy and I wanted to do, of course, was to hear the music, and as my villa contained no piano we all trooped down to the Casino, where there was one in a corridor leading off the gambling rooms. There the clicking of chips and the croupiers' calls competed with Cole's piano, bringing to our delighted ears the title song, 'You're the Top' and 'Blow, Gabriel, Blow'. Not only to *our* ears. Once, I recall, the door was pushed open by a pleasantly intoxicated young American socialite, who in his befuddled state concluded that Cole was a hired performer.

'Don't play that stuff,' he said. 'Play something good. Do you know "I Wonder Where My Baby Is Tonight"?' Cole did know it and played it without protest. Our visitor began to cry. 'That song hits me right here,' he said, thumping the region of his heart. 'Just been divorced, so can you blame me for wondering?'

We made sympathetic noises, and Cole played 'You're the Top'. The intruder came weaving back through the door.

'Forget that stuff,' he said. 'Do you know a number called "The Horse With the Lavender Eyes"? It drove us down from the Plaza to the church. Dawn said the horse had lavender eyes,' he continued brokenly, 'so we sang the song all the way down the avenue. Dawn O'Day, that was her stage name. Pretty, isn't it?'

He rose and laid a small column of 100-franc chips on top of the piano.

'What's that for?' we asked.

'For him,' he said, indicating Cole. 'He plays okay, but he picks out rotten numbers.'

Anything Goes was one of the most brilliant scores ever written for

Broadway, with Porter's art at its very apex. Even when one of his loveliest melodies, 'Easy to Love', was rejected by the leading man William Gaxton, Porter immediately wrote a replacement just as good, 'All Through the Night'. But he was at his most Porteresque in the compilation of two catalogue songs which have retained their currency ever since. 'You're the Top', a witty laundry list comprising all the symbols of excellence with which Porter had taken such care to surround himself, contained two flattering references to professional rivals, Irving Berlin and Vincent Youmans, besides nodding at Garbo, Mae West and Irene Bordoni. But the title song is the finer piece of the two because the less mechanistic in its musical structure, which in turn has released the lyric from the cage of rumpty-tump. The great model for all the accomplished lyricists of the century, beginning with Wodehouse and embracing Porter, Hart, Dietz and Ira Gershwin, had been W. S. Gilbert, who was, on his own admission, impervious to the subtler shades of musical feeling. Constricted by his inability to concern himself much with what his partner was composing, Gilbert very often produced light verse of the highest quality which is nonetheless doggerel in the sense that its rhythmic variations are minimal. It was here that Coward and Porter in particular had the advantage on their mentor, for they were able to conceive a lyric in the same moment that the first wisps of melody came to them. One of the most pleasurable parlour games connected with the Broadway musical has been detecting those convoluted lines which must surely have been born, words and music together, as an instantaneous idea. Porter has been explicit about the creative process:

> I like to begin with an idea and then fit it to a title. I then write the words and music. Often I begin near the end of a refrain, so that the song has a strong finish, and then work backwards. I also like to use the title phrase at the beginning of a refrain and repeat it at the end for a climax. . . . Writing lyrics is like doing a crossword puzzle.

The title song of *Anything Goes* offers a perfect example of how the ability to play Gilbert to his own Sullivan enabled Porter to break up his lines in a way more interesting by far than the rumpty-tumperies of the Savoy operas. The first four bars of the main theme deploy a rhyme-scheme unusual in the Gilbertian sense, since the rhyming words are placed at different points in their respective bars, so that a pleasing effect of syncopation is achieved:

> In olden days a
> Glimpse of stocking was
> Looked on as something
> shocking. But now God knows . . .

In *The Grand Duke*, Act Two, Gilbert's chorus, in a confidential aside to the audience, uses the identical rhyme but to less ingenious effect:

> And perhaps I'd better mention,
> Lest alarming you I am,
> That it isn't our intention
> To perform a Dithyramb.
> It displays a lot of stocking,
> Which is always very shocking,
> And of course I'm only mocking
> All the prevalence of 'cram'.

Gilbert's extension of the scheme to embrace a triple rhyme cannot conceal the fact that the verse would work perfectly well without any music at all, that he was in effect composing light verse which just happened to be set to music afterwards. Porter, in contrast, and even more strikingly Coward, extended the art by introducing into the tradition of light verse the elements of musical syncopation. Porter's awareness of the English versifying tradition dates back to childhood and to the trifles he concocted while at Yale. One of the shows he wrote for his fellow-students, *The Pot of Gold*, in 1912, included a piece called 'My Houseboat on the Thames', in which Porter refers directly to the source of so much of the deftest versifying of the period:

> . . .It's a jolly ripping vessel to relax on
> For it's deuced dull and deadly Anglo-Saxon.
> We'll have Punch on board, I think,
> one to read and one to drink. . . .

Further evidence of Porter's affection for English versifying generally and Gilbert's in particular turns up much later in the record, in 1941. *Let's Face It*, an army comedy, featured Danny Kaye and Eve Arden singing an exercise in polysyllabic virtuosity called 'Let's Not Talk About Love', which leaned heavily for its inspiration on that moment in *The Sorcerer* when John Wellington Wells makes his introduction:

> Then, if you plan it, he
> Changes organity
> With an urbanity
> Full of Satanity,
> Vexes humanity
> With an inanity
> Fatal to vanity,
> Driving your foes to the verge of insanity.
> Barring tautology

> In demonology,
> 'lectro-biology,
> Mystic nosology
> Spirit philology,
> High-class astrology,
> Such is his knowledge, he
> Isn't the man to require an apology.

More than sixty years on, Porter discovers that Gilbert's old wheeze is still as serviceable as ever; the lyrics which elevated Danny Kaye within a few nights of the show's opening into a star property included these lines:

> . . . bring a jeroboam on
> And write a drunken poem on
> Astrology, mythology,
> Geology, philology,
> Pathology, psychology,
> Electro-physiology,
> Spermology, phrenology?
> I owe you an apology. . . .

In fact the list song was a device which Porter used to telling effect over and over again. One of the earliest commercial successes he ever enjoyed, 'Let's Do It', is an ingenious catalogue of all the things in the universe which enjoy falling in love. Apart from the two laundry lists which enliven *Anything Goes*, Porter wrote at least one other famous list song, which has attached to it the most famous of all the anecdotal footnotes of his career. As the only person who could ever have verified the story was Porter himself, and as it portrays him performing sublime heroics, it might be excusable to question its literal truth, but whether it happened or not, it succeeded in its intended function, of drawing attention to a piece which was certainly deserving of it. In 1937 Porter went to stay with a New York socialite at a house party in Oyster Bay. When his fellow-guests decided to go horse-riding, Porter elected to ride with them, and is said to have selected a skittish mount. While riding along the bridle path with his friends, Porter lost control of the horse, which reared and threw its rider, falling on top of him and crushing one of his legs. Terror-stricken, the horse attempted to regain its feet, but instead rolled over and crushed Porter's other leg. According to the famous story, Porter contrived to make the pain bearable by starting work on a lyric in the agonizing time which dragged on until help came. The song eventuaally emerged as the brilliantly urbane 'At Long Last Love', introduced by Clifton Webb in the following year in a production called *You Never Know*. The anecdote ignores the fact that Porter was one of a group of riders when the accident occurred, so that he would certainly have been discovered instantaneously by the rest of the riding party. But perhaps when talking of the long lonely wait till his rescue Porter was referring to the lapse of time before a van from the local Fire Department arrived to take him to hospital? But no. Any faint chance of bestowing on the story a few shreds of credibility is destroyed by the simple facts. The riding accident occurred on 24 October, 1937. 'At Long Last Love' had been copyrighted on 6 October.

Why should Porter have indulged in all this foolishness, persistently melodramatizing what he, more than almost anybody else, knew to be an arduous craft demanding long hours of solitude? Apparently as a recourse to self-advertisement. All his life he was an insatiable gossip and a shrewd manipulator of the press, an egocentric who enjoyed publicity so long as he was at the centre of it and cast in a favourable light, and the episode of the riding accident makes a fitting bedfellow for the French Foreign Legion and French army tales which saw him performing the same sort of heroics. But the malaise cut much deeper. That Porter was dissatisfied with the body and the temperament with which he had been endowed was clear from schooldays, when he first began embellishing the facts, altering his date of birth to make himself seem more precociously brilliant than he was, telling little white lies concerning his musical erudition and education, resorting to stimulants when reality no longer seemed acceptable. Porter was constantly preoccupied with his physical appearance, studying himself in the looking-glass, nurturing his suntan with comic meticulousness. As his fame grew, so his professional conduct declined. He became notorious for inflicting countless discourtesies on those unable to defend themselves, and often walked out of a room in mid-conversation, sometimes even in mid-sentence. He even grew envious of the success of his musical contemporaries, and once explained to Richard Rodgers his theory that the secret of writing songs which had a mass appeal was to adopt what he defined as a 'Jewish' style, by which apparently he meant minor themes. That so sophisticated a plutocrat should have been so childishly naïve in relation to the one art of which he was a supreme master seems quite unbelievable, and Rodgers later confessed his own astonishment at what Porter had told him.

Not that someone like Rodgers would have appealed much to Porter as a coeval. Rodgers had never attended an Ivy League sanatorium, had never been raised in a climate of opulence, hobnobbed with no countesses. Porter's snobbery was the least likeable aspect of his convoluted personality. And yet when it was a question of earning large fees, he seems to have curbed his tongue when in the courts of the philistines. Especially unpredictable was his affection for Hollywood, which he visited regularly even when not engaged on a production. His experiences at the hands of an executive producer at MGM called Katz read less like life than one of the more outrageous inventions of P. G. Wodehouse in his tales of Jacob Z. Schnellenhamer at the Colossal-Exquisite Studios. In December 1935 Porter began attending conferences for the production eventually to emerge as *Born to Dance*. The plot was to be based on the current scandalous romance between the ancient John Barrymore and a young starlet called Elaine Barrie. Katz decided that the leading roles would be portrayed by Clark Gable and Jean Harlow, which must have come as alarming news for anyone about to write songs for the hero and heroine. At the next meeting Katz announced that, having investigated the situation further, he had reached a decision. Gable and Harlow could not sing. So out went the Barrymore theme. In the absence of even the faintest suspicion of a plot, Katz told Porter that there was no need to worry 'because I can spend $200,000 on authors to give you the right script'. A week later the two original scriptwriters were dropped from the team because of exhaustion. A new team announced its plans for a story about a boy and girl reporter who love each other but are rivals for the Pulitzer Prize for the best newspaper story of the year. Katz, who was by now a strong contender for the worst screen story of any year, thought this was wonderful, but after another week he announced that the newspaper story was out and so were the writers who had submitted it. Porter then took a hand himself, suggesting a story based on the various sections of a newspaper, exactly in the style of Irving Berlin's Broadway revue of three years before, *As Thousands Cheer*. Katz was so overwhelmed by what he considered to be staggering proof of Porter's genius that he advised him to 'go and rest for three weeks'. But the newspaper idea soon followed the others into the trash-can. A week later the picture was going to be about a six-day bicycle race, a blatant plagiarism of the Rodgers and Hart show *The Girl Friend*. A week later the production had put aside its bicycles and was concentrating on the theme of a radio show, a shameless burglary of the *Big Broadcast* series which had proved so profitable to Paramount Pictures. Another week and another plot, this time about some sailors on leave who become acquainted with the members of a Lonely Hearts club. Katz, inspired by the nautical theme to heights of creative euphoria, now gave his team an alarming command: 'I want a scene with two battleships, one covered in boys, the other covered in girls.' Porter began to work, probably in despair, completing a song called 'Goodbye, Little Dream, Goodbye', which moved Katz to dithyramb unprecedented: 'That song is so beautiful it's Jewish.' The next day Porter was informed that 'Goodbye, Little Dream, Goodbye' had inspired such ecstasies on the lot that the studio had decided to sign him for a second picture, raising his fee from $75,000 to $100,000. By May, when production was at last proceeding, Katz asked Porter for an ice ballet for Sonja Henie. As Miss Henie was not in the picture, Porter's disarray is understandable. The ice ballet was soon abandoned and so was 'Goodbye, Little Dream, Goodbye', but Porter was indeed signed for a second picture at the higher salary.

Sometimes the philistinism took a different form, when would-be songwriters decided to denigrate Porter's work in the obvious conviction that they could do better. The case of Ring Lardner is as odd as any in the musical annals. A renowned writer of comic tales in the vernacular, Lardner, like Damon Runyon an ex-sports columnist, began to nurture dreams of a career as a lyricist. Calamitously he also took upon himself the role of guardian of the morals of Tin Pan Alley. However, as Tin Pan Alley had never had any morals, nor had any intention of ever acquiring any, Lardner's posture was comically absurd, but evidently oblivious of the ridiculous nature of the position he had adopted, Lardner embarked on his campaign against what he took to be dirty songs, using the pages of *The New Yorker* as a platform. Among those items which he found deeply offensive were 'Paradise', 'As You Desire Me' and 'Let's Put Out the Lights and Go to Sleep'. In this regard the choice of the last of those three items in particular is interesting, because its weary rejection of the minor pleasures of life could be taken as a glimpse of puritanism, and it must have taken a mind of spectacular prurience to have divined in Herman Hupfeld's innocent lines even the tiniest seeds of pornography. The idiocy of Lardner's campaign embarrassed many of his friends, including Scott Fitzgerald, who later described it as 'an odd little crusade', and Hemingway, who remembered the articles as 'those pitiful dying radio censorship pieces'. But it was not until he persisted with an essay called *Night and Day* that Lardner reduced himself to something worse than absurdity. He had, he told his readers, become disillusioned by the works of Cole Porter, whose lyrics he compared with those of Primo Carnera. This was presumably one of Lardner's much-admired jokes, but it was not until he began attempting to improve on some of Porter's lines and amending his constructions that it began to be clear that what was troubling Lardner was not Porter's lyrics but his own septic ego. It may also have been that Lardner, a famous prude who once boasted of his inability to laugh at a dirty joke, knew something of Porter's private life and decided to express his repugnance through a critique of the songs. Whatever the motivation, Lardner took as his premise the judgement that the line in 'Night and Day' in which Porter maintains his syllabic consistency by inserting between the verb and the adjective a wedge of exclamatory padding:

There's an oh such a hungry yearning burning inside of me. . . .

was feeble, boring and easy to write. Lardner danced blithely into the brick wall of catastrophe by offering his own derisory alternatives, the best of which were:

Night and day, under the bark of me,
There's an oh such a mob of microbes making a park of me.

Having ignored or overlooked Porter's interior rhyme which matches
yearning to burning, Lardner has second thoughts, but replaces the
rhyme in the wrong place:

Night and day under my dermis, dear,
There's a spot just as hot as coffee kept in a thermos, dear.

Porter wisely ignored this outburst of dementia, but it is proof that there
is some aesthetic justice in the world that while 'Night and Day' shows
no sign of losing its charm after more than fifty years, Lardner's career
as a songwriter is totally forgotten. He died soon after mounting his
attack on 'Night and Day', and nobody in the profession knows or cares
that he once composed those bathetic pearls, 'How Far is Heaven From
Here?' and 'Teddy, You're a Bear', or even that long long ago in the
pages of *The New Yorker* he took up arms against Cole Porter and shot
himself in both feet. At least he was spared the chagrin of having to
stand by and witness the triumphal processional of Porter's subsequent
career; it would be especially diverting to know what the Lardner lobby
would have made of Porter's masterpiece when at last it came.

By 1948 Porter's self-confidence had been destroyed by a succession
of what he regarded as failures, by which he meant shows and films
which had not proved profitable to their investors. In retrospect it seems
surprising that he should not have realized that even the most
accomplished writers require some sort of dramatic structure within
which to perform their craft, and that when plot, characterization and
dialogue are witless, as they too often were in the golden age, then even
the most gifted melodist, even the most ingenious rhymer, is likely to
tumble. This explains why some of the very best songs in the popular
catalogue have emerged from dramaturgic disasters so colossal as to
appear comic in retrospect: Gershwin's 'Isn't It a Pity' from *Pardon my
English*, Kern's 'All the Things You Are' from *Very Warm for May*,
James Van Heusen's 'Here's That Rainy Day' from *Carnival in Flanders*
and the same writer's 'Darn that Dream' from *Swinging the Dream*,
Vincent Youmans's 'Time on My Hands' from *Smiles*, and so on. Porter
was no more immune than anyone else from the disease of rickety
librettos and crackpotted characterization, but he seemed to take most
of the blame for the ineptitude of others on to his own shoulders. In
1944 he had composed 'Every Time We Say Goodbye', a moving ballad
of parting which received some attention in America but which in
Britain, once the locals had discovered Ella Fitzgerald's recording,
became the best-loved of any of his songs. Among his other isolated
triumphs had been one of those huge commercial hits whose

background Porter for once had chosen not to publicize.

In 1934, in the wake of the spectacular success of *Anything Goes*, Porter had been contracted by Twentieth Century Fox to write the songs for a production entitled *Adios Argentina*, all about rivalry on the polo field. Because the plot embraced several cowboys suffering pangs of homesickness, Porter knew he would be required to write at least one convincing cowboy song, always assuming that there is such a thing. It so happened that the film's producer, Lou Brock, had recently received a book of poems from his friend Bob Fletcher, a Montana traffic engineer whose hobby was the composition of light verse. In return, Brock suggested to Fletcher that he write some verses with the title 'Don't Fence Me In', with a view to including the song in the new picture. Fletcher then wrote a song, which was sent to the Waldorf-Astoria in New York, where Brock was laying siege to Porter. One week after Porter signed, Brock wrote to Fletcher telling him to send his song to Porter:

> . . . one of our very best composers, who is rated as high as anyone on Broadway at the present time. Unlike most of the others, he also writes his own lyrics and does not as a rule have anyone collaborating with him. However, he was very much interested in your stuff, and what kind of a deal I can work out with him I do not know as these are matters to press somewhat delicately with a man of his standing.

Soon after receiving Fletcher's song, Porter told Brock he wished to buy the right to use Fletcher's title and some of the key phrases of the lyric. Brock arranged a deal for Porter to pay Fletcher $250 in return for the right to use what he wanted of the original lyric. Porter preferred to write a melody of his own, and promised that he would do everything he could to see that Fletcher received credit for his share in the creation of the song. In January 1935 the song was published, complete with a credit for Fletcher beneath the title. The film was then abandoned and the song laid away in the lost limbo of unwanted theatre relics. Ten years later Warner Brothers produced a jingo farrago called *Hollywood Canteen*. By now the Warners owned the publishing house of Harms, which in turn owned 'Don't Fence Me In', so it was perfectly legitimate for Warners to use the song in the new picture, where it was sung by Roy Rogers. It was then taken up by Bing Crosby, who combined with the Andrews Sisters to make a best-seller of this forgotten collaboration between Cole Porter and a highway engineer. But when the song was republished, Fletcher's name was nowhere to be seen, and as the piano copy sold over a million, as did the Crosby recording, it was only to be expected that Fletcher, who legally speaking had no rights to the song, should feel aggrieved. Porter then signed over a percentage of his royalties to Fletcher, and no more was heard of the matter. Fletcher's original later came to light, and was found to contain references to cottonwood trees, the rhyming of 'turn me loose' with 'on my cayoose', the evoking of Western skies, and the closing statement:

I can't stand hobbles and I can't stand fences, don't fence me in.

There was one other episode in the years leading to the consummation of Porter's career which he must have regarded with mixed feelings. In 1945 he had been subjected to the hideous honour which Hollywood bestowed on only a few choice victims: the biopic. What was unusual about the screen biography of Porter was that its hero was still alive at the time the crime was committed. When approached, Porter had agreed to endorse the picture on condition that the part of himself be played by Cary Grant, who instantly agreed. The result, predictably christened *Night and Day*, was no more dishonest than all the other composer-biopics of the period, but it is yet another revealing insight into Porter's idealized view of himself that he should so adamantly have insisted on Cary Grant, the dashing, handsome, debonair hero adored by beautiful women, as his alter ego. It is said that when the veteran publisher Max Dreyfus, mentor to Kern, Rodgers, Gershwin, Romberg, Youmans and Porter himself, was asked who he wished to portray him in a projected biopic, the octogenarian Max, a shrivelled little walnut of a man, replied 'Clark Gable'. But Dreyfus had been joking, whereas Porter when he called for Cary Grant was being perfectly serious.

Evidently the film *Night and Day* had done nothing to buttress Porter's sagging ego. When the writer Bella Spewack completed a script of a musical adaptation of *The Taming of the Shrew*, her first choice as composer was Burton Lane, still basking in the afterglow of the great success of *Finian's Rainbow*. But Lane announced that he was committed to other projects, which is mystifying in view of the fact that another eighteen years were to pass before he found himself free enough to compose another Broadway score, for *On a Clear Day You Can See Forever*. Miss Spewack, who could not wait that long, now demanded the services of Cole Porter, who, on first meeting, rejected the idea out of hand for a multiplicity of reasons. He felt no affinity to Shakespeare; his instincts told him that the whole idea was too highbrow for the commercial theatre of Broadway; he sensed that his style was unsuitable. But the real reason for his unwillingness to commit himself was the string of indifferent projects with which he had been associated over the previous few years. That he should have been so disheartened by failure is surprising, since most of the flops had come about through no fault of his own, certainly not from any significant waning of his powers. A current census to find the 35 most popular songs of all time in America had listed his work no fewer than five times: 'What Is This Thing Called Love?', 'Night and Day', 'I Get a Kick Out of You', 'Begin the Beguine', 'Just One of Those Things'. While he must privately have grieved over the omission of items like 'In the Still of the Night', 'I Concentrate on You' and 'Let's Do It', he ought surely have been encouraged to grasp the nettle being offered to him by Miss Spewack. She finally had her way by resorting to that most peculiar of devices, Porter's latent jealousy of his Jewish rivals. Still as firmly convinced as ever that the success of the Gershwins and the Kerns and the Rodgerses was in some obscure way linked to their Jewishness, Porter was prevailed upon to think again when the cunning Miss Spewack explained to him the overtones of the Yiddish theatre to be found in Shakespeare's plot. Spurious though the theory was, it was enough to galvanize Porter, who now produced his masterwork, one of the outstanding scores of the century for one of its best musicals.

He drew upon several sources for his songs. Some were vintage Porter and could have come out of any show, especially 'So in Love', a conventional romantic ballad, and 'Another Op'nin', Another Show', a typical backstage anthem. Others, like 'I've Come to Wive It Wealthily in Padua' and 'Where is the Life that Late I Led?' cleverly remind the listener of the story's Shakespearean roots, while 'Brush Up Your Shakespeare', delivered by a pair of illiterate slobs, is the irreverent schoolboy's dream of anti-bardolatry, with its perverse irreverence:

> If your blonde won't respond when you flatter 'er,
> Tell her what Tony told Cleopatterer.

Kiss Me Kate became by far the most successful as well as the best-crafted work of Porter's life. His longest previous run had been *Let's Face It*, with 547 performances. *Kiss Me Kate* ran for over a thousand, and has since entered the permanent repertoire of the musical theatre. Only once in the score of the show is there any suggestion of any other than Shakespearean sources, and that is in the song 'Always True to You in My Fashion', a dazzling piece of work which contains resonances of the English poet Ernest Dowson (1867–1900) whose most famous work, 'Non sum qualis eram . . .', contains the reiterated 'I have been faithful to thee, Cynara! in my fashion'. Dowson, who died in abject poverty as a young man, left to starve in the richest city in the world, has suffered the ironic fate of becoming one of the most famous posthumous one-liners in history. It may be that Porter read him at college, or perhaps was introduced to him during the furore attending the first and last novel of Margaret Mitchell, which borrowed its title, 'Gone With the Wind', from Dowson. Long after *Kiss Me Kate*, Johnny Mercer was to find himself writing the title lyrics for a picture about two drunks; the title was 'Days of Wine and Roses', again from Dowson. None of Porter's biographers and annotators has made any reference to Dowson, but the song whose title was certainly inspired by him incorporated one of Porter's most ingenious lyrics:

> Mister Harris, plutocrat,
> Wants to give my cheek a pat.
> If a Harris pat means a Paris hat, Bebe!

After *Kiss Me Kate* there were further, lesser triumphs, 'It's All Right With Me' and the last of the vintage catalogue songs, 'All of You'. He retired in 1958 and died six years later, having endured long years of agony as the surgeons performed one operation after another in a vain attempt to ease the pain in his shattered legs, one of which was eventually amputated. And so, at last, because of a temperamental horse at a weekend house party, Porter found himself cast as the stoic martyr to physical pain he had once pretended to be.

Porter's life demonstrates the proof of the proposition that a man's bank account will sometimes condition the manner in which he resolves a discord or selects his adjectives. There is such a thing as a Cole Porter song, a Cole Porter style, compounded of elements indefinable yet instantly recognizable: a certain soigné impudence, a smartness, a period sheen, and, in the love ballads, something deeply moving because of the sheer intensity of the passion expressed. Porter was what the songwriter becomes when he is far too rich ever to need to work, yet cannot resist the compulsion. For all his grandfather's millions, for all the generous subsidizing by his wife, Porter drove himself like a starving man, writing words and music for 27 musicals, numerous college shows, assorted films and dozens of individual songs. Why? Apart from the fact that his innate gifts were far too strong to resist, Porter was pursued by demons all his life, and one in particular. Raised among wealth by an over-solicitous mother and a cantankerous grandfather, the pride of a family in which his own father was little more than a cipher, Porter exchanged one mother for another by marrying Linda Lee Thomas, and confined his love-life to his own sex. On the surface his life and career were triumphant. He became world-famous, a man celebrated by his peers, one of America's greatest artists. The evidence suggests that all this was not enough. There was something badly wrong somewhere. The times were in some way out of joint. In the 1920s, while still a young man, he wrote an unpublished piece significantly titled 'Poor Young Millionaire', yet another catalogue, but this time of all the things which had already lost their appeal to him:

> Tired of sporting, tired of flirting,
> Tired of courting, tired of racing,
> Tired of yachting, tired of loafing,
> Tired of rotting. . . .

The goblin which stalked him was boredom. One of the greatest of all popular songs, written in 1934, opens with these lines:

> My story is much too sad to be told,
> But practically everything leaves me totally cold.
> The only exception I know is the case
> When I'm out on a quiet spree
> Fighting vainly the old ennui
> And I suddenly turn and see
> Your fabulous face.

It is only a song, and songs, we understand, are not meant to be taken very seriously. But it would be a gross misjudgement to assume that because a writer puts his emotions into a song, they are not his emotions. Johnny Mercer's perceptions of approaching death were certainly synthesized into his later verses. Alan Lerner's belief in the paranormal glows behind half the songs he ever wrote, and Porter in his songs expresses the moral dilemma of a man to whom one of the most unfortunate misfortunes has occurred: he has got what he always wanted and is no longer sure he ever really wanted it. The persistent reiteration of the themes of boredom, of ennui, of disenchantment, of disillusion with the minor pleasures of life, was what gave his work that distinctive essence. The last song of his life, written for a televised version of *Aladdin*, with a libretto by S. J. Perelman, was delivered by Basil Rathbone, who must have been aware, like the rest of us, that the songwriter was speaking from the heart:

> Wouldn't it be fun not to be famous.
> Wouldn't it be fun not to be rich.
> Wouldn't it be pleasant
> To be a simple peasant
> And spend a happy day digging a ditch.
> Wouldn't it be fun not to be known as an important V.I.P.
> Wouldn't it be fun to be nearly anyone
> Except me, mighty me.

P. G. Wodehouse observed of those songwriters who specialized in pieces about going back to the farm, that had anyone taken them at their word they would have asked for police protection. And no doubt if someone had offered to grant Cole Porter his dearest wish and divest him of his wealth, he too would have recoiled in horror. Even so, it seems likely that the villain of the piece may well have been old J.O., who, by dying in 1923, turned his gifted grandson into a millionaire several times over. As Frank Sinatra and Celeste Holm ask each other in *High Society*, who wants to be a millionaire?

CHAPTER FOUR

Noël Coward

There is nothing which so disconcerts thc English as a man with two professions, unless it be a man with three. Noël Coward, who mastered at least six and dabbled in several others, has caused the entire critical battalion to retire in comic disarray. There has been a price to pay for this virtuosity. Coward remains underrated even by his most dedicated boosters, whose range of appreciation, being less comprehensive than Coward's, has disqualified them from any attempt to see their man whole. The playgoer who revels in the badinage of the first act of *Private Lives* has no faint suspicion of the harmonic subtleties of 'Mad About the Boy', and the musicians who never stop to think what Coward was doing in that tank of oily water at Denham Studios in *In Which We Serve* knew nothing of the short stories. The fortunate few who witnessed his late flowering as a consummate cabaret artist were never much interested in his portrayal of Shaw's Caesar or King Magnus; those who thrilled to the sentimental charm of Coward the leading man in his own plays never thought of him as the successor to Gilbert as a purveyor of comic verse whose lightness of touch often concealed a cutting edge of acute social comment. Coward's careers as director, dramatist, performer and writer fall far beyond the confines of the popular song, but even had he written nothing else but the songs he would have been a dominant figure. He remains almost the only Englishman to bear comparison with the best American songwriters, and certainly the only one able, like Porter and Berlin, to provide words to his own music, His nearest rival, Ray Noble, who composed half a dozen memorable melodies and sometimes added his own words, and who enjoyed a brief hour of thespian glory playing a silly ass in the Astaire picture *A Damsel in Distress*, was far adrift of Coward in most respects and, being an engagingly modest man, would have been embarrassed by the comparison.

Coward's songs fall into three categories: those in which the melody

NOËL COWARD

is no more than a pleasant accompaniment to a set of scintillating lyrics, those whose sumptuous melodic allure remains in the mind when the words have faded, and a third group in which the writer achieves the perfect synthesis of words and music to create that elusive entity, the classic standard song, qualifying their creator for inclusion among the élite of his profession. The items in all three categories are world-famous, but what is less widely appreciated is the intuitive nature of Coward's art, its freedom from the trammels of academic law either literary or musical. To locate its roots we need to excavate territory not often concerned with the genesis of popular song: the live theatre. Most of his rivals were abject performers. Kern, Warren and Berlin ranked among the great deadbeats of the keyboard, and Porter made commercial recordings as a singer-pianist which were bad enough to make nonsense of the claim of one of his biographers that had he not taken to songwriting he could have earned a comfortable living as an entertainer. This remarkable theory was once expounded to André Previn, who observed, 'If that's true, then Porter must have had a great magic act he was hiding from everybody.' Of the major songwriters, only George Gershwin and Johnny Mercer could have been successful as performers. However, George could play but not sing; Mercer could sing but not play. Coward, on the other hand, was one of the great performers of his day, for which reason it becomes impossible to distance his songs from the way he interpreted them.

All his music bears the vivid signature of the man responsible for it. This is true to some extent of all composers, all lyricists, but especially so of Coward, who took so much trouble, and devoted so much energy and ingenuity to the building of a public persona compounded in equal parts of flippancy and sincerity, elegance and slapstick, wit and gravity, romantic fervour and wicked derision. Each of these qualities might imply the contradiction of all the others, wherein lies the essence of Coward's attraction as a songwriter. One moment he is the rampant jingo patriot of *Cavalcade*, the next the derisory chronicler of the loony empire-builders. When he waxed romantic few lyricists could match the intensity of his passion, yet he could be gloriously vulgar about the ludicrous nature of love. It is terrifying enough attempting to digest his complete oeuvre, but even within the frontiers of a single province of his career, the contradictions can be bewildering. George M. Cohan shared with him the convention of composing only those songs which had been filtered through the mannerisms of his performing style; Cole Porter sometimes suggested Coward in his leaps from fervour to frivolity. But Cohan painted only in primary colours, and Porter in his lighter moods was being no more than facetious. Neither man aspired to the satiric social comment of which Coward was the consummate master. He has no parallel.

The most impressive fact of all about Coward in the musical theatre is his lack of a formal education. Most of the composers of standard songs managed very well without the impediment of academic quackery, but the lyricists have often been men like Hart, Dietz, Porter, Wodehouse and Hammerstein, whose exposure to the English curriculum endured at any rate into their late teens. No more erudite or technically accomplished versifier than Coward ever devoted his talents to the popular song, yet if his account of things is to be believed, he spent hardly any time in the schoolroom at all. Instead he received a much more valuable education, in the performing arts. Considering the bald facts of his heredity and early environment, it is impossible to imagine him in any role in life other than man of the theatre. Born into the shabby-genteel stratum of turn-of-century Teddington, of a mother who came from 'a good family' but had no money, Coward found himself cushioned from birth by the cameraderie of amateur music-making. His parents and all his aunts and uncles were pillars of the local church choir; one of the group, Aunt Hilda, transcended the rest in vocal glory and became renowned as 'The Twickenham Nightingale'. His father worked for a music publisher and later became a piano salesman. The parents conducted a choral courtship born out of an amateur production of *The Gondoliers*. Their son was encouraged to perform even as a tot, and made his public debut when he was seven; the occasion was a school concert, at which two revealing facts emerge. The song he sang was 'Coo' from *The Country Girl*, and he accompanied himself at the piano. The choice of aria reflects the musical conditioning in genteel English operetta to which he was already being exposed, and the identity of the accompanist suggests a freakish aptitude, considering his tender years and apparent lack of any instruction. Neither Coward nor any of his biographers mentions childhood piano lessons, yet clearly the young Coward displayed extraordinary affinity with the instrument. The most thorough of his biographers, Cole Lesley, says this of his subject at the age of fifteen, on returning from a musical matinee:

> He had developed the extraordinary gift of being able, as soon as he got in the door, to rush to the piano and play by ear most of the score complete with verses and the correct harmonies. With the aid of a booklet of the lyrics which you could in those days buy for sixpence he was able to play and sing them, words and all, straight away. He never forgot those much-loved scores, and forever after would gladly play and sing them for us at the drop of a hat.

Lesley mentions among other works which affected Coward in this way Oscar Straus's *A Waltz Dream* and *The Chocolate Soldier*, Lehar's *The Merry Widow* and Lionel Monckton's *The Quaker Girl*; Monckton had also composed the song with which the infant Coward had made his debut at a school concert, and there is no question that all these writers and several others were strong influences on Coward in his intermittent ventures into operetta.

By the time he was ten Coward was a professional actor, having emerged from a brief course of dancing lessons in time to accept the role of a small fish in a fairy play called *The Goldfish*, a work with no relevance today apart from Coward's involvement and the coincidence that the first words he ever uttered on a professional stage were 'Hello Dolly'. Once launched as a precocious child actor there was no stopping him, and even so powerful a figure as Charles Hawtrey was obliged to endure his young protégé's cheeky intrusions on his privacy. The first emergence of the songwriter is dated by his biographers as 1916, when he wrote a song comically world-weary for so untried a sprig. It was called 'Forbidden Fruit' and hinted at the pointlessness of existence:

> Ordinary man invariably sighs
> For what cannot be.

Having served notice of one musical mood for which he was to become notorious, within a year he had introduced another. In August 1917 he writes to his mother from the Gaiety Theatre, Manchester, where he is appearing in a play called *Wild Heather*. The letter is feverish with the excitement of expectations about to be fulfilled at last; he is writing a song in collaboration with another aspiring composer, Max Darewski. Although the song came to nothing, the friendship endured to the extent that Max passed Coward on to his publisher brother Herman, who, in his dealings with this unknown young man, displayed a fetching combination of generosity and dementia. Coward was always to find the business conventions of Tin Pan Alley quaint to the brink of lunacy, and nothing more vividly exemplifies this than the episode of his contract with Darewski:

Through the influence of Max, I signed a three-year contract with his brother Herman, who at that time was head of a music publishing firm in Charing Cross Road. The contract was for lyrics only, and I was to be paid fifty pounds the first year, seventy-five pounds the second year and one hundred pounds the third year. I appeared dutifully every week or so for the first few months, armed with verses and ideas for songs. I waited many hours in the outer office, and sometimes even penetrated into the next-to-outer office, but seldom if ever clapped eyes on Herman Darewski, and nobody seemed at all interested in my lyrics. At the end of the first year I began to get a little anxious about the second instalment of seventy-five pounds. But I needn't have worried because it was paid to me without rancour, on the day specified. During the third year of my contract I was too busy with other affairs to go near the office until the last day, when I called to receive my cheque for a hundred pounds. Herman Darewski's third or fourth secretary handed it to me with a charming smile, and, after a brief exchange of social amenities, I had a cup of tea in the outer office and went home. Soon after this, the Herman Darewski publishing firm went bust, a fact that has never altogether astonished me.

Among the promising items which Darewski and his regiment of secretaries overlooked was one which establishes the comic Coward with unmistakable style. The Gilbertian device of concocting a convenient real name to rhyme is the only outside influence on this otherwise typical piece of Coward lyric-writing:

> Annabel Devigne
> Had a flat at Golder's Green,
> And her ways were really most endearing.
> She desired to learn a bit
> And she thought she'd make a hit
> If she did a little auctioneering.
> On a box she'd take her stand
> With a hammer in her hand
> And a firm resolve to keep from skidding.
> But don't think that she fell,
> She went most awfully well
> With the men who came to do her bidding.
>
> Anna was an auctioneer
> Though what she sold is not quite clear.
> And as a business woman she
> May never quite have shone.
> She discovered young men's choice was
> To hear how nice her voice was –
> Going, going, gone.

Something just as typical as the ballad of Annabel Devigne emerges from Coward's account of the Darewski connection. In his short stories as well as in some of his revue sketches and verses, Coward proved to be the annalist of a peculiar subsection of domestic seediness, the theatrical boarding house. Groomed by long experience for connoisseurship of the aromatic implications of cabbage soup and only slightly soiled bedlinen, of flyblown prints of *The Stag at Bay* and its uncanny resemblance to the landlady who had placed it over a grease-stain on the parlour wall, Coward enjoyed the sentimental joke of the professional darlings looking back to their apprenticeship in provincial digs. Insulated by fame and money from the horrors of the bad old days, they are able to look back and sigh over them with a very real affection:

> Touring days, touring days, what ages it seems to be
> Since the landlady at Norwich
> Served a mouse up in the porridge
> And a beetle in the morning tea.
> Touring days, alluring days, far back into the past we gaze.
> We used to tip the dressers every Friday night
> And pass it over lightly when they came in tight,
> But somehow to us it seemed all right,
> Those wonderful touring days.

Coward knew all about that sort of life while he was still in his teens, and has left just such an affectionate portrait of slatternly making-do as lights the lyric of the song and others like it. While working on the piece with Max Darewski, Coward was staying with a Mancunian chatelaine called Mrs Wood in Lloyd Street:

> She waited up every night for me and brought me my supper on a tray. It was usually Heinz baked beans, or welsh rarebit or something equally delicious, and she used to sit on the edge of a large feather bed and gossip with me while I ate it. It was a bright room with a permanently crooked Venetian blind veiled demurely by white lace curtains. There was an incandescent gas bracket with the mantle broken at the end, which shed an acid yellow glare over everything and almost succeeded in taking the colour out of the eiderdown. There was a fire-screen ornament in the grate made of crinkled paper, and on the mantelpiece several photographs of Mrs Wood's sister as Sinbad the Sailor in tights leaning against a log of wood. The bathroom was down one flight of stairs and contained a fierce geyser which blew up occasionally, and once completely destroyed the fringe of a well-known character actress.

The researcher who goes to the source looking for early pieces like 'Annabel Devigne' and 'Touring Days' will not find them. Late in life, when compiling his collected lyrics, Coward amended them into selected lyrics, remarking in his preface that 'it is not that I am ashamed of having written them, even the worst ones; it is merely impractical to overweight an already weighty book with a lot of repetitious and inferior work for the dubious reason that I happened to have written it.' For the first indications that his musical gifts were maturing, there was the revue *London Calling*, which included a fetching exercise in sentimental whimsy called 'Parisian Pierrot'; soon after came a second revue, *On With the Dance*, which echoes with the resonance of childhood days in the church choir, and which includes the first of those Coward songs with the curious knack of evoking the distinct flavour of a certain passage in London post-war life, when those who were enjoying themselves included that group of monumental dullards the Bright Young Things. 'Poor Little Rich Girl' retains its currency more than sixty years after the event, although its contents are apt to surprise those who might hardly be aware that it has any contents at all. The sentiments of the song are fiercely puritanical, waving an admonishing finger at those for whom the temptations of loose living are irresistible. The song has usually created the diametrically opposite impression, of a writer celebrating the tipsy abandon of the period. The same is true of the song's companion piece, 'Dance Little Lady', which delivers the same sermon, sugared with the same surging sophistication of its rhythmic patterns, an ironic invitation to the very dance of which the lyric so sternly disapproves. Each song stands as a well-intentioned warning to reckless youth, and each harps on the theme of Time racing by. Coward was certainly not the only writer of the period to adopt this stance; it may be found in the early novels of Evelyn Waugh and in some of the rhymes of John Betjeman, whose 'Varsity Students' Rag':

> We had a rag at Monico's. We had a rag at the Troc:
> And the one we had at the Berkeley gave the customers quite a shock.
> Then we went to the Popular, and after that – oh my!
> I wish you'd seen the rag we had in the Grill Room at the Cri.

might almost be the text of a revue song, except for its inability to stray from its own well-beaten rhythmic path. What saved Coward from the rhythmic limitations of light verse was his musical range. Betjeman's lyric is Gilbertian, not Cowardesque, a distinction which Coward took considerable pains to define. In describing the verse of a lady friend of his teens with whom he dabbled in collaboration, he has this to say:

> Being a natural musician, I found it easier to write tunes jangling in my head than to devote myself to mastering iambics, trochees, anapaests, or dactyls. If a tune came first I would set words to it. If the words came first I would set them to music at the piano. This latter process almost invariably necessitated changing the verse to fit the tune. If you happen to be born with a built-in sense of rhythm, any verse you write is apt to fall into a set pattern and remain within its set pattern until it is completed. This is perfectly satisfactory from the point of view of reading or reciting, but when you attempt to set your pattern to a tune, either the tune gives in and allows itself to be inhibited by the rigidity of your original scansion or it rebels, refuses to be dominated and displays some ideas of its own, usually in the form of unequal lines and unexpected accents. This is why I very seldom write a lyric first and set it to music later. I think that the best

lyrics I have written are those which have developed more or less at the same time as the music.

As this is the most coherent exposition of the hoary which-comes-first question, it is a pity it ranks among its author's more esoteric statements, but what might appear complex becomes simple enough through reference to Coward's texts. In 'Poor Little Rich Girl', the reader of the selected lyrics will find:

> Though you're a child, dear,
> Your life's a wild typhoon . . .

which is in fact a beautifully balanced rhyming couplet, even though there is a syllabic disparity between the lines; the rhymed couplet is built on two four-syllable statements, with the apparent imbalance adjusted by a delightful extension on the musical phrase to accommodate the word 'typhoon'. Coward found this kind of writing simple enough, but that was because he was his own collaborator. Wodehouse has testified that whatever felicities might be found in his lyrics were due entirely to the melodies provided for him by Kern, without whom, according to Wodehouse, none of the charm of the songs they wrote together would ever have existed. The enigma of collaboration becomes of paramount importance in assessing the talent of a songwriter who has worked with two contrasting stylists, as in the case of Richard Rodgers. For Coward, like Berlin and Porter, the problem simply did not exist.

As he was still under thirty when he wrote 'Dance Little Lady', he was perhaps rather too callow to be handing out sage advice to the younger set, but as nobody took the advice or even realized what it was, the point was overlooked. In any case, Coward's reputation by now was of such a nature as to have nullified anything he might have said on behalf of the virtues of self-denial. In November 1924, a few days before his twenty-fifth birthday, he had starred in his own play, *The Vortex*, a work which was, by the standards of the day, candid beyond the bounds of discretion. Its twin themes, drug addiction and the love of an older woman for a much younger man, though commonplace enough in the real world, seemed outrageous when exposed to a fashionable theatre audience. The Lord Chamberlain defined the play as 'unpleasant', Gerald Du Maurier dismissed it as 'filth', and business at the box-office had never been brisker. Overnight *The Vortex* flung Coward into that category of freaks whose every action, every word, every whim, is considered newsworthy. For the rest of his life it was to be his fate to be lit by the lurid lamps of celebrity. From now on there would always be crowds waiting at the stage-door, reporters snooping at the tradesman's entrance. Suddenly his greatest creation, himself, had become transmuted into a symbolic figure of the age. Among those who expressed this idea was the novelist Stella Gibbons:

> I was present at the very first performance of *The Vortex*, in a little kind of converted drill-hall in Hampstead, and remember how shocked I was at the drug-addict boy (he would have been called a Drug Fiend in those days by ordinary people), and ever since I have had so much enduring pleasure and laughter from his songs and jokes. He seems to me to incarnate the *myth* of the 'twenties (gaiety, courage, pain concealed, amusing malice) and that photograph . . . with prised fingertips held to hide the mouth, with the eyes delightfully smiling, is an incarnation in another form, even to the extreme elegance of the clothes.

Although neither *The Vortex*, nor indeed almost any of Coward's plays has any relevance in the context of his musical career, one effect they did have was to dub him the mouthpiece of the reckless self-indulgence of the young. Like the newspaper proprietor who boosts his circulation by publishing salacious gossip which he pretends disgusts him, Coward had suddenly emerged as a key figure of his generation by daring to mention the dramaturgically unmentionable, so that from now on anything he wrote, acted or said was taken to be scandalous. In fact Coward's motive for writing *The Vortex* appears to have been sternly moral, a passion inspired by his affection for the mother of one of his friends, Grace Forster, who was once subjected, within Coward's earshot, to abuse because of her age. The private Coward retained a lifelong abhorrence for those indulgences which deprive the victim of self-control, whether drugs or alcohol. But the gilded reputation carried with it a huge audience determined to see in this oddly untypical young man an argument for well-mannered, meticulously dressed and manicured debauchery. Yet a glance at his early song lyrics shows how absurd all this was. His advice to his poor little rich girl includes the remark 'the role you are acting, the toll is exacting, soon you'll have to pay'. To his dancing little lady he issues an even more peremptory warning: 'Laughter some day dies, and when the lights are starting to gutter, dawn through the shutter shows you're living in a world of lies.'

It is revealing that as early as the mid-1920s Coward's integration of a high intelligence into the frame of the popular song was exposing his work either to misunderstanding or bowdlerization. When, in the composition of 'Poor Little Rich Girl', he ended with:

> You're weaving love into a mad jazz pattern
> Ruled by Pantaloon.
> Poor little rich girl, don't drop a stitch too soon.

he could have given no thought to his reference to a stock character from Venetian comedy. The London theatre audience was well able to digest the reference, even if it was not able to quote the relevant chapter and verse. But what of American audiences? Coward was a successful songwriter whose reputation was mid-Atlantic. How might Broadway and Hollywood react to such comparative erudition in the popular song: In the event, by excising it. The Judy Garland recording of 'Poor Little Rich Girl' finds us listening to a spirited and tuneful interpretation marred by the ending, which has now been reduced to gibberish:

> You're weaving love into a mad jazz pattern
> Ruled by Sun and Moon.
> Poor little rich girl, don't drop a stitch too soon.

Whether or not Miss Garland's advisers took the reference to mean one half of a pair of knee-length trousers and, having reached that conclusion, decided that for the world to be ruled by half a pair of pants was ridiculous, we will never know. What we do know is that Coward was always meticulous concerning the structure, vocabulary and execution of the popular song, whether his own or those of others, and the insertion of Sun-Moon, always assuming he was aware of it, must have given him some pain. Nor was it the only occasion on which his American friends took his beautifully crafted lyrics in not quite the right way. *This Year of Grace* became newsworthy for several reasons, one of which was Coward's amazing exhibition of virtuosity. It was the first time he had been allowed to write everything: words, music, sketches; the effect was to extend his reputation into the realms of infallibility. And, to consummate the process, a delicious element of snobbery intruded in the form of the heir to the throne, who let it be known that one of the show's musical items, 'A Room With a View', was his special favourite. In spite of this, the song is quite pleasant, but it did not always inspire such enthusiasm among Coward's associates. When *This Year of Grace* arrived on Broadway, among those who took exception to the lyrics of 'A Room With a View' was Alexander Woollcott, an elephantine drama critic whose fame was sustained only so long as he remained alive to sustain it, and who would be forgotten altogether were it not that immortality was bestowed upon him at one remove when Kaufman and Hart used him as the model for Sheridan Whiteside in *The Man Who Came To Dinner*. During his career, Woollcott was an excessively opinionated and narcissistic man who believed in express-ing his prejudices in as flamboyant a way as could be devised. What particularly incensed him about Coward's song was the cloying couplet:

> Maybe a stork will bring
> This that and t'other thing. . . .

Taking his own dissent as an opportunity for self-advertisement, Woollcott hired a box for one of the performances, filled it with cronies who included Harpo Marx, and did what he could to disrupt Coward's performance of the song by noisily reading a newspaper, no doubt containing one of his own reviews. As his entire journalistic output consisted precisely of the gushing euphemism to be found in the offending lyric, it is hard to see what animated Woollcott's foolish behaviour, which was by no means excused by the fact that Coward agreed with him about the song. Not long after the incident he told his producer, C. B. Cochran, 'I can't go on singing those terribly slushy words. It's more than I can bear, and more than one should expect of the audience.' The onus of delivering the words was passed over to another member of the cast, leaving Coward free to resume the triumphal processional of his career. Because that career incorporated the writing of several plays, he was in the unique position of being able every now and then to provide his characters with musical diversions. One of the stark differences between characters on the stage and their real-life counterparts is that real people are forever singing, playing, whistling, humming, tapping. Just as Wodehouse was to take advantage of his own duality to tell us what the characters in his novels are singing and whistling, so Coward on one famous occasion allowed the audience at one of his comedies to hear the most intimate thoughts of his hero and heroine put to music. *Private Lives*, his most renowned play, features a pair of lovers played in the original production by Coward himself and his favourite actress, Gertrude Lawrence. At one stage in the story, the pair of them converge on the piano and perform 'Someday I'll Find You' in a style which perhaps owed more to romantic intensity than to musical brilliance. Miss Lawrence, a formidable virtuoso in the art of musical comedy, was a vivid example of personality overcoming the limitations of nature. One of the other distinguished composers who wrote for her, Kurt Weill, told Alan Lerner, 'Gertie Lawrence has the greatest range between C and C sharp of anyone I know', but as Lerner added, when she sang she somehow made music. Coward, too, was a singer who invented his own style. After the first performance of *Private Lives*, Mrs Patrick Campbell entered his congested dressing-room and inquired of the friends assembled there: 'Don't you love it when he does his little hummings at the piano?' Coward was by no means always aware of the origin of these little hummings. Like Arthur Schwartz, who was confronted by the melody of 'You and the Night and the Music' while on board ship thinking of quite other things, Coward knew the deep pleasure and gratification of serendipity as it applied to his own work. In 1929, having completed the book of *Bitter Sweet* with his usual ease, he was struggling to finish the score while appearing in the New York run of *This Year of Grace*:

After a matinée, driving across town in a taxi to get his precious, sacred rest between the shows, the tune of 'I'll See You Again' dropped into his head in its entirety during a long traffic jam, with drivers honking their klaxons all around him. This was one of the miracles which forever mystified Noël and which no one, least of all himself, could explain: 'How can a theme come to me complete like that? How can it be accounted for, and where does it come from?' Stuck in the taxi he had no time to question the miraculous but went over and over the melody in his head for fear of losing it. When he did get to his apartment (he could not write music down and this was long before the days of tape recorders) he had to play it over, over and over again on the piano until 'I'll See You Again' was fixed in his memory.

It comes with the shock of revelation to be reminded once again how utterly innocent of all instrumental artifice Coward was. As with Berlin, the simplicities of musical notation were beyond him. Yet he was able to conjure rich melody and harmony over a forty-year period. The lack of any connection between musical ability and musicality, between a knowledge of music and the ability to create it, comes home even more forcibly in the case of Irving Berlin, but Coward's case is almost as stupefying. Much more mysterious to him was another visitation whose circumstances are stranger by far than those applying to 'I'll See You Again'. In 1934, he fulfilled a long-standing ambition by writing an operetta for his idol Yvonne Printemps. Retiring to his farm near Romney Marsh, Coward began writing the songs for this new show, to be called *Conversation Piece*, but made the mistake of confiding his plan to his producer, Cochran, who instantly informed the newspapers. The fever of expectancy which followed put pressures on the composer which, just for once, cramped his style. For ten days he laboured to find the major waltz theme without which none of his musical works as complete. Nothing came. At last, in deep despair he decided to advise Cochran to postpone the opening for six months:

I poured myself a large whisky and soda, dined in grey solitude, poured myself another, even larger whisky and soda, and sat gloomily envisaging everybody's disappointment and facing the fact that my talent had withered and that I should never write any more music until the day I died. The whisky did little to banish my gloom, but there was no more work to be done and I didn't care if I became fried as a coot, so I gave myself another drink and decided to go to bed. I switched off the lights at the door and noticed that there was one lamp left on by the piano. I walked automatically to turn it off, sat down and played 'I'll Follow My Secret Heart', straight through in G flat, a key I had never played in before.

Coward evidently believed that the unfamiliar key, which was the only one in which Irving Berlin ever composed, and which may be more familiar to amateurs as F sharp, the home of the black notes, only compounded the mystery. In fact, it may go some way towards explaining it. The unfamiliar alignments of a strange new key can sometimes have a most inspiriting effect on the executant, and it would not be stretching the truth too far to say that any musical piece, when transposed into a different key, becomes a different composition. This is a truism familiar to every instrumentalist. But that was the point. Coward was not an instrumentalist. If he had been, he would surely have explored the possibilities of modulation before giving up the ghost. Instead he remained overcome by the perversities of his own muse. There is a strong case to be made that 'I'll Follow My Secret Heart' is the loveliest of all Coward's pieces, the perfect marriage of words and music, the ravishing upward swoops of the melodic line matched by the deeply moving unspoiled sincerity of the words, proclaiming the resolve to defend the purity of romantic dreams from the inroads of reality. It is one of that group of Coward compositions which transcends its environment, its time and place, to become one of the great standard songs of the modern era, its musical beauty melting into the depth of its poetic emotion, and a far cry indeed from the world of the Bright Young Things. Only marginally less moving was the song from *Bitter Sweet* which for a long time was eclipsed in the popularity stakes by 'I'll See You Again' but which has a far maturer set of words. 'If Love Were All' is the *cri de coeur* of what the verse defines as 'a humble diseuse', whose life has been a long succession of romantic disappointments, and whose quiet, brave desperation is expressed at the end of the first chorus:

> Heigho, if love were all
> I should be lonely.

If 'I'll Follow My Secret Heart' expresses the idea of romantic idealism at the outset of its long journey, then 'If Love Were All' tells of the end of that journey, ending in defeat and loneliness but not quite complete disillusion. Yet again, Coward was elevating the pretensions of the popular song to a plane of expression hardly ever attempted; there were even occasions when, having arrived at his melody, he found himself tempted by several contradictory lyric moods and succumbed to all of them, as in *Words and Music*, the revue of 1932 which ranks alongside *The Bandwagon* as the outstanding example of the genre. Apart from being one of his very best tunes, 'Mad About the Boy' sees Coward deploying his lyric virtuosity to startling effect. The heroine of the song exists in four personas. She is the streetwalker who feels 'there's maybe something sad about the boy'; the society woman who suspects 'there are traces of the cad about the boy'; the cockney housemaid who admits she's 'got it bad about the boy'; and the schoolgirl, who is convinced that 'Housman really wrote "The Shropshire Lad" about the boy'. Alan Lerner, one of the very few of Coward's contemporaries to possess a comparable command of the English language, has suggested that the closing statement by the society lady constitutes 'the essence of Cowardiana':

> Will it ever cloy,
> This odd diversity of misery and joy?
> I'm feeling quite insane and young again
> And all because I'm mad about the boy.

There remain the songs for which Coward is likely to be remembered the longest, those items which have gone into the dictionaries of quotations to become part of the English poetic heritage, although as no more than a versifying footnote. There is a precedent for this repertoire. In his Savoy operas W. S. Gilbert castigated one sacred cow after another, using the unlikely receptacle of Sullivan's Mendelssohnian strain to pour out his genial contempt for English art in *Patience*, English law in *Trial By Jury*, English politics in *Iolanthe*, the English theatre in *The Grand Duke*, until with *Utopia Limited* he flung the largest of his custard pies at all these aspects and several others. Coward's campaign at the expense of the foibles of his countrymen was less sustained but no less deadly. It could even be said that by collecting all Coward's best comic songs, we might reconstruct a sort of history of the British and their Empire in the twentieth century. Coward was born on 16 December 1899, just as the early reversals of the Boer War, known as Black Week, were beginning to unfold. No moment could have been more auspicious for a lampooner of the jingo imperialists. By the time Coward died in 1973, that huge empire had gone, British power had shrunk, the days of greatness were to be found only in the history books. Coward was born just in time to witness one of the most melodramatic retirements the world had ever known. His experience spanned the euphoria of enlarging the empire and the pains of withdrawing from it, and the comic songs reflect varied aspects of this withdrawal and some of the social changes taking place in Britain across the century.

The most famous item of all, 'Mad Dogs and Englishmen', had first appeared in *Words and Music*; by the time, more than twenty years later, when he took to the cabaret stage in search of ready money, Coward was disenchanted with the song, compromising with himself by singing it as fast as possible, which somehow only made it sound more risible than ever. He had lived through the phase when the bookshops were full of memoirs from the farflung outposts, in which, undeterred by the tropical climate, the pioneers of Empire had supped their mulligatawny, retained their heavy suitings, refused to acknowledge that in a different continent a different life-style is vital to success, and perspired their way to a sort of dotty glory. The song is a wonderful example of how a musician-lyricist can break up his lines and rescue himself from the charge of doggerel:

> Hindus and Argentines sleep firmly from twelve to one
> But Englishmen detest a
> Siesta.

Cole Lesley tells us that, flattered though Coward was by the inclusion of the song's title in the 1953 edition of the *Oxford Dictionary of Quotations*, he remained faintly uneasy that the phrase was not quite original Coward. The vigilance of his admirers was bringing through the letterbox assorted scraps of evidence to the contrary, beginning with a work which sounds exactly like the sort of chortling lunacy satirized in the song, 'Rough Leaves from a Journal', by Lieut.-Col. Lovell Badcock (1835), in which the reader, provided he can stay awake, will find: 'It happened to be during the heat of the day, when dogs and English alone are seen to move.' Coward himself subsequently encountered an unlikely item called *Guide to Malta, 1874*, compiled by an optimistic divine called G. N. Goodwin, chaplain to the British forces on the island. Describing the intensity of the heat, the reverend wrote: 'Only newly-arrived Englishmen and mad dogs expose themselves to it.' Nonetheless, Coward has thoroughly earned his entry into the dictionaries, for having so brilliantly crystallized the essence of a vague idea into a rich comic pearl.

In 1938 came another classic, in an otherwise unpopular play called *Operette*. Ever since the tail-end of the Victorian era, Liberal elements in the British legislature had been chipping away at the privilege of the landed aristocracy, safe till now behind the palisades of their vast acreage. The campaign had begun in 1889 with Goschen's imposition of a duty of one per cent on all estates exceeding £10,000. Five years later Sir William Harcourt had one of the few amusing ideas of his interminable career when he decided to strip the nation's rich corpses of their posthumous assets, or, as the Oxford History of England puts it: '. . . take substantial toll of the capital wealth left by deceased persons'. In 1909 came the hardest blow of all, Lloyd George's controversial budget which planned for an increase in the booty from Death Duties from £2.5 million to £4.4 million. Slowly but surely, inch by inch, younger son by younger son, the landed aristocracy was being flushed out of its holes. The effect of the new taxes, compounded by the inevitable national asset-stripping of the Great War, caused the country retreat to become a retreat of quite a different kind, which steadily grew into headlong flight. Countless landowners found themselves no longer able to maintain the vast draughty marble halls of their inheritance. The long process of inbreeding had produced a sub-species best defined by Wodehouse's Clarence, Earl of Emsworth, who is never quite sure what or even who he is. As Lady Bracknell had announced as the twilight of the Victorian age closed in, 'What between the duties expected of one during one's lifetime, and the duties exacted from one after one's death, land has ceased to be either a profit or a pleasure. It gives one position, and prevents one from keeping it up.' At which point enter four young men whose titles have been chosen with some care, Lord Elderley, Lord Borrowmere, Lord Sickert and Lord Camp, who sing of 'The Stately Homes of England'.

Again the ringing title phrase was not quite Coward's. It had been coined by Mrs Felicia Dorothea Hemans (1793–1835), whose gift for the bathetic expressed itself in an even more famous line, 'The boy stood on the burning deck'. Nor was Coward the first writer of his generation to borrow Mrs Hemans's splendid cry. Virginia Woolf, nine years before the opening of *Operette*, had published *The Common Reader*, which incorporated the observation: 'Those comfortably padded lunatic asylums which are known euphemistically as the stately homes of England.'

But no matter who had resorted to the phrase before Coward, his song made certain that nobody would ever resort to it again after him, unless with reference to his song, which in its successful attempt to cover every aspect of *dégringolade*, switches from lampoon to pastiche to slapstick, from the elegance of the best light verse to music-hall facetiousness, until at last nothing is left standing but a few mortgage debts. He refers to the sale of the Van Dycks, the pawning of the Bechstein Grand, the renting of the old ancestral home to rich Americans; jeers at the decrepitude of blueblood plumbing, hints at skulduggery linked to the fire insurance, and ends with the suggestion that the only resort left to the younger sons is to marry for money, although the absence of an intellect may well scotch even that plan:

> The Stately Homes of England
> In valley, dale and glen
> Produce a race of charming
> Innocuous young men.
> Though our mental equipment may be slight
> And we barely distinguish left from right,
> We are quite prepared to fight
> For our principles,
> Though none of us know so far
> What they really are.

The third comic masterpiece of the 1930s was not written for a stage production at all, which suggests that it simply suggested itself as a likely theme. During Coward's lifetime the phenomenon had occurred of the Drama School. After the knighting of Henry Irving, the acting profession had struggled from disgrace to toleration and finally to some sort of acceptance. The establishment of an Academy of Dramatic Art in Gower Street had been a symbolic step forward, but the smaller schools which mushroomed in the wake of the Academy suddenly made it fashionable for the children, and especially the daughters, of the well-to-do, to play the theatre game for a while, and, in a few freakish cases, to take the challenge of the Stage seriously. Because in Coward's day any donkey could buy his or her way into a drama school, the student body tended to be more financially secure than artistically endowed, and many an anxious parent, confronted by the challenge of one of his children determined to become a thespian, wondered how to respond. It may be that Coward picked up the germ of his idea from a letter sent to Bernard Shaw in 1917 by a gentleman from Wimbledon called Mr McCarthy, who wanted advice as to whether or not to allow his daughter to take to the stage. Shaw's reply reads like a paraphrase of the song which Coward was to write:

> . . . to strength of mind must be added a considerable strength of body. The life is sometimes very hard, and touring requires the constitution of a horse . . . Your daughter is beginning too late . . . The best way to begin is to go through the Academy of Dramatic Art in Gower Street . . . I hope what I have said will enable you to see more clearly what your daughter's decision means in practice.

The counsellor in Coward's song, beseeched not by Mr McCarthy, but by an insistent gorgon called Mrs Worthington, is far less patient than Shaw. Indeed, the joke lies in the steady drift from weary politeness:

> How can I make it clear
> That this is not a good idea

to the rising gorge of the first chorus, with its references to an over-developed bust, to the brutal mention of 'the width of her seat' in the second, the bitter candour of the third:

> Though they said at the school of acting
> She was lovely as Peer Gynt.
> I'm afraid on the whole
> An ingenue role
> Would emphasize her squint

to the climactic irascibility of the closing candour, which explodes at last in a complete loss of composure:

> One look at her bandy legs should prove
> She hasn't got a chance.
> In addition to which
> The son of a bitch
> Can neither sing nor dance.
> She's a vile girl and uglier than mortal sin.
> One look at her has put me in
> A tearing bloody rage.
> That sufficed, Mrs Worthington,
> Christ! Mrs Worthington,
> Don't put your daughter on the stage.

The 1940s produced two further imperishable items, the duet for two dropsical old Indian army veterans, 'I Wonder What Happened to Him?', and one of Coward's contributions to the Realpolitik of wartime, 'Don't Let's Be Beastly to the Germans'. Looking forward to the prospect that a second military victory might be followed by a second disastrous peace, he implied that had it not been for the stupid and ignoble policies of Appeasement there might not have been any second war at all:

> Let's soften their defeat again
> And build their bloody fleet again
> But don't let's be beastly to the Hun.

There were other, lesser comic wartime gestures: 'Could You Please Oblige Us with a Bren Gun?', which hits off with masterly exactitude the blend of admiration and derision in which the British held the Home Guard; 'Imagine the Duchess's Feelings', a little-known treatment of the problem of the communistically-inspired younger son who sometimes surfaced on the muddy waters of the social life of the times; and a curiously affecting song called 'Three White Feathers', about the pawnbroker's daughter, married into the peerage but still nostalgic for the good old days.

By the mid-1950s Coward's stock was slumping, as contempt in some circles for the well-made play seemed to shove him back into the quaint and distant past. A new generation of writers began to hog the headlines just as he had once done. But he continued to write with undiminished skill, and gave a pointed title to a book of poems published in 1967, *Not Yet the Dodo*. The Britain of those years, shell-shocked into some sort of realization of its own diminished role in world affairs, began to wonder what the future might hold, now that the umbrella of Empire had been blown away and the days when there were twenty shillings in the pound and nobody had any were little more than a dimly recollected dream. 'There Are Bad Times Just Around the Corner' is one of the funniest as well as one of the most perceptive songs by Coward or by any versifier. Using as its structure a gazetteer of the towns of Britain, it paints a picture of woe and chaos stretching from Devon to the Firth of Forth, from Windermere to Woking, from the Cotswold Hills to the Yorkshire dales. All the familiar bromides are turned upside down, from 'with a scowl and a frown we'll keep our pecker down' to the inspiration of the second refrain, which opens with the splendid facetiousness of:

> There are bad times just around the corner,
> The horizon's gloomy as can be.
> There are black birds over
> The greyish cliffs of Dover. . . .

As the 1960s drew on, Coward's rehabilitation gradually gathered pace. He wrote all or part of three new musicals, *Sail Away*, *High Spirits* and *The Girl Who Came to Supper*. Several of his comedies enjoyed acclaimed London revivals. In 1970 he accepted the knighthood which should have been his at least a generation earlier. It was in the early 1970s that the British belatedly acknowledged that the true heroes of their race are those who possess the gift of unmalicious laughter; three years later P. G. Wodehouse and Charlie Chaplin were similarly encumbered. By then Coward had gone. He died in March 1973 at his Jamaica home, leaving so vast a legacy of words and music that the songs represent only a small though intrinsic part of his life's work.

At least two other items among his musical works deserve to be noticed: 'London Pride', a wartime song of affection and defiance with mocking melodic overtones in its opening phrase of 'Deutschland über Alles'; and 'Let's Do It', his risqué version of Cole Porter's renowned catalogue song. The two items define as neatly as any the opposing poles of his songwriting persona, the rhetoric of deeply felt sentimental regard, and the irrepressible mischief of the sprite who enjoyed jokes at everyone's expense including his own:

> Grey city,
> Stubbornly implanted,
> Taken so for granted
> For a thousand years.
> Stay, city,
> Smokily enchanted,
> Cradle of our memories and hopes and fears.

* * *

> The most recherché cocottes do it
> In a luxury flat.
> Locks, Dunns and Scotts do it
> At the drop of a hat.

Among several other things he was the most dextrous versifier and composer of popular airs produced by his country in the twentieth century, a truly national asset who was advised by Winston Churchill in 1940: 'Go out and sing "Mad Dogs and Englishmen" while the guns are firing. That's your job.' But by far the greatest of all his creations, more ingenious than any of his rhymes, subtler than any of his dialogue, gallant, inspired and original to the point of genius, was his invention of himself. The son of a stage-struck mother and an ineffectual father, raised in a small suburban house where they took in boarders in a pathetic attempt to retain hold of their own gentility, an unschooled child actor who began the most auspicious theatrical career of the age by portraying a mussel, this nobody contrived somehow to impose upon the outside world a vision of himself he must have glimpsed somewhere in infancy, the vision of an urbane, slightly superior, impeccably accoutred soigné lounger who worked harder than ten other men with the aim of appearing idle. Perhaps he found the germ of his own astonishing transmutation in the sophistication of Charles Hawtrey, the first panjandrum of the English stage to notice his existence. Perhaps he dreamed up the whole idea for himself. But whatever the roots of his ambition, it took prodigious energy, great moral courage and an irrepressible imagination to pull off this most astounding of all gambits, the re-creation of oneself in a new image. That he left a permanent mark there can be no question. Sometimes one of his phrases comes back to us in an unguarded moment, a line, perhaps, or a rhyme, especially a snatch of melody suddenly recalled, and instantly a certain indefinable aura is evoked. What he seems to have yearned to be was the beau ideal of a certain type of gentleman, the type who is said to have flourished during his childhood, in that period before the Great War when he warbled Picardian thirds in the churches of Twickenham. He wished to remould himself in the image of his own ideal. To acknowledge that he succeeded is to record the last howling truism of his life.

Above: ARTHUR SCHWARTZ. *Below:* HOWARD DIETZ.

CHAPTER FIVE

Schwartz & Dietz

Two of the most revealing items of correspondence to be found in the archives of popular music are those which passed through the mails between February and March 1924. The first letter, dated 24 February and headed: 'Arthur Schwartz, Counselor at Law', ran as follows.

My Dear Dietz,

    Beans Cerf, a friend of yours and mine, promised to introduce me to you, but he is such a busy publisher these days, I fear he has totally forgotten me.

    This is what's on my chest. I'd love to work with you on songs for the Neighbourhood Playhouse annual show, the Grand Street Follies. I am developing contacts which are, I think, going to lead to something worthwhile. As I told Beans, I think you are the only man in town to be compared with Larry Hart, and from me that's quite a tribute, because I know almost every line Larry has written. I think that three or four tunes of mine will be riots in the Grand Street Follies this year IF they have lyrics such as only Larry and you can write.

    Don't be too amused at the fact that I speak of tune-writing under a lawyer's letterhead. I'm giving up the law in a few months to spend all my time at music.

             Sincerely, Arthur Schwartz.

The overture performed, thirteen days later came the brush-off:

My Dear Schwartz,

    As I have written a first show in collaboration with a well-established composer, I don't think that our collaboration is such a good idea.

What I would suggest is that you collaborate with an established lyric writer. In that way, we will both benefit by the reputation of our collaborators, then when we both get famous, we can collaborate with each other.

It's nice to hear from you,

Yours, Howard Dietz.

This deft rejection suggests that Dietz was already accustomed to receiving unsolicited offers of partnership from unknown songwriters, but his comically high-handed spurning of Schwartz's offer, and particularly his claim that he had worked with a 'well-established composer', make ironic reading in the light of what subsequently occurred. It was quite true that at the time Schwartz's letter arrived, Dietz was deep in a project involving no less than Jerome Kern, although the realities of that unlikely pairing were rather less imposing than Dietz evidently believed. The show, *Dear Sir*, was an American-ized version of a European property called *The Polish Wedding*, which had arrived in New York heavy with the prestige of a 700-performances run in Berlin. Kern wrote only five songs for the show, and Dietz provided only some of Kern's lyrics. Not all of these were found acceptable to the management; all that survives of what came to be known as the authentic Dietz style is a song about the Mormons which resorts to the triple rhyme: polygamy–bigamy–pig o' me. At the time Schwartz wrote his letter, the fate of *Dear Sir* still hung in the balance; had he waited a little longer, he would have read in his morning newspaper that the show had folded after only two weeks. Still, a collaboration with Kern was something to brag about, and Kern certainly spoke well of this brash young man who had been sent to him laden with fulsome endorsements from mutual friends. On what evidence Schwartz had formed his acutely perceptive assessment of Dietz's ability it is hard to imagine. Like all aspiring young versifiers Dietz had published a few squibs in newspapers, and had placed at least one song in an obscure show, but for Schwartz to have discerned resemblances to Hart was more than generous, especially as there already existed a Schwartz-Hart connection which the young lawyer inexplicably omitted to mention in his beseeching letter.

Rarely could two more compatible partners have ever found each other than Schwartz and Dietz, who were products of the same university in the same town in the same epoch, and who shared the same social and ethnic backgrounds, the same experience of the popular arts, and more or less identical views as to what might or might not divert the average musical comedy audience. Dietz's father was one of that vast vociferous army of Russian-Jewish fugitives from unholy Russia whose children were so drastically to amend the sight and sound of American popular art. But young Dietz was unfortunate in one regard. Unlike most of his contemporaries he was saddled with a father crippled by a calamitous lack of a sense of humour. Dietz in his autobiography describes his father as a domestic tyrant with little desire to understand what his children were hoping to do. He writes that his mother was 'too good' for his father and quotes her as telling her children with her dying breath: 'The ten years since your father died have been the happiest of my life.' Dietz was a bright, precocious boy with the physique of an athlete and the appearance, according to one of Kern's biographers, of 'an amiable tough guy'. If the tone of his autobiography is anything to go by, he also tended to a certain youthful intellectual conceit which he seems never to have outgrown. Having worked his way through Columbia by performing menial chores for local newspapers, he was drafted into the armed forces in 1917 and, after a landlocked spell in the navy, joined Samuel Goldwyn as a publicity writer; two years later he placed his first lyric in a professional show, and two years after that came the call from Kern and the letter from Schwartz.

Born in 1900, four years after Dietz, Schwartz never quite lost a certain element of hero-worship towards his partner. The age-gap was just too wide for them to have shared the same campus, and when Schwartz arrived at Columbia, Dietz's aphorisms still hung on the air. Long before arrival at Columbia, Schwartz had received a thorough if pragmatic education in the whys and wherefores of the Broadway stage. Although throughout his long life he never had so much as an hour of musical instruction, he was a natural musician who remembered being able to play the piano by ear from the age of four: 'If I didn't know the right harmonies, I made up my own.' The influences upon him were the predictable ones in a family which patronized the New York musical theatre. Lehar, Kalman and, in Schwartz's considered opinion the most talented of all the Viennese, Leo Fall. Then came the group of European Americans who began the progress of Americanizing the nuances of the continent, Herbert, Friml, and Romberg and, most influential of all, the man who in Schwartz's opinion consummated that process, Jerome Kern:

Kern broke away from the European tradition with a style of his own. 'They Didn't Believe Me' is a melodic song in a new frame. What has that song got that Romberg and Friml and Herbert don't have? The word that occurs to me is — Intimacy. It is non-pretentious, not flamboyant, not to be sung loudly, not to be shouted.

Like George Gershwin, Schwartz was so bowled over by the grace and originality of Kern's theatre writing during the Wodehouse period at the Princess Theatre that he aspired, if not to the same profundity, then at least to the same profession. But Schwartz's father was a lawyer, and it was understood that his sons would follow him, especially Arthur, who from his earliest years showed all the signs of scholastic aptitude. He went on to become what might be termed a born student, academically the most over-qualified of all the popular writers, becoming a Bachelor of Arts, Master of Arts and Doctor of Jurisprudence. The irony of his situation was not lost on Schwartz, intensely educated in a profession he never pursued, not educated in even the rudiments of another which was to obsess him all his life and over which he was to acquire a mastery never in dispute among his peers. By the time he began to study Law he had already caught the fever:

> I was studying for a Master's degree at Columbia, and they had a recreation hall with a piano. I remember vividly sitting at that piano, afternoon after afternoon, trying to write something that I felt was good, and never doing it. Not till three years later did I write the first melody I thought was any good.

It must have been around this time that Schwartz took the first steps towards making the acquaintance of one of his greatest heroes, surprisingly not a composer but a lyricist. In Schwartz's youth one of the pillars of adolescent life was the annual summer Boys' Camp, which enabled parents to rid themselves temporarily of their responsibilities in return for the payment of a fee to cover food, board and the healthy outdoor life for two months:

> When I was in college I got a job as counselor in a Boys' Camp, and I heard at this camp that working as a counselor at a different camp was Lorenz Hart. There was a man at my camp who knew all Hart's lyrics, none of which had been heard professionally. I recall one song, 'Don't love me like Othello, I'm much too young to die', which intrigued me. I told this man I'd love to meet Hart, and he said that next year I ought to go to Brant Lake Camp, where Hart worked, and get a job there. So I worked out this plan to edit a Camp newspaper, and the next summer I went to Hart's camp, and we wrote songs for the Camp show.

Hart had been filling in time at the camps for some years by the time Schwartz caught up with him. Brant Lake was the last of his summer retreats, and it was now that Schwartz's emergence as a composer began, although he remained unaware of it for a while. The lyrics which Hart wrote for Schwartz's first song that he thought was 'any good' have a special interest, as all lyrics must which have subsequently been replaced by verses much more familiar. They are also the only lyrics of any consequence written by Hart to any songwriter other than Richard Rodgers:

I love to lie awake in bed.
Right after Taps I pull the flaps above my head.
I rest my head upon my pillow –
Oh, what a light the moonbeams shed.
I feel so happy I could cry,
And tears are born within the corner of my eye.
To be at home with Ma was never like this.
I could go on forever like this.
I like to lie awake a while
And go to sleep with a smile.

This example of early Hart, apart from being a fascinating specimen in itself, gives the student of such affairs a rare opportunity to measure the craftsmanship of one versifier against another, for within a few years Dietz had rewritten this song and transformed it into a major hit, the first in Schwartz's career. This is not to say that Dietz did the better job, merely that the setting for Schwartz's melody had become rather more auspicious than high jinks at a Boys' Camp, and that by integrating the piece into the frame of a Broadway revue, Dietz had switched the approach of the words from the particular to the general, which is of course the first requisite for any song aspiring to a life beyond the theatre walls. In 1929, five years after the *passade* at the camp, Schwartz and Dietz wrote their first New York score, for a revue called *The Little Show*, featuring Fred Allen, Clifton Webb and Libby Holman. Dietz had been hired to provide the lyrics for one hundred dollars a week and half of one per cent of the gross. His first act after signing was to suggest to the management that it recruited Schwartz as their composer. The new partners now hired rooms at a hotel near the theatre and wrote into the small hours, a situation which provided an opening for Dietz's much-vaunted gift for the funny line:

> Working into the night, the sound of the piano, however muted, endlessly repeating the same strain, penetrated the walls to an unwilling audience. We worked on borrowed time waiting for the manager to knock at the door. We became wandering minstrels, moving from room to room, hotel to hotel, the Warwick, the St Moritz, the Essex House.
> 'They don't like what I'm playing,' said Arthur sadly.
> 'That must be it,' said Dietz. 'They never complain about the lyrics.'

Schwartz and Dietz were not the only team working on the project. Kay Swift and her husband James Warburg contributed 'Can't We Be Friends?', and the pianist in the pit band, one Ralph Reichenbach, wrote 'Moanin' Low' to fit the peculiar moaning style of Libby Holman.

Reichenbach was soon to transmute himself into Ralph Rainger, the Oscar-winning composer of 'Thanks for the Memory' and one of the outstanding contract writers in Hollywood. But in the face of this fierce competition, Schwartz and Dietz could fairly claim to have made the biggest impact on audiences, with their revamped Camp song, which now told a very different story, of an ill-advised love affair:

> I guess I'll have to change my plan
> I should have realized there'd be another man.
> Why did I buy those blue pyjamas?
> Before the big affair began.
> My boiling point is much too low
> For me to try to be a fly Lothario.
> I think I'll crawl right back and into my shell,
> Dwelling in my personal hell,
> I'll have to change my plan around,
> I've lost the one girl I found.

According to Dietz, the impact of the revamped song appeared to be nil: 'We thought it was lost in that Sargasso Sea of songs that have popular quality but no popular success.' But three years later a rumour began to circulate that in London a nightclub act called De Lys and Clarke was featuring it under the title 'The Blue Pyjama Song'. Soon De Lys and Clarke were booked into a New York venue called the Place Pigalle. Schwartz and Dietz attended the opening, and before the act began De Lys came over to their table and told them that the act incorporated an English song which he thought they might enjoy. Schwartz then asked De Lys who wrote it, to which the singer replied, 'I don't know. It dropped in from nowhere. Someone like Noël Coward.' After the song had been performed and flattened the audience, De Lys returned and asked what the two writers had thought of it. Schwartz replied, 'I think it's the best song someone like Noël Coward ever wrote.'

Meanwhile the song's American publisher, being like all publishers in a constant state of disarray, began being plagued with requests for the sheet music of 'The Blue Pyjama Song'. In desperation he telephoned the scholarly Schwartz to ask him if he knew of such an item. Schwartz told him that he and Dietz had written it, and complimented him on 'the effortless way you go about making a song hit'. But in preparing the song for the open market, Dietz now altered the lyric once again. The line referring to the plot-laden pyjamas was replaced by 'I overlooked the point completely', and the second half of the song rewritten:

> Before I knew where I was at,
> I found myself upon the shelf and that was that.

> I tried to reach the moon but when I got there
> All that I could get was the air.
> My feet are back upon the ground,
> I've lost the one girl I found.

And so, after so many vicissitudes of fortune, after being born as 'I Love to Lie Awake' and then breaking loose as 'The Blue Pyjama Song', the first authentic Schwartz-Dietz hit finally began to flourish under the title 'I Guess I'll Have to Change my Plan', one of those enterprises which blossomed in spite of everything its publisher did on its behalf. But the real interest of the song is a stylistic one. The Hart version shows a complete independence of the conventions of Hapsburgian fustian which had been laying so heavy a hand on the emergent American musical. On the other hand, somewhere just behind the scenes of Hart's verse may be discerned the benign influence of Wodehouse, even down to the images of the schoolboy sensibility. The eventual lyric too shows the mark of Wodehouse, which is hardly surprising, for Dietz at the end of his life remembered that on that first terrifying meeting with Kern, he had attempted to establish some sort of bona fides by claiming to know 'everything you and Mr Wodehouse have written', later included Wodehouse in his list of the ten most influential lyricists in the evolution of the American musical, and at last defined the creator of Jeeves and Wooster as 'the lyric writer I most admire'. The idolatry is noticeable not only in Dietz's rhymes but in his comments upon them. His description of the early failure of the pyjama song to register in the open market is amusing enough. It is also vaguely familiar. There is a sense that the writer is not quite the first member of his profession to invoke the particular image he does. Then we suddenly remember the cricketing prodigy Mike Jackson, who, on agreeing to perch on the high stool of clerical servitude in the New Asiatic Bank in Lombard Street, wanders the purlieus of Dulwich in search of bed and breakfast. At last he encounters a landlady whose absurd appearance reminds him of the music hall clown Wilkie Bard. This apparition leads him upstairs to show him his bedroom:

> It was a repulsive room. One of those characterless rooms which are only found in furnished apartments. To Mike, used to the comforts of his bedroom at home and the cheerful simplicity of a school dormitory, it seemed about the most dismal spot he had ever struck. A sort of Sargasso Sea among bedrooms.

The existence of Schwartz's first successful song in two different forms was a freak which was to repeat itself more than once in his early years. Clearly his problem was an eagerness to find a collaborator with whom he could feel comfortable, and before the forging of the perfect partnership with Dietz there had been other candidates. When the two young men began work on a new revue to be called *Three's a Crowd*, their success was by no means guaranteed. A concurrent attempt to repeat the success of *The Little Show* by presenting *The Second Little Show* had ended in disaster, and now Schwartz, faced with the challenge of providing Dietz with something memorable, produced from the bottom drawer a song which he had taken to London at some unspecified date and given to one of the very few British writers with experience of working with American songwriters. Little is known of Desmond Carter, except that he was a London writer who worked on the staff of the local headquarters of Chappells, who published most of the best Broadway material. Not even his date of birth is known, and the nearest thing to a statistic has been provided by the Russian émigré composer Vernon Duke, who remembered him as 'a gentle, sloe-eyed, wonderful lyric writer who died young in 1939'. Although he worked on more than thirty musicals, Carter's work remains virtually unknown in America, even though he was thought highly of by the Gershwin brothers and contributed to their musicals on those occasions when their importation to London required a certain localizing of the rhymes. George always regarded Carter as 'a promising young lyricist', and Duke describes a glimpse he once caught of the two of them working together, George at the keyboard chewing on a cigar, Carter in an easy chair, 'a model of tact and reticence'. When not engaged with the lions of Broadway, Carter expended much energy on collaborations with the British composer Vivian Ellis, who tells us that Carter had a house at Selsey and that his wife was 'an attractive redhead called Betty'. Carter's tendency, when he was not constrained either by the promptings of a composer or by a libretto, was to be facetious, a point which emerges strongly from his brief passage with Schwartz. At the end of his life, whenever he gave a recital, Schwartz would make a point of demonstrating how a tune might be transformed by the work of the lyricist. The song he had offered to Carter was treated in a way that might suggest that the lyricist had found himself confronted by a difficult task. The result was an ingenious blend of impudence and facetiousness:

> I have no words to say how much I love you,
> That's my excuse, I have no words.
> I've got a cottage and a room with a view,
> And H and C, but I've no words.
> I would beg for you,
> Lay an egg for you,
> Break a leg for you, like the birds up in a treetop.
> I wrote a song to say how much I love you,
> I've got the tune but I've no words.

Dietz certainly did have words, and he now halved the song's tempo, dropped Carter's half-serious pose and produced a sentimental little hymn verging on self-parody. The essential difference between the two lyrics is symbolized by the middle section. Where Carter had pursued the slapstick triple rhyme of beg, egg and leg, Dietz drops the third rhyme in the cause of convenience, and waxes passionate:

> Though I'll pray for you,
> Night and day for you
> It will see me through like a charm,
> Till your returning.

The upshot, 'Something to Remember You By', is remembered by a later generation as one of the less distinguished weepies of the period. Its fate on Broadway was to be eclipsed by the only song by another team of writers to be included in *Three's a Crowd*, the masterpiece 'Body and Soul', composed by Johnny Green and a small army of lyricists. *Three's a Crowd* ran for 271 performances despite the calamitous effect on Broadway box-offices of the Great Depression, and it was now inevitable that the partnership would continue manufacturing revues. In 1931 it surpassed itself, creating what has since been accepted as the finest revue ever to be produced in New York.

This time the ingredients were different. Instead of emergent stars like Allen and Holman, Schwartz and Dietz found themselves writing for Fred and Adele Astaire. The producer of all the revues in the series was Max Gordon, an entrepreneur who seems to have spent most of his professional career looking for the money to put on his next show. In his autobiography Gordon casts himself as the Hollywood stereotype of a Broadway producer: picturesque, eccentric, always panicked but with a heart of gold. He was a man prone to anxieties on all manner of themes, several of which existed only inside his own head. Among his phobias was a fear that if he entrusted Schwartz with a full score, the result would be disaster. Only the insistence of Dietz procured for Schwartz that exclusivity which every stage writer of the period coveted. The song which changed Gordon's mind was one of the lesser items from the score, but it impressed the distracted Gordon out of all proportion to its merits:

> I shall never forget the Sunday Schwartz telephoned. . . .
> 'Max,' he yelled, 'we just finished a knockout.'
> 'Sing it for me,' I said, 'I can't wait.'
> Schwartz sang 'I Love Louisa.' I nearly jumped through the mouthpiece. In my exuberance I proclaimed, 'Boys, it's a pleasure to go broke with you.'

This anecdote points the problem facing a later generation interested in the truth of how classic songs emerge. Clearly Gordon is intent on playing a role, shoring up his chances of survival by reducing himself to a series of funny lines and melodramatic excesses. Schwartz and Dietz too were liable to gild the lily for the same reasons, which brings us to the masterpiece which came out of the new revue, *The Bandwagon.* In his book Dietz is rather offhand about it, dismissing it in a few words:

> When we wrote 'Dancing in the Dark' I thought it was a good song but I thought it was dull. I debated whether or not we should use it in the show. There seemed to be no way of staging it. It was sung by John Barker in evening clothes. There were mirrors all round so that Tilly Losch could dance with her reflection. Time and applause have taken the dullness out of it.

In retrospect it seems incredible that Dietz should have found so profoundly beautiful a song dull, that he should have committed the solecism of allocating it to a man in evening dress, and positively insane that nobody, from Gordon down to the stagehands, should have seen instantly that here was the ideal material for Fred Astaire. In later years Astaire repaired the damage by commandeering the song and making it his own, but at the time there must have been a very real danger that the song might disappear through sheer ineptitude on the part of the production team. What is most striking of all about the history of the song is the unbridgeable abyss between Dietz's recollection and the Schwartz version of how the song came into being. In his later years Schwartz was a resident of London with the mad itinerary of a week a month in New York, where he helped administer the financial and legal affairs of ASCAP. One afternoon in the early 1970s I sat with him in his Knightsbridge home in a room pleasantly cluttered with books and music. On the grand piano were piled songbooks and manuscripts, and on the shelves against the wall was a long neat row of bound collections of Schwartz compositions. To meet Arthur in those later years was an experience which never failed to astonish the suppliant Englishmen who were granted an audience. The extraordinary thing was his physical appearance, especially his face. The reference books all agreed that he had been born in 1900, yet here he was, with the features of a man far too young to have written a Broadway show before the Wall Street Crash. When I left after the first meeting, I confirmed the relevant dates and was reduced to wonder. There seemed little doubt that unless something dramatic and unfortunate happened, Arthur was all set to follow Irving Berlin and Eubie Blake into his nineties at the very least. Everything about him seemed spry, alert, a man in full command of his powers. When I asked him to talk about 'Dancing in the Dark', this is what he said:

One night at Dietz's house he said he wanted to write a song that had more than just a romantic meaning, something that said more than 'Darling I love you', something about Man and his existence. He said to me, 'I don't want to be pompous about it, but let's try to think of the mood of such a song.' By now it is one o'clock in the morning, and Howard started to look along the spines of the books in his library, hoping to get the germ of an idea. Suddenly he stopped at a book called *Dancers in the Dark*. 'That's it,' he said, ' "Dancing in the Dark",' and I got his meaning immediately. I said, 'You mean that in a sense of all of us on the planet are dancing in the dark.' 'Yes,' he said, 'that's exactly what I mean.' I told him I would try to think of a melody and I went home. It was very late by now, but I went straight to the piano and I played this melody as if I had known it all my life. It took one minute or so to play. There was no music paper in the room, so I thought, 'I have got to keep playing this so as not to forget it.' Then I took out some bits of paper and wrote out the melody so as not to forget it. It took me one minute to write the tune and it took Howard two or three weeks to write the lyrics. I'll tell you what I was aware of. Not that it was going to be a hit, in fact I didn't regard it as a hit. I regarded it as something fascinating and different, different from what I had heard anywhere else in form and in mood.

It is impossible to accept the truth of Schwartz's scenario if what Dietz is saying is accurate, impossible to accept Dietz's recollection if what Schwartz is saying is the truth. While the anecdotage cannot affect the indisputable quality of the song, it does offer insights, if Schwartz's picturesque little fable is indeed an accurate account of events, of how the great popular works can be conjured up. Having voiced my misgivings in various radio programmes over the years, I was diverted by one letter from a listener confirming that in 1931 a novel was published in America with the title *Dancers in the Dark*, which, while it does nothing to substantiate Schwartz's story, at least keeps it within the bounds of the feasible. It is also true that 'Dancing in the Dark' expresses ideas of Man's place in the cosmos almost never hinted at throughout the entire range of twentieth-century popular music, true also that even had Dietz been maladroit in his expression of the idea, the allure of the melody might well have carried the enterprise to acceptance. The structure of 'Dancing in the Dark' has the same resilience and strength which characterize a more famous example, 'The Man I Love'; what the two compositions have in common is a harmonic structure so impressive as literally to become part of the melody. In the Gershwin song the main theme is underpinned by a descending line, moving down in semitones. In 'Dancing in the Dark', the descent of a semitone under the main theme on the threshold of the third bar, and again at the start of the seventh bar, have become as much an essential part of the tune as Schwartz's match to the words.

But sumptuous though Schwartz's melody is, it is never in danger of eclipsing, or detracting from, Dietz's lyric, which contrives to express an elusive idea with great technical skill and refinement. In the predicament in which Dietz found himself, the problem was to define a vague philosophic abstraction in very few syllables. Concision is always the hardest taskmaster of all in the lyric-writer's world, but in 'Dancing in the Dark' the challenge was doubly difficult because the lyricist had chosen to embroil himself in nebulosities. Dietz's triumphant mastery of the problem is now world-famous; what has gone less remarked is the even greater ingenuity of the verse, which reduces the art of concision to 33 one-syllable words. Here is how Dietz resolves his difficulties:

> Dancing in the dark.
> Till the tune ends
> We're dancing in the dark
> And it soon ends.
> We're waltzing in the wonder of why we're here.
> Time hurries by — we're here
> And gone.
> Looking for the light
> Of a new love
> To brighten up the night,
> I have you, love,
> And we can face the music together,
> Dancing in the dark.
>
> What though love is old?
> What though song is old?
> Through them we can be young.
>
> Hear this heart of mine,
> Make yours part of mine.
> Dear one,
> Tell me that we're one.

The two partners were to express very similar sentiments in their next revue for Gordon, *Flying Colours*. By this time Dietz was finding the routines required for revue increasingly wearisome to concoct, and was especially distressed by the ordeal of sitting through the endless casting auditions:

One day I was sitting with Helen Broderick at an audition watching a man whose act was to do a violent and comic prizefight with himself. He actually made his nose bleed. Incredulous, I asked if he made his nose bleed at every performance. 'Oh, no,' replied Helen, 'only at auditions.'

As usual, Schwartz looked back into his collection of old songs, unfinished songs, rejected songs, in his efforts to complete the score for *Flying Colours*. He recalled that years before, during preparations for the bar examination, he had begun whistling in the classroom, much to the displeasure of Harold Medina, the eminent master of jurisprudence who was lecturing to the class. Schwartz now refined this fragment, which became 'A Shine on My Shoes'. But the outstanding song in the score was another of those haunting speculations on the possibilities of romantic love, this time with the self-contradictory title of 'Alone Together'. More melodramatic both as a melodic contrivance and as a set of verses, 'Alone Together' so clearly evokes the mood of 'Dancing in the Dark' that its writers often referred to it as 'Dancing in the Schwartz', the word 'schwartz' being a German-Yiddish term meaning 'black'. Although it ran for 188 performances, *Flying Colours* was not a financial success, and Gordon later took perverse pleasure in insisting that it had never recouped a single dollar of its production costs.

At this point Schwartz entered the first crisis of his career as a musician. Between February 1933 and June 1934 he could not think of anything to write. Unable to rely all the time on Dietz, who had his other career as a film publicist to sustain him, Schwartz decided to give himself until September. If, by then, nothing had occurred to him, he would return to the Law and forsake music once and for all. He was saved by a product called Ivory Soap, which was to be advertised on radio in a 39-week series called *The Gibson Family*. In the climate of the Depression the prospect of regular employment attracted Schwartz, just as it was attracting George Gershwin, about to embark on a radio series advertising Feenamint, a chewing-gum laxative. When Schwartz agreed terms, the middle-man said to him, 'The price is right, but you'll have to write at least three songs a week. Won't that take a lot out of you?', to which Schwartz replied, 'Yes, but it will also take a lot out of Bach, Beethoven and Brahms.' Further inspiration arrived when he and Dietz embarked on an operetta based on Alarcon's *The Three-Cornered Hat*, to be entitled *Revenge With Music*. This show ran quietly for a while before disappearing, but not before it had established another Schwartz-Dietz song in the standard catalogue, 'You and the Night and the Music'. Yet again we encounter a melody by Schwartz living two independent lives.

The version featured to great effect in *Revenge With Music* is still favoured more than fifty years later by superior singers of standard songs, and once again Schwartz had a scenario which went along with the song:

I was on a ship coming to England, and on the ship were Maurice Chevalier, Georges Carpentier the prizefighter, Helen Morgan the musical comedy star, and one or two other people. Chevalier and Carpentier and Morgan were doing a concert for the passengers, and one morning I was standing on the deck while a rehearsal was going on nearby. Suddenly this melody came to me. It always sounds phoney when a composer says a melody 'came to him' but that's the only description I can give you. I had made no effort to write it. I wasn't sitting trying to find something. I was just standing there on the deck when the complete melody came to me. I was afraid I would forget it, so I burst into this rehearsal of Chevalier and the others and said, 'Would you let me play something on the piano before I forget it?' They must have thought I was some kind of a nut, but they knew I was a songwriter. I played the melody four or five times and they all said, 'What is that? That's great! What is that?' I told them it was just something I had composed. Later I found some music paper and put it down.

The secondary version of the melody which flew into Schwartz's arms on a ship's deck has utterly vanished, and were it not for a few surviving copies of the sheet music, might have left no trace at all. But in 1934, the same year that *Revenge With Music* opened at the New Amsterdam Theatre, Anna Neagle starred in a parochial film called *Queen's Affair*, which included a piece called 'Tonight' which may be sung with complete confidence to the tune of 'You and the Night and the Music':

> Love can be ours if we choose it,
> Here is an hour of delight.
> Are we to take it or lose it tonight?
> Patience is nothing to boast of,
> Why should we wait for the light?
> Why shouldn't we make the most of tonight?
>
> For just one wonderful hour we can borrow
> A treasure to keep in our hearts.
> One little dream of tomorrow
> In case this love departs.
>
> Prove that you mean what you've told me,
> Morning is still out of sight.
> Live for this moment and hold me in your arms tonight.

It comes as no surprise to discover that the writers of the song were our old friends Desmond Carter and Arthur Schwartz, who somehow contrived to use the identical melody concurrently in the West End and on Broadway with two different collaborators.

From now on the Schwartz-Dietz partnership became fragmented, as Dietz pursued his lunatic career in Hollywood and Schwartz was obliged to work with a variety of different partners. In 1935 the pair of them worked on yet another revue, *At Home Abroad*. The topicality of its score long ago yellowed into history, but 'Love is a Dancing Thing' retains a certain faded charm. In 1937 came the last of the vintage collaborations between the two friends. After *Between the Devil*, it was to be eleven years before they worked together again. *Between the Devil*, Schwartz recalled,

> . . . was about a bigamist, played by Jack Buchanan. He was married to an English woman played by Evelyn Laye, and to a French woman played by an English girl who had a very good French accent, Adele Dixon. It was for Broadway, but I came over to London to cast it, as Howard couldn't come over. What happened was that in the second act Buchanan the bigamist was trapped and was about to be sent to jail. As he had to go away all by himself for a while, we wrote this song, and the way we staged it, there was a policeman standing behind him, and as Buchanan sang and danced, the policeman danced along with him in the background like a shadow.

The song, 'By Myself', was another which Astaire was subsequently sensible enough to acquire as an unforgettable part of his repertoire, just as years later Sinatra did the same with a haunting song of unrequited love from the show, 'I See Your Face Before Me'. There was also a brilliant comic song into which Dietz neatly inserted a reference to his own double life. Although acknowledged as one of the most gifted lyricists of his generation, Dietz was content that his paymasters should remain the moguls at the head of MGM studios, whose famous trademark, the roaring, blinking lion, had been another of Dietz's wheezes, hence the couplet in 'Triplets':

> MGM has got its Leo
> But mamma has got a trio. . . .

By now rising through sheer force of levity through the movie ranks, Dietz was one of the most adept of those concocters of moonshine, garbage and asininity which characterized the publicizing of feature films. When Goldwyn became part of the conglomerate Metro-Goldwyn-Mayer, Dietz's duties became more demanding, especially as he was still trying to maintain his other profession, the real one, as a writer of song lyrics. One day Nick Schenck, the power behind Mayer and company, noticed Dietz's erratic office hours and barked at the offender, 'You come in late,' – to which Dietz responded with 'Yes, but I go home early.' Dietz records the exchange in his autobiography, and evidently takes great pride in his own witticisms. The only time in the book when he is bested comes when he asks Greta Garbo if she will come to have dinner with him on Monday. Miss Garbo, no doubt using a well-tried defence, replied, 'How do I know if I'll be hungry on Monday?' But it remains astonishing that the man capable of the delicacy of the words he put to Schwartz's music should have been content to sink, as he eventually did, to the degradation of Vice-President in charge of Publicity at the studio.

When Dietz was too busy dreaming up gibberish for Mr Mayer, Schwartz was obliged to find other partners. Among the successes he enjoyed with Dietz in absentis were 'Then I'll Be Tired of You' with Yip Harburg, several songs from his three musicals with Dorothy Fields, and a few enlightening moments in his 1946 alliance with Ira Gershwin, *Park Avenue*. But he came back to Dietz in the end with a show called *Jennie*, which included 'When You're Far Away From New York Town'. That was the last Broadway experience for the partnership, and it was in the years of retirement which followed that Arthur made his home in London. From his conversations it was clear he had not given up completely, and at one point he became excited over a musical version of *Nicholas Nickleby*, into which he had poured much energy. One day in 1980 he suggested that I take the ten or twelve most famous and successful of his songs and concoct around them a libretto, thereby placing old songs in a new dramatic context. The idea was not quite so outlandish as it sounds, especially in a period when the composition of literate, melodious musical scores has become very nearly a lost art. But there was another reason why the suggestion astonished me. It had already been taken up and done with dazzling success. In 1953 Betty Comden and Adolph Greene had written a screenplay called *The Bandwagon*, in which Astaire is an ex-Broadway star who has spent the fat years in Hollywood and come home to find the old days and the old ways apparently buried forever. The screen version of *The Bandwagon*, packed with cryptic allusions to Astaire's past, is one of the most memorable ever made, not least because of the score, which includes all the Schwartz-Dietz classics and one new piece, written by the partners while production was proceeding, 'That's Entertainment'. I told Arthur that his excellent idea had been acted upon years ago, to which he said, 'Well act on it again.' So I said I would but never did. The last time I came to his house I asked him why he did not write his autobiography. His response was the most revealing thing I ever heard him say: 'Howard has already written it.' It was this period when the obituarists were crouched at the starting line, awaiting the imminent news of Dietz's death. He had been in ill-health for some years, until at last the expectation was that it was now a matter of days rather than weeks. At which point Arthur telephoned me and said we should have lunch, just to make sure that when I came to write an obituary of his old friend, I would not get anything wrong.

We lunched at a restaurant in St Martin's Lane. It was a summer day and we were both feeling the heat. I noticed that when Arthur reached out for the menu his forearm seemed scrawny, the forearm of a very old man. Yet he was only 83, and we all knew that Arthur was destined for a century. I soon realized that when he said he had not wished me to get anything wrong, what he had meant was that I must not leave out the jokes. 'Howard was a very funny man. You know, when he was at Columbia, they held a competition among all the students at the Journalists' School to see who could write the most sensational short headline. Howard won with "Pope elopes" – how about that?' Arthur told me the Dietz jokes at the expense of Sigmund Romberg's plagiarist tendencies. He told me about the time Dietz, having been sick during a dinner at one of the moguls' houses, placated the hostess by assuring her he had brought up the white wine with the fish. He told me all the stories, and throughout the recital the light of a deep affection lit his face. At the end of the lunch Arthur surprised me by saying that he was selling up and going back to New York, and that if we were to meet again it would have to be in his home town and not mine. Howard Dietz died on 30 August 1983, and my obituary duly appeared, incorporating many of the things Arthur had told me. After he had returned to New York, I enjoyed one or two telephone conversations with him, in which he spoke optimistically of a new show he was putting together, and explained that this was why he had decided to sell the London house. I kept seeing the wasted forearm and the decrepitude of his movements when we started to get up from the table in the restaurant. I could not help feeling that he had gone home to die. He finally did, on 4 September 1984.

Left: ALAN LERNER. *Right:* FREDERICK LOEWE.

CHAPTER SIX

Lerner & Loewe

THE ART OF PUTTING WORDS TO music is so riddled with imprecision that it cannot even agree on its own terminology. Ira Gershwin, that most erudite of all practitioners, confessed in his writings on the subject that although throughout his life he had been described as a lyricist, he was very much afraid that so far as purists like himself were concerned, the term was a solecism, and that the true word was 'lyrist'. He also acknowledged that lyrist, for all its correctitude, was a lost cause, defeated by the world's refusal to deploy it. Lyrist, then, is correct but spurned, lyricist wrong but familiar. For those who feel uncomfortable in the face of controversy, there is always solace to be found in the evasions of 'lyric writer'. But whatever the term, Alan Jay Lerner certainly ranks among the six greatest toilers in the field. As to the worth of that eminence, Lerner himself was given to whimsical disparagement, on one occasion telling a New York audience that although lyric-writing was an art form, 'it's only a minor one, somewhere a little above photography and woodcarving'. But that was only the comically false humility of a highly sophisticated man who knew it would amuse the informed audience he was addressing, which it did. So far from being a casual, slapdash sort of business performed by cigar-chewing philistines in bowler hats and utterly lacking in real creativity or literary finesse, writing words to music was for Alan Lerner, as it was for Cole Porter, Lorenz Hart, Noël Coward, Ira Gershwin and Johnny Mercer, a process so subtle, so intricate, so demanding, so severe in its exercise of the art of concision, that he was, on more than one occasion, known to have agonized for a week over a single line, and not always to his own satisfaction, a demonstration of his aesthetic morality which comes out in the background to 'Wouldn't It Be Luverly?'.

During the preliminary stages of their work together on *My Fair Lady*, Lerner and Loewe received an inquiry from Mary Martin, who expressed her desire to hear the songs. Privately embarrassed by this intrusion of so mature an actress for the role of the girlish Eliza Doolittle, but acting on the precept of Lorenz Hart that if a star expresses interest, do not say no for at least 24 hours, the partners agreed to play some of the score to Miss Martin. The recital encompassed five pieces, after which Miss Martin hastily departed. After a week of silence Lerner contacted Miss Martin's husband, who sadly informed the lyricist over lunch that his wife had 'walked the floor half the night saying over and over again, "How could it have happened? Those dear boys have lost their talent." ' The effect of this piece of opinionated idiocy, delivered by someone irrelevant to all the issues raised by *My Fair Lady*, was catastrophic so far as Lerner was concerned. When Loewe handed him the melody of 'Wouldn't It Be Luverly', Lerner observed his habit of never beginning a lyric until early morning, and waited a few hours, keyed up to the pitch of excitement which told him that he and Loewe were about to achieve their finest hour. The next morning 'at six-thirty I locked myself up and plugged in the coffee-pot'. Twelve hours later not one word had been written down. Lerner persevered, but at the end of a week, still not one word. After four weeks he had lost eight pounds in weight and, in his own words, 'had become a basket-case'.

> In desperation I went to see Dr Bela Mittelmann, a psychiatrist whom I had gone to for a spell eight years earlier. Besides being one of the nation's most respected analysts, he was also the only psychiatrist I had ever encountered who had a sense of humour and did not have modern furniture in the waiting room.
>
> Collapsing on the couch, I poured out my tale of woe. In the course of the hour I remembered him saying to me, 'You know, you write as if your life depends on every line.' 'It does,' I replied. Passing that by, he continued to explore my recent past. Suddenly, from nowhere I found myself spilling out the incident with Mary Martin. In the most sympathetic way imaginable, he began to chuckle. In an instant I saw that that brutal lunch had shaken me more profoundly than I realized.

Within two days, the lyric for 'Wouldn't It Be Luverly' was finished and Lerner was eating once again, although he later wrote that 'the words "those dear boys have lost their talent" are forever engraved on the walls of my duodenal lining'. This fierce dedication to the Flaubertian ideal of *le mot juste* might surprise those who have never had dinner with a good lyricist, but certainly there was no more fanatically dedicated servant to the art of the lyrist, or lyricist, or lyric writer, than Alan Lerner.

And yet, in the everyday sense in which the term is applied, he was not a songwriter at all. He would often make this point, especially when some well-meaning entrepreneur invited him to write a song for some momentarily prestigious event, a theme song, perhaps, for a television series, or a title song for a picture. Alan's answer was always the same. He wouldn't do it. He couldn't do it. He never had been able to do it. He never would be. He was, from start to finish, a dramatist who wrote part of his plays in rhyme. The distinction is profound, even though unnoticed by most of those who professed to understand his work. (He once said, 'Over the years I've been constantly amazed at the number of people who think that Lerner and Loewe wrote the music and somebody, the actors perhaps, made up the lyric as they went along.') Before he could begin to conceive even the vaguest shadow of a shape of a lyric, he had to be intimately familiar, it would seem, with the character's past life, present predicament, future prospects. He had to know what tensions lay behind the scene and which factors had brought them about, what the character was wearing and what the nature of the backdrop. After all, how can it be possible to put words into a person's mouth without some knowledge of that person's likely vocabulary? Lerner's Guinevere says 'ergo' instead of 'therefore', and would, no doubt, in defining her station in life, have talked of being fortunate. Alfred Doolittle on the same theme refers to his 'bloomin' luck'. The point is almost too obvious to need making, yet is overlooked consistently in assessments of versifiers labouring in the musical theatre. Professor Higgins displays in his songs a correctitude verging on the pedantic which befits his professorial pretensions; the lady in *Love Life* defines her dream man as 'Mr Right' and babbles of cocktail shakers and Tyrone Power; when the minstrel chorus in *1600 Pennsylvania Avenue* explain why the poor get poorer, they sing, 'Cuz Dey's Dum'. The classic definition of a song in a musical production is of a set of verses put to music which serves as a device for thrusting forward the action of the plot. The lyrics do not describe or embellish the action. They *are* the action. If not, there is no point in using the song at that juncture. When Henry Higgins admits he has grown accustomed to Eliza's face, the confession comes as a revelation to him if not to us. It is not an amplification of what has been said or will be said. A song lyric is part of the dialogue: the phrase 'I've grown accustomed to her face' is not just a paraphrase of, but a replacement for, the moment in *Pygmalion* when Higgins tells Eliza, 'I have grown accustomed to your voice and appearance', which is excised from the text of *My Fair Lady* because there is no further need for it now that the identical sentiment has been expressed in song. Therein lies the essence of the art of adaptation. Merely to insert songs would be to elongate the evening to an insufferable length, calling to mind the remark of a New York critic: 'I quite liked the first two years of Act One.' Lerner's consummate skill as an adapter lay in his ability to strip down the text and repair the damage so skilfully with his lyrics that the seams become invisible.

Of course he acknowledged readily enough that there were some lyric writers with the ability to knock off something brilliant or moving without foreknowledge of any personality or dramatic context. He revered the best of these men, referred to them as songwriters and, intending that definition to indicate high praise, once told me he believed the greatest American songwriter of the twentieth century was Johnny Mercer, because Mercer could conjure an 'Early Autumn' or a 'Goody Goody' literally out of thin air. It comes back to me how he gave a laugh of delight when I told him of the music hall writer of Max Beerbohm's recollections who, on being asked by a County Court judge how much he earned in a year, replied without hesitation, 'Three hundred and sixty-five pounds', and on being asked to explain the exactitude of his figures, said, 'I write a song a day and I receive one pound for each song.' That was what you called a songwriter. Lerner belonged to the other group, the versifying dramatists whose place was neither in Tin Pan Alley nor the halfway house of Hollywood, but in the living theatre. In his autobiography Lerner has hardly begun before he defines his own status:

> I am a librettist. However, whenever I fill out a form which asks that I identify my profession I do not say I am a librettist, I say 'playwright-lyricist'. Until a few years ago, it was not even proper to say 'lyricist' because there was no such word in the dictionary. A man who wrote words for a song was officially called a lyrist. Popular usage finally defeated tradition and lyricist became accepted. One of the reasons I dislike the word librettist is best illustrated by a famous Mrs Malaprop of New York who a few years ago, when asked where she had been the night before, said, 'To the opera.' Asked what she had seen, she replied, 'It was some Italian opera called *Libretto*.' A librettist has always seemed to me someone associated with opera and operetta and who specialized in unintelligibility and anonymity. Nevertheless, that is what I am. A librettist.

In the light of this definition of himself, Lerner is disclosed not as an artist who was first inspired by the popular jingles of the day, but as a member of the theatre audience, in which regard he was singularly fortunate in his choice of parents. His mother had in her teens aspired in a genteel sort of way to a vocal career, and at one time had as her accompanist the mother of Richard Rodgers. His father, by all accounts an extraordinary man, seems to have inspired his son without actually performing any practicalities as a mentor. A dentist manqué, the old boy built up a successful chain of stores and, by the time his son was old enough to notice, was indulging his two great loves, prizefighting and love itself. With regard to women, Lerner opens his autobiography with a sentence which contrives in only 23 words to borrow a famous quote from the Gershwins, define the state of the family fortunes and make the whimsical confession that the marriage of his parents had speedily collapsed:

> My Pappy was rich and my Ma was good-lookin', but by the time I was born my father no longer thought so.

Lerner writes: 'My father's influence on me was indelible and my love for him as alive as it was on the day he died in 1954, but there were many issues where we parted company. Principally they were politics and women.' Two other aspects of Lerner senior which had relevance to his son's attitudes were his atheism and his wit, which at times coalesced to produce a memorable phrase. Two days before his death he confirmed to his son his adamant atheism. By now a veteran of a different kind of theatre from the one to which his son aspired, and about to undergo his forty-ninth bout of surgery, he filled in the form sanctioning the next operation and wrote underneath: 'When it gets to fifty, sell.' Alan recalled that although he started studying the piano at the age of five, he had resolved on a career in the theatre by the time he was twelve and was already writing songs in his early teens, yet his father 'paid no attention'. What he did do was to express his reverence for the English language by shipping his children to England to learn it, and never failing to apply to their range of knowledge the most stringent tests and measurements. Not very long after Alan had won a Drama Critics Award for his work on *Brigadoon*, he received from his father, whose struggle with cancer had finally deprived him of the power of speech:

> Alan – I have counted the words you have used this weekend and you have an active vocabulary of 297 words. I don't see how you can make a career as a writer with an active vocabulary of 297 words. However, I believe you have talent and if you would like to return to school and study, I would be more than happy to subsidize you.

But they both knew that there was a sense in which Alan had never left school, never stopped studying. His alma mater was Broadway, his campus the theatres and rehearsal rooms, his fellow-students the performers and technicians who made the productions possible. In this most demanding of all universities, Alan worked tirelessly all his life, never deterred by failure, never rendered complacent by success, never disillusioned by the numberless hordes of jackasses with which the administrative ranks of the entertainment world are staffed. After *Brigadoon* had been acclaimed, a friend remarked to Lerner senior on the beach in Florida that 'Alan certainly is a lucky boy', to which the old man scribbled the reply, 'Yes, it's a funny thing about Alan. The harder he works the luckier he gets.' And Lerner adds his own postscript: 'I know the story is true because the man sent me the slip of paper.' Apparently not till the very end of his life did the old man come close to expressing his pride and admiration. One day, when the son was wheeling his father into the operating theatre, the patient handed him a note which read: 'I suppose you're wondering why I want to live.' Alan read the note and nodded. The second note read: 'Because I want to see what happens to you.' The sad irony was that Lerner senior never did find out. He died one month before his son started to write *My Fair Lady*.

He bequeathed to his son among other things a love of England and the English which animated every word he ever wrote and was the inspiration for his finest work. In his indispensable history of his craft, *The Musical Theatre, a Celebration*, published posthumously in 1986, he prefaces his tribute to W. S. Gilbert with these sentiments:

> It is my biased opinion that the British society is the most civilized on the planet Earth. One of the most prominent reasons for the civility of the English is their possession of that most precious of all human traits – a sense of humour. The French may be witty, but there is no appreciation of civilized silliness. Lots of aphorisms but no giggles. George Bernard Shaw, for instance, who, although born in Ireland, spent more than seventy years of his creative life in England, is the only major humorist who ever lived who was not bitter.

The passage tells us as much about Lerner as it does about Shaw. Of all the men I ever knew, Lerner was the one who exulted most in the entertaining absurdities of anecdotal recollection. His hero Shaw once told Florence Farr: 'It is by jingling the bells of a jester's cap that I, like Heine, have made people listen to me. All genuinely intellectual work is humorous.' The remark is doubly significant in the context of Lerner's career because, as well as proclaiming the golden rule of the librettist, it nods obliquely in the direction of one of Lerner's much-loved mentors, as we shall see. Lerner's history of musical comedy is that very rare thing, an erudite work shaking with silent laughter. The prose is crisp, the thinking crystalline, the verdicts judicious. But bubbling away beneath the scholarship are the springs of comedy, bestowing on even the harshest judgements the benison of charitable good humour. For instance, knowing perfectly well that his readers knew of his eight divorce cases, he wrote: 'When one recalls how many lawyers left the profession for the theatre – W. S. Gilbert, Oscar Hammerstein, Cole Porter and Arthur Schwartz – one cannot but speculate what a more pleasant and civilized world this would be if the rest of the legal profession followed suit.' And this from the gifted lyricist Howard Dietz on the theme of Sigmund Romberg's tendency to lean a little too heavily at times on Tchaikovsky and company: 'I don't like composers who think. It gets in the way of their plagiarism.' But Dietz could turn a pretty compliment when sufficiently moved. When Alan sent Dietz his introduction to Dietz's autobiography, he received this response:

Dear Alan,
     When I received your introduction to my book I was in the hospital.
     When I finished reading the introduction I went home.
                   As ever, Howard.

In discussing some of the dramatic follies of 1931 Alan recalls that the shortest run of the year, a calamity called *The Singing Rabbi*, opened on the Thursday and never saw Monday. He adds: 'I do not know if they gave a performance on Saturday.' And in recalling the problems of piecing together his early musical *The Day Before Spring*, he tells how the choreographer asked Fritz Loewe to compose twelve minutes of ballet music depicting Paris at five o'clock in the morning. Fritz then locked himself away for a week, wrote the music and invited the choreographer to hear it. When the recital was over the choreographer complained, 'It sounds more like six in the morning,' to which Fritz replied, 'Yes, I see what you mean. Come back next week.' When the second recital took place the choreographer said, 'Just right,' and that was that. Lerner confesses he thought they were both mad.

I recall one blissful Sunday lunch in the hospitality lounge of a television company. Lerner, André Previn and myself were to appear on a show to do with the popular arts and had, as always, been called hours too soon. So we beguiled the time by amusing each other. Lerner knew of my appetite for the comically absurd, and told of an episode in the later, decrepit years in Hollywood of John Barrymore. It was at a stage in his career when the great actor was no longer able to remember even the briefest snatches of dialogue, a handicap he was bravely attempting to overcome with the device of the cue-card. One day they were shooting a scene in which Barrymore, alone in his room, opens the door to a stranger and asks: 'Yes?' Fearful that he would forget what to say once he opened the door, he had arrived at the studio armed with a huge sheet of cardboard on which was scrawled the word 'Yes'. At first the director indulged Barrymore's whim, but at last, after several unsuccessful attempts to locate the sheet of cardboard in a place where Barrymore could see it but where it was out of camera range, he asked Barrymore if he was quite sure he needed the card. 'Certainly I need it,' Barrymore is purported to have replied. 'Without the card I might open the door and say "No" – and then what would happen to the plot?' But the stories Alan liked best of all were those in which the goons from Front Office were done down by the witty artist, for which reason he delighted in the tale of how in 1944 the impresario Billy Rose commissioned Igor Stravinsky to write a fifteen-minute ballet for the Broadway production *Seven Lively Arts*. After the opening in Philadelphia, Rose sent Stravinsky a telegram:

> Your music great success stop could be sensational success if you would authorize Robert Russell Bennett retouch orchestrations stop Russell orchestrates even the work of Cole Porter stop.

Stravinsky wired back:

> Satisfied with great success.

Of all the wits and jokers who crossed Alan's path, the most resourceful and entertaining seems to have been Fritz Loewe, his longest-standing partner. Alan once launched on a description of a few of Fritz's extra-cultural exploits, and was so diverting on the theme that finally I interrupted him and asked why he hadn't written it all down, guessing even before I asked the question what the answer would be. By this time Loewe was a semi-invalid in splendid retirement. As I anticipated, Alan explained that too many of the stories, for instance the one about Fritz and the lady critic from Boston, could not be made public till after Fritz's death. Nobody, least of all Alan himself, suspected that Fritz, fourteen years the older of the two and in a frail physical condition, would survive the longer.

The partners had come together in the oddest of ways, through the vicissitudes of fortune both of them had suffered in the boxing ring. As a child Alan had often accompanied his father to Madison Square Garden on Friday nights to watch the fights. The experience left him with such an appetite for the Noble Art that while at Harvard he strove to get into the university boxing team. One day an opponent caught him with a left hook so potent that it damaged his sight permanently. After several operations he emerged with only one good eye, a disability he contrived to mask from the world with remarkable success. Once or twice in my association with him, when the word was about that some charlatan of a director was giving him a hard time in the revival of one of his works, I wondered why Harvard's ex-featherweight prospect did not succumb to the temptation to give the fool a shot in the head and quieten down his pretensions. But Alan was far too much of a gentleman ever to have done such a thing, more's the pity.

Fritz Loewe's boxing career was much more spectacular and actually reached the professional arena. Nothing Alan ever told me about anything or anyone astonished me more than the revelation that Fritz had once stepped into the same ring as Tony Canzoneri. For the benefit of the insular and the uncultured, I had better explain that Tony Canzoneri was once to the featherweight and lightweight divisions what someone like Vincent Youmans or Arthur Schwartz would be to the art of composing melodies. Canzoneri was an Italian-American artist of the Realist school who came out of New York to win world titles in the early 1930s in the most brilliant and ruthless fashion. It has been a source of incredulous astonishment to many people that the composer of such felicities as 'The Heather on the Hill' and 'How To Handle a Woman' should have been a professional boxer. That he had once dared to challenge the great Canzoneri was much more incredible. 'What happened when they met?' I asked Alan, hardly daring to hear the answer. 'Well,' said Alan, 'if Fritz had got a decision against Canzoneri I wouldn't have written *My Fair Lady*. Fritz had a strategy for the Canzoneri fight, to box on the retreat and keep out of Canzoneri's reach. He was convinced he could have danced all night. Canzoneri's reach turned out to be just a little more extensive than Fritz had figured. Fritz was stopped in the first, and the music profession gained a new recruit.' I have pondered that story ever since, hoping fervently that Canzoneri, a childhood hero of mine and a great professional, might have been able to find solace after his eventual dethronement by Barney Ross from the knowledge that at any rate Ross could never claim to have KO'd the composer of 'On the Street Where You Live'.

Like his partner, Frederick Loewe could be said to have been influenced profoundly by his father. Edmund Loewe was one of Europe's most celebrated singer-actors, among whose dubious cultural distinctions was to have been the first man to appear on the Berlin stage as Count Danilo, the well-dressed nincompoop who finally amends the status of the Merry Widow. His son was already a music student by then, studying under Busoni. In 1915 he made his concert debut as a pianist with the Berlin Philharmonic; a year later he wrote a million-seller called 'Katrina', and a year after that, still only sixteen years old, he was awarded the Amsterdam Medal for the best young concert pianist in what was left of Europe. In 1923 Edmund responded to the overtures of the American impresario David Belasco by sailing for New York with his wife and young Fritz. While rehearsing his first production in the New World, Edmund collapsed and died. In the ordinary way of things, so successful a performer would have left his family reasonably well provided for, but Edmund had been an addictive gambler, and it was left to Fritz to keep himself and his mother alive. He barely managed to do this by taking a succession of jobs which sound impressive on the dust jacket of a biography but nowhere else. According to Lerner he became the first Hapsburg cowboy in the history of the West, before becoming a gold miner. Having mined no gold he then turned to the professional boxing ring; after the Canzoneri debacle he became a riding instructor, followed by a job playing the piano in one of New York's several simulations of a German beer garden. From this musical nadir he rose to the modest glory of rehearsal pianist for a Broadway production of *Die Fledermaus* entitled *Champagne Sec*. This hybrid opened in October 1933, and it is not until 1936 that his name surfaces once more on the brackish waters of the Broadway life, when his composition 'A Waltz Was Born in Vienna' appeared in a short-lived revue. The record then becomes blank until in December 1938 we find him collaborating with one Earle Crooker on a production called *Great Lady*, which survived for only three weeks. Loewe's songs for this calamity find him remaining true to his origins, for the score included an item called 'There Had to Be the Waltz'. There follows another blank until in August 1942, Lerner, lunching at the Lambs Club, is accosted:

A short, well-built, tightly strung man with a large head and hands and immensely dark circles under his eyes strode to a few feet from my table and stopped short. His destination was the men's room and he had gone the wrong way. He turned to get back on the right road and suddenly saw me. He stared for a moment. I knew who he was. He came to my table and sat down. 'You're Lerner, aren't you?' he asked. I could not deny it. 'You write lyrics, don't you?' he continued. 'I try,' I replied. 'Well,' he said, 'would you like to write with me?' I immediately said 'Yes.' And we went to work. We began in Detroit in 1942 working in a stock company, rewriting old plays and adding a few songs. When I say old plays I exaggerate. The stock company closed after one old play.

Their first Broadway collaboration was a revue called *What's Up*, which survived for 63 performances thanks mainly to the prestige of its leading man, Jimmy Savo; one of its songs, 'My Last Love', incorporated the most microscopic of straws in the wind with an image later to become world-famous:

My last love never danced with me all night.

Two years later came *The Day Before Spring*, starring Irene Manning and Bill Johnson. This time the partners achieved the respectable run of 165 performances, although Lerner later reflected that it had been 'a succès d'estime, meaning a success that runs out of steam'. Already Lerner's view of the matrimonial condition was adapting itself to circumstances. In a lyric called 'My Love is a Married Man' there occurs the following verse:

I'd like a nest in
Some clandestine

> Hide-away on a hill.
> Though passion sweep me
> Heaven keep me
> For I know he never will.

Then came Lerner's expression of his affection for the whimsy of James Barrie, *Brigadoon*, the story of a highland village which becomes visible to the naked eye only one day in every century. After suffering the indignity of several rejections, the partners then endured the even worse indignity of being accepted by the regrettable Billy Rose, whose attitude proved so impossible that Lerner recalled, 'The contract he wished us to sign negated Abraham Lincoln's Emancipation Proclamation that freed the slaves.' At last the show was produced by Cheryl Crawford and established the fame of the two ex-boxers once and for all.

Although *Brigadoon* is set in Scotland, *Paint Your Wagon* in the Wild West, *My Fair Lady* in Edwardian London, *Gigi* in pre-Great War Paris, and *Camelot* in medieval England, Loewe's music never lost its faint aroma of the continental nuances of his father's theatre. The musk of Vienna pervades more than one of his more popular pieces. Most strikingly, there is the wordless waltz to which the transmuted Eliza swirls at the embassy ball, evoking instant images of one of Lehar's heroines doing her stuff. In fact its origins lie closer still to home. In 1865 Franz Von Suppe, pioneer of the Viennese operetta, enjoyed great success with a version of the Pygmalion myth entitled *The Beautiful Galatea*, whose overture took the musical world by storm:

> Starting buoyantly, then becoming almost Wagneresque, it ended with a waltz so potent, so Viennese, that Frederick Loewe must unconsciously have paid homage to it when he composed the Embassy Waltz for *My Fair Lady*.

It was to be Loewe's curious fate that in the act of crowning his career so triumphantly with *My Fair Lady*, he was fashioning melodies for a hero he knew would never quite attempt to sing them. The essence of Professor Higgins is that, confronted by the most voluptuous melodies, he will talk his way through them because he insists he cannot sing in the accepted sense of the word at all. Rex Harrison's creation of the role was quite faultless, but it must have been hard sometimes for Loewe to hear his happiest configurations being flung aside in the cause of characterization. Nowhere is this more striking than in 'A Hymn to Him', an inspired exercise in misogynistic doggerel which never gets to be sung at all. If we wish to acquaint ourselves with what Loewe has written, we are obliged to resist the performance and concentrate on its accompaniment, where may be discovered, in the middle passage to which Lerner has fitted a lyric beginning 'One man in a million may shout a bit', the most perfect evocation of genteel Edwardian England in the whole score, a sedate four-bar measure which then echoes itself a tone higher, raising as it does so the ghosts of long-dead brass bands whose tarradiddles once wafted out across the esplanades of England's fashionable watering places, the kind of music possessing the power to evoke specific costumes, manners, banter and choreography, all of which belong to the lost world in which Shaw's play was conceived. 'A Hymn to Him' is the triumph of Higgins at the expense of Loewe.

Whatever posterity may find to say about the partnership, it will certainly concede that it was the most accomplished songwriting team, pugilistically speaking, in the history of the American theatre. It will also take note of Lerner's account of how his father deployed his own love of boxing in the cause of the Noble Art of Self-Indulgence, and how, through a careless miscalculation regarding the latest boxing information, he crashed to matrimonial disaster. Sometimes when Lerner senior said he was off to the Friday night fights, he was not being strictly accurate; as his son put it, 'On many occasions his taste for combat drew him to other, more quilted arenas.' Alan continues:

> In those days people worked on Saturdays, and one Saturday morning, my father later told me, as he was preparing to go to the office, two things happened that had never happened during his entire married life. The first was that while he was dressing my mother woke up. The second was that as she opened her eyes she said, 'Who won the fight?' Alas, that Friday happened to have been one of the nights my father's ringside seat was empty. I do not remember who fought in the main bout, but we will call them Smith and Jones. My father, taking a chance, said 'Smith'. My mother turned over and went back to sleep. My father went into the dining-room and opened the *New York Times* at the sports page. Jones had won.

That both Alan's parentage and his professional partnership should have been so profoundly affected by a sport which figures nowhere in his collected works may bemuse as well as amuse many of his admirers, but I can assure them that his interest in and admiration of the great gladiators of his boyhood never left him; as proof of his enduring loyalty I can cite his exasperation when the English edition of his autobiography, which mentions the fights between Joe Louis and Max Schmeling referred to the challenger as Schmelling and then unbelievably compounded the error in the index by omitting all reference to Louis and listing instead a mysterious figment of the indexer's imagination called 'Schmelling, Louis'. Whether he retained much interest in the techniques of the latterday champions I couldn't say, but I suspect that, like most of us, the real giants for him were those of his childhood. I never quite reconciled myself to the streak of controlled pugnacity which must once have been visible in the temperament of one of Harvard's up-and-coming nine-stoners, for he was in all things sweet and gentle in his worldly relations. Yet there must once have been a time when hitting people was a prime interest in his life. Were there moments, I wonder, when the two partners, the sucker for a left hook and the sacrificial offering to Mr Canzoneri, ever beguiled the longueurs between shows by boxing a few rounds? Probably not. They were both pianists, and a pianist must always care for his hands. In their long friendship, the only time there was any faint danger of bellicosity was during the trying time when *Camelot* desperately needed the hand of a capable director when Moss Hart was too ill to carry on. Lerner offered himself as a stopgap. Loewe insisted on a search for a replacement for Hart. The difference of opinion grew into a dispute and the dispute into a breach:

> Irritations and differences between us that had been long forgotten and were of little consequence at the time had now become the subject of questions by interviewers. Our replies travelled from mouth to mouth and by the time they reached us they were unrecognizable distortions. If we had stayed steadfastly and constantly together as we always had in the past we would have laughed, rowed or shrugged but in the end gone about our business. We did not. I do not know why we did not. I may have thought I knew then but whatever I thought, I am certain I was wrong. I have a feeling the reason was something far more insidious, something which neither of us was aware of and which affected us in different ways. I have a feeling it may have been too much success. . . . Perhaps I misinterpreted our differences as lack of support and he misinterpreted mine as heroics. Perhaps. Perhaps not. I will never know. Too much was never said. In the end we were a little like the couple being discussed in one of Noël Coward's early plays. 'Do they fight?' said one. 'Oh, no,' said the other, 'they're much to unhappy to fight.'

As this is the only statement about the break-up of a songwriting partnership by one of the participants which is both candid and coherent, it deserves to be studied in some depth. Whether or not Lerner was right about the corrupting effect of his success, there is no question that the breach was in artistical terms a tragedy for both men as well as for the modern musical. Loewe was tempted out of retirement only once, when Lerner prevailed upon him to resume the collaboration for a Hollywood version of *The Little Prince*, a work whose deplorable message that death is a good thing for children made it a surprisingly maladroit choice for someone as sensitive and intelligent as Lerner, who later blamed the fiasco on the 'cinematic bigfoot' who directed the picture. As for Lerner, the rest of his life was an unfulfilled search for a partner who could complement him half as well as Loewe had done. The only man who came anywhere near achieving this impossible task was Burton Lane, a teenaged prodigy in the 1920s who had graduated to Hollywood, where he had composed dozens of successful songs before returning to Broadway in 1947 to collaborate with E. Y. Harburg on *Finian's Rainbow*. Then there followed an eighteen-year silence from Lane, who explains his virtual retirement by claiming that although during this period he read hundreds of scripts, nothing appealed to him until the day he received a telephone call from Lerner outlining the premise of *On a Clear Day You Can See Forever*. Lane says he accepted instantly and never had cause to regret the decision.

On a Clear Day You Can See Forever may not be the best-known of Lerner's works, but it is certainly the one which comes closest to expressing his personal beliefs. Like his father, he was what might be called a secular Jew, a man born into the religion who never practised its rituals but who never rejected its roots. In his autobiography he describes the following incident:

> Two days before his death, my father looked up from his hospital bed and wrote to my younger brother Bob: 'What religion are your children?' Bob replied good humouredly, 'I don't know. Whatever church is on the corner I'll send them to.' My father nodded approvingly and wrote: 'It's all a lot of apple sauce.'

But if Alan was not religious in the conventional way, he was certainly sustained by what could be called a supernatural belief. He was convinced that none of us dies in the accepted sense:

> Nothing outside of the theatre has intrigued me and sustained my unflagging interest more than the occult, extra-sensory perception, reincarnation and all that is called metaphysical until it is understood and becomes physical.

And on the night when he was honoured by a one-man show in New York, he told his audience at the outset, 'Fundamentally I suppose I'm more interested in the dreams of Man, which are eternal, than in the temporary perversions of those dreams called reality.' At this point we are not a million miles away from the belief in the Life Force which so animated Alan's great intellectual hero Bernard Shaw, nor are we very distanced from Shaw's remark about all serious work being humorous. *Brigadoon* disclosed Alan's fascination for the paranormal, but it was not for nearly twenty years that he explored in a musical work his unshakeable faith in reincarnation.

The heroine of this unusual work is one Daisy Gamble, who regards her own psychic gift as a toy which she cheerfully deploys in such harmless pursuits as inducing flowers to blossom by talking to them. Unhappy about her habit of chain-smoking, she visits a psychiatrist who quickly perceives her alarming powers of extra-sensory perception. She knows instinctively where things are hidden and seems to be able to know the gist of telephone conversations before they happen. Under hypnosis her voice changes and she becomes metamorphosed into a nineteenth-century English orphan who has married a peer and cuckolded him for the love of a blue-blooded gambler. The doctor falls in love, not with Daisy but with her Victorian alter ego, which reduces Daisy to despair. She is being upstaged by her own former self. The tangle is eventually resolved when the doctor uses telepathic communication to implore Daisy to come back to him, which she eventually does. Lane was not the first composer propositioned by Lerner. In 1961 Alan had made a formal arrangement to collaborate on the saga of Daisy Gamble with Richard Rodgers. The working title was *I Picked a Daisy*, a prophetic title in view of what became of it. The collaboration was a disaster. Lerner recalls Rodgers telling him one day that Oscar Hammerstein had been known to disappear for three weeks before coming up with a lyric. Lerner, who had been known to take longer than that, comments, 'I should have realized at once our collaboration was doomed.' The Rodgers account is unintentionally comic. In his own autobiography, Rodgers complains that Lerner would make an appointment with him and not keep it, or, if he did show up, usually with only half a lyric. He concedes, 'It wasn't all Alan's fault. Perhaps he felt uncomfortable working with someone he found too rigid.' Perhaps also he felt uncomfortable working with someone whose tunes he found unappealing. Whatever the truth, Rodgers seemed to have the idea that lyrics could be written to office hours, and indeed thought so little of the craft that at one stage he appointed himself, with predictable results in *No Strings*. The episode can be seen in retrospect as a narrow escape for both men.

Lane proved to be more understanding than Rodgers, and very much more resourceful musically, even though he had misgivings based on his misunderstanding of the premise of the plot. Even the show's title bewildered him. He says that at first he took it to be a fanciful variation of a cliché current at the time, 'On a clear day you can see Catalina Island'. Yet it seemed to imply something more complex. He finally decided that if he were to write a tune and then Lerner wrote a lyric which made sense, then the show itself might make sense:

One night I sat down and wrote a melody. I wrote half a melody really. I didn't have the middle section or the ending but I had half a melody, and what was going through my mind was that at no point should he give away the title until the very end of the song. I didn't have any words, but I tried to illustrate it by saying, 'On a blue day diddle da-de-dah-dah, on a grey day . . . on a happy day, whatever, but on a clear day, on that clear day you can see forever' – saving the title for the very end.

Lerner found that writing this lyric was one of the toughest chores of his life. He spent two weeks in the attempt before realizing that if he waited till he completed it the rest of the show would never be written. So he moved on, allowing himself three hours a morning, seven days a week for working on the title song. And that was the schedule to which he adhered religiously. It took him eight months, and he remembered writing 91 complete sets of words and discarding them all. Of the 91 all but eight were thrown away and never even seen by Lane, who recalls going through the eight surviving versions of the song, each one worse than all the others. 'Alan, who is a genius, took eight stabs at the lyric and they were awful. I mean, you cannot conceive that someone with his kind of ability could come so far off. You'd say to yourself, whoever wrote this lyric never wrote a lyric before. It's hard to conceive, but one day he came in with the lyric that we now have, which is absolutely stunning. It's magic.'

What Lerner had at last succeeded in doing was to express his sense of the paranormal. Where Lane had assumed a conventional set of words expressing various moods through the colours of the day, Lerner used Lane's melody to state his belief, held with perfect sincerity that

The glow of your being outshines every star.

He brought the same intensity of emotion to the other lyrics in the show. The plea of the psychiatrist that Daisy return from her Victorian bolthole crystallizes into 'Come Back to Me', with its invocation:

If a date waits below
Let him wait for Godot.

Most involuted of all, and so brilliantly executed, is the song in which Daisy expresses her jealousy of her own previous incarnation. Here is that rarity, an original love triangle. Girl loves boy who loves another girl who is the first girl. Lerner defined this song as 'a puzzler':

No matter how many times I wrote it, it never sounded right. Finally I realized that the melody had a peculiar strength that demanded words of one syllable. Not only words of one syllable but strong words like 'knack of', 'lack of', harsh-sounding words.

Lerner's perception that here was a song which demanded something diametrically opposed to the kind of polysyllable fireworks with which he was associated by those who recalled 'Why Can't the English' and 'A Hymn to Him', must have filled him with foreboding. For, as every lyricist knows, it is the short words that give the most trouble, a fact of life confirmed by Alan in a memorable moment. He was ever the lyricist, never the bore about lyrics. One night, in the car park of the Chichester Festival Theatre, a small group of us were chatting idly about the musical we had just endured, when one of the company happened to make a flattering remark about the polysyllabic vanities of Henry Higgins. I think it may have been the passage which runs:

> Exasperating, irritating, vacillating, calculating, agitating, maddening and infuriating.

Alan listened to the recitation and then, turning to give me a sidelong conspiratorial glance, said, 'They're the easy ones. It's the short ones that give the trouble.' It was his look at me in the half-light of the swirling car headlights around us, which I treasure as yet another of his little compliments to somebody who was after all no more than a passing acquaintance. I knew what he had in his mind when he made the remark, because he had once described to me the long search for a rhyme to fit into Daisy's song about her rivalry to herself. 'What Did I Have That I Don't Have Now?' has two full choruses; in the first, halfway down, there occurs the neat interior rhyme:

> Something in me then, he could see then.

The difficulty was to match it with something as neat, with a touch of wit, something which expressed the same idea with a different image. Daisy saw her own existence as the sequel to a previous life. Lerner eventually solved the problem with the pairing of two common two-syllable words. The whole thing takes only nine syllables.

> Why is the sequel never equal?

But in spite of the agonies to which he submitted himself every time he started to compose a new lyric, he never lost the impish suspicion that somewhere at the bottom of it all there was hidden a huge joke. Some years after writing 'On a Clear Day', he was told by a friend that the lyric was to be used as the text of a sermon at a local church. Lerner responded wryly: 'Tell the minister not to wait for the second chorus.' Unlike some of his professional colleagues, Alan was a great historian of the genre. The last book he published was proof of his knowledge, and it was proof too of his belief in the importance of song-with-words to all of us. The denouement of his history of the musical is this:

In the musical *42nd Street*, the director of the play says, in an ecstatic moment, 'The two most glorious words in the English language, Musical Comedy.' Quite right.

It follows that any man who contributed to that much-loved form would have been among Alan's heroes:

> In the 1930s , when I was at school, I was induced into trance by the pipes playing 'Dancing in the Dark', 'Just One of Those Things', 'Where or When' and 'Embraceable You'. To me, an exotic aphrodisiac was a great pair of legs on a girl in the front line. And the gurus who led me on to the next plane of happiness had nice Occidental names like Gershwin, Rodgers, Porter, Hart, Berlin, Dietz and Schwartz. I knew every song and every lyric they wrote, including the verse and second chorus.

Notice that Alan has taken especial care to place Lorenz Hart among the great masters of his chosen art, by naming not only the writer but the title of one of his loveliest and metaphysically profound ballads. Lerner had a special affection for Hart. The two men were friends in the last years of Hart's tragic life, and the older man never failed to encourage and advise the apprentice. And then, having described the sad end of his hero, he writes:

> I believe in reincarnation, and I pray the next time he returns he is six feet tall and that he will be repaid in kind for the joy he gave and never shared.

It would be taking discretion to absurd lengths to attempt any appreciation of Lerner without referring to his relationships with women. He was famous as the most-married gifted man in the Western world, and although I felt that a man's private life is his private business, and that nobody has the right to publicize either his fortunes or his misfortunes in this area, I have to say that he had a delightful sense of the unorthodoxy of his situation sometimes and expressed it with typical whimsicality. The first time I ever met him he was staying with his then wife, the penultimate incumbent, as he later put it, at the Berkeley Hotel in London. I forget now who arranged our meeting or on what pretext, but whatever the circumstances, there is always a great difficulty on these occasions in breaking the ice. I, a local nobody, find myself alone in a room with some great practitioner of his art. We have never met. He knows nothing about me. What am I to say? I have faced the dilemma a hundred times, with every sort of celebrity from Orson Welles to Frank Sinatra, from Joe Louis to Denis Compton, from Neville Cardus to Compton Mackenzie, but never was I disarmed so humorously or so painlessly as on my introduction to Alan. He emerged from the bedroom, extended his hand and said, 'I believe you know my father-in-law', a remark of such stupefying incongruity that I backed into an armchair and started laughing. We both knew that I was by some years the younger man, and yet, with this eccentric opening gambit, Alan was aligning himself with unbarbered youth, prepared for an encounter with a member of the older generation. The facts were that someone had briefed him about my jazz background, and that he had inferred from what was told to him that I must at some time have come across the well-known jazz pianist whose daughter was the current Mrs Lerner. 'But he's younger than you are,' I blurted out. 'I know,' responded Alan, 'and so's his daughter.' When I asked him how the piano player had reacted to news of the nuptials, he told me that the father-in-law's initial impulse had been to go out and find a child-bride of his own. By this time we were laughing at and with each other like old friends, and it had been all his own work, the first of many small kindnesses and courtesies he was to show me.

My only other recollection of any observation by him on the vexed question of the battle of the sexes takes me back to an afternoon when we had been discussing the details of a recital we were to give, appropriately enough at the Shaw Theatre, the idea being that my dissertations on the art of the theatre lyric should be interrupted periodically by Alan, who would recite words without music. The fate of the eventual recital falls outside the bounds of this narrative, but on the afternoon when Alan and I met to find out what he might care to select for recitation from his own works, he was pressed for time because of rehearsals at the Adelphi Theatre for a revival of *My Fair Lady*. I can see him now, leaning on the sill of a first-floor window watching me thread my way towards the front door, after which he displayed great patience for an hour or so as we discussed possible items. He then announced his imminent departure for the theatre, inviting me to share his taxi. Along Knightsbridge we found ourselves locked in a spectacular traffic jam, at which point he suddenly took to chatting about femininity in general and his own experiences in particular. After reflecting that the disappearance from the musical theatre of Julie Andrews had been a calamity for writers like himself who required the inspiration of interpretative virtuosity every time they embarked on the long haul of a new show, he went on to define his present situation. I sensed that he might not altogether be content with his prevailing arrangements, and that his present preoccupation was very much with Eliza Doolittle, but his talk was so amusing and so utterly lacking in any taint of self-pity that I was not sure whether to laugh or to commiserate. Suddenly we found ourselves inching through the afternoon traffic of the Strand and approaching the end of the journey, at which point he cut off his ruminations and announced his final conclusions on this most enigmatic of riddles. 'What can you do with them?' he asked, and then, glancing at me with just a shade of uncertainty, as though fearing I might find him guilty of self-idolatry, he quoted his own wonderful words: 'Their heads are full of cotton, hay and rags.' And then he darted out of the taxi leaving me laughing on the pavement and asking myself if he had ever considered playing the role of Henry Higgins. That evening, the London papers carried the story of his engagement to the beautiful singer-actress playing the role of Eliza, Liz Robertson. After that, judging from his demeanour whenever I saw him, I deduced that he had found his perfect partner at last.

I remain uncertain whether his rejoicing in the slapstick procedures of his profession did not occasionally tempt him to gild the lily. Whenever he was not engaged on one of his wars of attrition with some recalcitrant rhyme or maladroit metre, he was the most diverting of raconteurs. His view of the musical stage was of unqualified delight at the antics of his fellow-workers, and there may have been moments when the artist in him embellished the facts a little in the cause of a good story. I can never be sure, but there is the business of his work on a 1952 MGM production called *Royal Wedding*, for which Burton Lane wrote the tunes. The story he wrote for Fred Astaire was most unusual in the degree to which it incorporated facts into its fiction. Like Comden and Green's *The Bandwagon* a year later, *Royal Wedding* was very much a *roman à clef*, and there must have come moments during the period when Astaire must have wondered where his own life stopped and make-believe started. Just as *The Bandwagon* has much to do with the 1931 stage production of that name, incorporating Fred's eternal quest for a dancing partner of the desired height and poundage after the retirement of his sister Adele, so *Royal Wedding* reconstructs the details of the process by which Adele dwindled into a wife. In the summer of 1929, at the last night of the Gershwin musical *Funny Face* at the Princes Theatre in London, Adele was introduced to Lord Charles Cavendish, son of the ninth Duke of Devonshire. For the next two years Cavendish, conducting himself like the traditional Wodehousean hero, wooed Adele in several cities, finally taking a job with a New York banking house in order to be strategically well-placed while Adele was co-starring with Fred in *The Bandwagon*, which the brother and sister were agreed would be Adele's last appearance before marrying Cavendish, which she did, contriving to live happily ever after in the style of the most improbable musical comedy libretto.

In *Royal Wedding* Astaire and Jane Powell play Tom and Ellen Bowen, who close their Broadway run of *Tonight and Every Night* and bring it to London, where Ellen meets, falls in love with and eventually marries Lord John Brindale, played by Peter Lawford. The picture stands towards the bottom of Astaire's merit-list and is remembered today only for the sequence in which Fred, by resorting to trick photography, dances all over the ceiling in a gravity-defying dance to a song called 'You're All the World To Me'. In this song Lerner matches Lane's romantic tune with a catalogue of romantic symbols, which, for the purposes of illustrating the anecdote, had better be quoted:

> You're like Paris in April and May,
> You're New York on a silvery day.
> A Swiss Alp as the sun grows fainter,
> You're Loch Lomond when autumn is the painter.
> You're moonlight on a night in Capri,
> And Cape Cod looking out at the sea.
> You're all the places that leave me breathless,
> You're all the world to me.

Lane's professional apotheosis had come in 1934 when, as a 22-year-old, he wrote a song fated to be dismembered by Joan Crawford in a picture called *Dancing Lady*, in which Astaire appeared as himself. Lane and his partner Harold Adamson, having produced in 'Everything I Have Is Yours' a song so performer-proof that not even Miss Crawford's voice could altogether conceal its quality, were now assigned an Eddie Cantor picture produced by Sam Goldwyn, for which most of the songs were to be written by Walter Donaldson and Gus Kahn. Lane and Adamson were required to write a bright number for a scene in which the blacked-up Cantor plays the star of a simulated minstrel show. At one point he is flanked by the juvenile Nicholas Brothers, who dance a dazzling routine to the strains of a song called 'I Want to Be a Minstrel Man'. The lyrics run as follows:

> We always love a minstrel man.
> He thrills us like nobody can.
> The way he dances sure is dandy,
> And sings the songs about his sugar candy.
> He's learned to love the minstrel ways,
> Oh, bring them back, the minstrel days,
> Give us a man like George M. Cohan,
> We want a minstrel man.

As to how he decided to revive the melody of 'I Want to Be a Minstrel Man' and get Lerner to transform it into a romantic piece by slowing the tempo and writing a new lyric, Lane's recollection is vague, but he leaves no doubt that the whole thing was done in the full view of everyone:

Astaire was introduced in a film which was my first film, *Dancing Lady*. We were asked to do one or two songs for it, and they liked this song we wrote; which had no lyric. We were then told the tune would suit Eddie Cantor, so I agreed. Adamson then wrote a lyric which I never felt realized everything the tune could have. It limited it. I was never very happy with the result, but it worked in the picture. Many years later, working on the *Royal Wedding* assignment, I remembered this tune and decided to try to get the rights back from Sam Goldwyn, because this is the tune I always dreamed would be good for Astaire. And when I played it for Astaire, he flipped.

Lerner's recollection of the episode was very different, in that he had no recollection at all. He had assumed that Lane wrote the melody for *Royal Wedding*, and told me he had no knowledge of any previous incarnation. Perhaps, knowing how I relished the idea of any songwriter being paid twice for the same piece of work, he pandered to my sense of humour and pretended that Lane had duped everyone, himself included. Perhaps on the other hand Lane really did pull off a daring subterfuge without anyone noticing. Whatever the answer, the anecdote underlines the terrible handicaps under which researchers in the muddy waters of the songwriting profession are obliged to labour.

I miss the presence of Alan Lerner in London. Even after long spells without meeting, his proximity seemed to make the theatre a more interesting place. I shall miss his 'Dear boy' as he greeted you, and the full-hearted boyish laughter which followed the recitation of one of his absurdly true stories. If his conviction regarding the paranormal possibilities of the human race turn out to have been an inspired guess, then I venture to suggest that even as I type this memoir, he is off in some cool corner of paradise arguing his case before a jury consisting in its entirety of George Bernard Shaw, and insisting that it was right and proper for Eliza to get her Henry Higgins in the end. In the meantime, we have his lyrics to console us.

CHAPTER SEVEN

Frank Loesser

ONE TIME, DAMON RUNYON ADVISED his old crony Gene Fowler, 'To hell with plots, because nobody remembers much about the plots of Dickens and Mark Twain, they remember the characters.' Coming from one of the supreme masters of the surprise ending, this is rich, but richness apart, there is nothing particularly perceptive or unusual about the remark. What distinguishes Runyon from all the other modern classics is not the preoccupation with picaresque characters, but the lengths to which he was prepared to go to find them. No writer ever flouted the unwritten code more blatantly in the quest for quiddity of temperament, and none showed more eagerness to explore where other men were not prepared to go, far beyond the charted limits of the literary life. Runyon was like a traveller who disappears one day down a deep dark hole and returns years later with fabulous tales to tell.

He was a small-town boy – symbolically the place was called Manhattan, Kansas – born on 8 October 1880, the son of an itinerant drunkard, gambler, printer and Indian fighter. He sold his first piece to the *Pueblo Evening Post* when he was seventeen, drifted through the ranks of scattered newspapers in Mississippi and Colorado, settled at the *Denver Rocky Mountain News* in 1906 for four years, and by 1910 was working for Hearst on the *New York American*. Within a year he was making enough money from his bizarre baseball reporting to marry a would-be socialite called Ellen Egan. From this moment the choice confronting him was stark. Like Twain, he had chosen a wife who much preferred gentility to the typewriter, but, unlike Twain, Runyon plumped for the typewriter every time, wrecking his own marriage, estranging his own children, and winning an awesome reputation, even among his press-box cronies, as a loner, a dedicated, dispassionate observer who kept his emotions to himself and went around looking for stories he could tell.

FRANK LOESSER

But although Runyon was, and still is, one of the most elusive figures in popular literature, he has left us an oblique portrait of himself. He is the faceless 'I' of the Broadway fables, the little man who drifts helplessly in the wake of hoods and hoodlums because they insist on having him around. When, in the tale 'Blood Pressure', the narrator is invited for a night's sport by the monstrous Rusty Charley, he is too terrified to refuse, but once the escapade begins, nothing shocks him, not even Rusty Charley's feat of knocking an iceman's horse cold with one punch. It does not do to cross such characters, and the narrator takes care never to do so. The real Runyon was friendly with a lot of real Rusty Charleys, all of whom he was careful not to offend, and whom he immortalized in stories which would never have come to be written at all had it not been for his taste for low company. Poor bewildered Ellen Egan, the frustrated socialite, once said, 'If he should die, I wouldn't know a soul at the funeral.'

Of course Runyon paid a price for this freedom. There is a distressing philistinism about his attitude to life and letters. In *Bred for Battle* we are given to understand that either a man is musical or he has courage, one or the other. And when in 1926 the Shavian Gene Tunney outboxed the saloon slugger Jack Dempsey, Runyon could never quite convince himself that the fight hadn't been fixed. All his life he had idolized rough, tough prizefighters, Rusty Charleys in silk drawers, and that the roughest and toughest of them all should be outpointed by a milksop who read poetry was too much for him. After all, fights were fixed every day of the week, a few of them by Runyon himself, so why take Tunney's science for granted? Again, Runyon's stance on literary ethics is revealing. He had none. 'Get the money,' he used to say; and again, 'My measure of success is money'; and yet again, 'Money is not everything, it is only 99 per cent of everything.' This is to reduce the writer's morality to the level of the hoodlum, but then he never seems to have had much professional pride. When the Hollywood moguls mangled his scripts, he not only went quietly, but actually praised them for it, saying that if the picture made money, then the moguls must have known a thing or two when they butchered his stories. And it was this crude approach to manners and morals which eventually led Runyon into a fatal impasse.

For who were the most successful moneymakers of all? The criminal element. There is something risible about Runyon's ambivalence in the face of the murderous criminality with which he consorted. Men who dealt in homicide, prostitution and kidnapping, who lied, thieved and counterfeited their way to huge fortunes, who bought judges and congressmen, police chiefs and city mayors, all of them were fine fellows in Runyon's book. He was the confidante of Arnold Rothstein, the racketeer and drug pedlar who rigged the 1919 World Series. He was a good friend to Al Capone, the biggest gangster in America. He even became an apprentice scoundrel himself, helping to fix the very gladiatorial contests whose outcome he had thrilled to as a boy. Irony of ironies, he does not appear even to have been a very competent fixer; the fiasco of the notorious Young Stribling–Tommy Loughran match of 1924, when Runyon apparently forgot to explain to Loughran that it was Stribling's turn to win, does irreparable damage to the portrait of himself which Runyon liked to advertise, of the Big City wiseacre schooled to perfection in the arts of skullduggery. Perhaps he was never aware of the contradictions. Perhaps he was aware and didn't care, adopting a kind of perverse moral imbecility born of artistic need, because without the acquiescence of the underworld, where would his fictional material come from?

And so in his stories Runyon apotheosizes the criminal classes of America, cleansing them with the whimsy of vocabulary and literary style. His Big Black Marrio is an idealized sketch of Capone, who had come out of Runyon's report of the 1931 trial smelling of roses. Dave the Dude is based on Frank Costello. Rothstein becomes The Brain, and George McManus, the professional assassin who murdered him, is bowdlerized into Daffy Jack. Walter Friedmann, who 'discovered' that monumental pugilistic mutt Primo Carnera, and who so ruthlessly abetted in the criminal exploitation of that pathetic man, becomes genial Good-Time Charley Bernstein. Miss Missouri Martin is the mirror-image of Texas Guinan; Waldo Winchester is a too thinly disguised Walter Winchell. And the likeable Dancing Dan, who gives the Mob the slip one yuletide night by disguising himself as Santa Claus, is a projection of one Ratsy Tourbillon, alias Dapper Don Collins, shakedown virtuoso who, after a lifetime dedicated to the gentle art of seduction, arrived at the Byronic conclusion that 'between the ages of 16 and 60 no man is completely sane except for the ten minutes immediately following an orgasm'. If he was right, and if what we are told of him is even half-true, then Ratsy must have been sane a great deal of the time.

These strong links with reality extend to the remarkable musical comedy distilled from the stories. Sky Masterson was drawn from the life, the life of Bat Masterson, one-time sheriff of Dodge City, who went east one day and playfully forgot to leave his guns behind. Nathan Detroit owes much of his flair to that colourful gambler and cabaret partner of Jimmy Durante, Lou Clayton. Lieutenant Brannigan looks back to the renowned John Broderick, the most feared strong-arm plainclothes cop in the New York of Runyon's time. Angie the Ox is really one Ciro Terranova, a gangster who endeared himself to all but vegetarians by cornering the New Jersey artichoke market. Hot-Horse Herbie is a salute to Horse-Thief Burke, Runyon's Florida chauffeur and part-time tipster. The unforgettable Regret, one of Runyon's favourite creations, was in real life a mathematical genius called Abba

Dabba Berman, who worked the numbers racket for Dutch Schultz, and who got his, by proxy as it were, one night in 1935 at the Palace Chop House in Newark, when his employer concluded a discussion with some business associates by being carried out by the handles. And Harry the Horse, a fictional projection of a certain Benjamin Caplan, is said to be 'a noble sport who is about as good an off-hand liar as there is in the United States', and who echoes his creator by dropping the most famous of all the Runyon philosophical bon-bons, 'All horse-players die broke.' The words may have been Harry's but the rueful wisdom behind them was Runyon's. He was one of those suckers who try to play both ends against the middle, as the saying goes, squandering a fortune on a stable of three-legged thoroughbreds and simultaneously betting thousands on other suckers' horseflesh. We spare a thought for poor Ellen, who was taken to the Saratoga racetrack once and took a solemn oath never to go again. And we recall miss Cutie Singleton, whose affecting destiny it was to see her wedding day postponed indefinitely because Hot-Horse Herbie had blown the money for the ring on an unambitious nag called Naishapur.

Endowed with this extraordinary material, Runyon needed only to find a suitable literary convention to give it shape. He found it in the use of the Historic Present tense and by imposing on his gallimaufry of roughnecks a comically euphemistic mode of expression. Nobody in a Runyon tale is ever scared, only nervous; never murdered, only eliminated; never hates his enemy, merely does not wish him well. A gun is not a lethal weapon, only an equalizer; events are never remarkable, only more than somewhat. It was a demanding convention requiring endless rewrites. Runyon junior defined his father as 'an agony writer'. And Runyon himself, giving the lie to the myth of the happy columnist casually knocking off the tales in his spare time between big fights and football games, said, 'Good writing is simply a matter of application, but I learned years ago that the words will not write themselves down on paper in dreams or in conversation.' The seventy-two Runyon stories, then, are essentially literary compositions, describing a compact world with its own physical, ethical and psychological laws, its own pace and its own imposing style. How then, to set this peculiar world to music, to make it sing and dance, to orchestrate its nuances without destroying them utterly? When Runyon died of cancer, on 10 December 1946, had anyone confronted him with the name of the man who would do for Harry the Horse and Nathan Detroit what Alan Lerner later did for Henry Higgins and Alfred Doolittle, he would have winced and quoted the nominee as a rank outsider at a nice shade of odds. But then Runyon always was a poor judge of form, and would not have been all that surprised when the outsider romped home.

His misgivings would have been perfectly understandable, because the case of Frank Loesser is freakish even in the crazy world of the musical theatre, a processional from hack to master which was not only triumphal but utterly unexpected, and, in the context of Loesser's life, bizarre and irrational. Born in New York in 1910, the year that Runyon arrived there, Loesser, as late in the day as 1942, had no professional record as a composer at all. As a writer of melody he literally did not exist, having established himself exclusively as a lyricist in an age which had known only three men since the bombastic vaudevillean George M. Cohan to have acquired complete virtuosity in writing both words and music. These three were Irving Berlin, Cole Porter and Noël Coward, each of whom had been playing Gilbert to his own Sullivan virtually from the outset. Loesser, brilliant though everyone inside the profession acknowledged him to be in his appointed task of setting rhymes to music, seemed the very last person to add his name to that exclusive list. He had had no musical training, his attempts to sing in public had ended in debacle, and he had been obliged to endure the most inauspicious beginnings as a man of the theatre, sitting on stage making lightning sketches of members of the audience. Apologists endowed with the wisdom of hindsight could point out that Berlin had had no musical training, that Porter's attempts to sing were calamitous, that Coward's first professional engagement had been as a mussel in a fairy play about fish. But neither Berlin, Porter nor Coward had ever doubted his own ability as an all-purpose songwriter, whereas by the time he was into his thirties the idea of becoming his own collaborator had apparently not occurred to Loesser except as an idle daydream. To express it in terms of Nathan Detroit, he appeared to have no chance of winning the race because it had never struck him that he might enter it. After the familiar succession of jobs, as newspaper reporter, caricaturist in a vaudeville act, editor of a trade paper, and even as a food-taster for a string of restaurants, he had published his first lyric in 1931, a song written in collaboration with a Mr Schuman, later to become a distinguished academic at the Juilliard School of Music. The song was called 'In Love With a Memory of You', and the only recorded comment regarding it has come from its composer: 'I gave Frank his first flop.'

Not till 1936 was Loesser able to luxuriate in the feverish glow of witnessing the spectacle of his own words being performed on a public stage, in a production called *The Illustrators' Show*. No trace remains of this modest turkey, which survived only a few nights, yet its text would surely reward the diligent researcher, who would find within it not only Loesser's words for a whimsically named song called 'Bang – the Bell Rang', but also a melody called 'A Waltz Was Born in Vienna' which died in New York, much to the chagrin of its composer, an ex-boxer and very nearly an ex-songwriter called Frederick Loewe. There are times in the theatre when nothing succeeds like abysmal failure, and soon after *The Illustrators' Show* had buckled under the weight of its own idiocy,

Loesser and his partner, one Irving Actman, were brought out to Hollywood by Universal Studios. By the time the studio executives realized their error, it was too late. Loesser had implanted himself in the film colony and was going briskly about the business of building himself a remarkable reputation as a writer and even more as a character.

At this stage Actman falls out of the reckoning, although he was to return in another role later on, at the psychological moment in Loesser's life. The new partner was Burton Lane, who had been a teenaged prodigy and, although only twenty-four years old by the time Loesser encountered him, had already written hundreds of songs and three Broadway revues, and had contributed to twelve musical pictures. His reputation stood mainly on his 1934 song composed for Joan Crawford to ruin in *Dancing Lady*, a ballad which has retained its currency ever since, 'Everything I Have Is Yours'. Lane had been shuffling between several studios since arriving in Hollywood, and by 1937, when he met Loesser, had still not settled at any one of them. Loesser's work impressed him greatly, and because he was himself involved in negotiations with Paramount, he procured a contract there for Loesser also. It is from the reminiscences of Lane that we get our first clear picture of Loesser the reckless egotist, unabashed by the indifference of the outside world to what he was doing:

> I thought he had great talent as a lyric writer. He had more lyrics he wanted to show me, so he invited me over to his apartment. He was living on Sunset Boulevard, where you either have to walk down seventy-five flights or up seventy-five flights to reach the apartments. So I came over after dinner and he said that he and his wife were having dinner and did I want some. I said I had already eaten, so I waited while he and his wife cooked a can of beans and shared an apple. They were penniless. So then he gets the Paramount contract, and the day after he signs the contract I walk into the office and there's a guy measuring him for shirts and suits. He was off to the races.

In view of what was eventually to happen, it is interesting that Lane recalls Loesser as 'a wonderful fresh kind of Runyonese character'. More revealing is a conversation between them which Lane never forgot:

> He said to me once, 'Burt, what do you think of a simple melody like this?' and he starts singing 'The Best Things in Life Are Free'. I said I thought it was a lovely tune, very simple but lovely. And he says, 'Oh, I could write tunes like that.' I said 'You could? Well go ahead and write them, you don't need me.' Well, the son of a gun went off and did it.

Burton is vaulting over the few hectic years in which Loesser served his apprenticeship as a lyricist, years in which he seemed able to produce witty, original verses no matter what the dramatic situation or who his collaborator happened to be. Lane found his working methods peculiar:

> In the days when I was working with Frank, I had to sit at the piano and play the tune constantly until he remembered it well enough to write a lyric to it. There was no way in those days except for the composer to play the song for the lyricist. Now Frank was very secretive. He would sit across the room from me, a pad held very high so that all I could see was his eyes. He would write very small, and then he would suddenly start to smile, and I'm dying to know what he's writing. I would say, 'Frank, what is it, what did you get, what made you laugh, what's tickling you?' And he'd go on writing till he'd finished, and then he'd put what he'd written up on the piano. His handwriting was terrible, and I'm supposed to sing the song and read his handwriting at the same time. Now I really adored Frank, but if I blew a line because I couldn't understand his writing, he'd say, 'God damn it, what's the matter with you, can't you read?' and he'd get upset. But finally he would settle down and I would ask him to type it out. He was wonderful to work with, great fun.

In the next three years Loesser worked on every kind of story with a bewildering variety of composers. His first picture with Lane was a dreary fishing epic called *Spawn of the North*, and it is certainly symbolic that the star, Dorothy Lamour, remembered it as the worst-smelling production in which she was ever involved. By the time he joined the armed forces as a writer of army shows, he had established himself as the most promising of the younger school of lyricists. Among the songs from this period which are well remembered are:

> 'Moon of Manakura', with Alfred Newman.
> 'See What the Boys in the Back Room Will Have', with Frederick Hollander.
> 'Kiss the Boys Goodbye', with Victor Schertsinger.
> 'Small Fry', with Hoagy Carmichael.
> 'The Lady's In Love With You', with Burton Lane.
> 'They're Either Too Young or Too Old', with Arthur Schwartz.

In retrospect, we see that there were other Loesser lyrics which deserved better than the oblivion which has obscured them ever since. 'Dancing on a Dime', written with Lane for a B-picture named after the song, and 'Snug as a Bug in a Rug', a collaboration with the violinist Matty Malneck for a trifle entitled *The Gracie Allen Murder Case*, are two among many. But his most impressive achievement in these emergent years was something written in collaboration with Hoagy Carmichael in 1939, a lyric which demonstrates both the deftness of Loesser's technique and the ease with which he could assimilate the intricacies of plot and characterization which are inevitable with an inherited property. In the previous year Paramount had signed up an ex-vaudevillean who had graduated to musical comedy but whose appeal to the studio lay in his success as a radio comedian. This artist, the London-born Bob Hope, was now teamed up with a former dance band singer named Shirley Ross and featured in one of those pot-pourri B-pictures of the period, *The Big Broadcast of 1938*. The vestigial plot concerned an ocean race between two luxury liners, with Hope and Ross portraying a young divorced couple who enjoy an accidental encounter on one of the boats. There were to be several songs, written by the successful team of Leo Robin and Ralph Rainger. The original intention had been to play the big encounter scene between the divorcees in dialogue, but after recruiting half a dozen writers and rejecting their work in despair, the producer, one Harlan Thompson, was visited by the one useful idea of his life and decided on the ingenious tactic of dropping the problem into the laps of Robin and Rainger, who were instructed to write a song in which the estranged couple tell each other they still love each other without actually mentioning the fact. The lyricist, Robin, now enjoyed his finest hour by composing the verses of 'Thanks for the Memory', one of the very few songs in the popular repertoire with claims to the status of a short story. The song triumphed, becoming an international hit and enjoying an evergreen distinction which still applies half a century later. But Robin, the astonished recipient of an Academy Award for his lyric, went to his grave incensed at the obtuseness of his employers, who had obliged him to rewrite what they took to be a prurient line. The offending reference was to the remembered honeymoon trip when 'we journeyed to Niagara and never saw the Falls'. It was the work of a moment for an experienced writer like Robin to rinse away the innuendo by substituting 'hardly' for 'never', but for the rest of his life he remained irate in his own meek and mild-mannered way that the success of his most famous song had very nearly been scotched by the philistines in Front Office. Those philistines, realizing that they had accidentally produced a highly profitable film which included a highly profitable song and a potentially highly profitable new star, now did what all studios did in those days whenever they had blundered into a moneymaking production. They produced it again. In the following year Paramount again featured Hope and Ross as a young loving couple and again sweetened the dish with some new songs. They could not very well use Robin and Rainger's big number so soon after the event, but they did the next-best thing by naming the follow-up production after the song, even though it never appears in the picture and has nothing to do with it. The film *Thanks for the Memory*, although it did not incorporate the song 'Thanks for the Memory' was even more profitable than *The Big Broadcast of 1938*, and yet the tactics deployed by the studio seemed then and still seem today to be deranged. Hoping to duplicate the success and prestige of the production, and hoping to confuse the public into buying tickets by implying that it actually *was* the first production, they borrowed the title of its big song but then hired different writers to provide the music.

By this stage in his career Loesser had already collaborated to some effect with Hoagy Carmichael, producing at least two pieces still remembered, 'Heart and Soul' and 'Small Fry'. The team was now assigned to do what Robin and Rainger had already done to perfection, conjure up a flippant piece whose unspoken sentiments, delivered in an elusive compromise between talk and song, imply a passionate romantic attachment expressed with the comic levity for which Hope was already becoming renowned. No two songwriters could ever have inherited a less rewarding job, for however well they performed, their new song was doomed to unfavourable comparison with Robin and Rainger's small masterpiece. And yet, due largely to Loesser's brilliant lyric, the song which eventually emerged from the confusion could stand comparison with the earlier piece. 'Two Sleepy People' has come over the years to be bracketed with 'Thanks for the Memory' as the best romantic duet of Hope's career, and it still seems surprising that in a year when 'Over the Rainbow' ran off with the Academy Award, and songs like 'Faithful Forever' and 'I Poured My Heart into a Song' received nominations, 'Two Sleepy People' was not so much as mentioned, since which misguided moment whenever topical parodies have been required for one of Hope's television shows or concerts, it is always 'Thanks for the Memory' rather than 'Two Sleepy People' which gets the dubious privilege of dismemberment.

But it is in his last grand gesture as a lyricist pure and simple that Loesser displays those qualities of Runyonesque chicane which were so affectionately remembered by Lane. In 1940, Jule Styne, working as a vocal coach at Twentieth Century Fox, was told by the head of the studio that he was wasting his time and ought to be concentrating on songwriting. Styne agreed, and soon found himself farmed out to the ultima thule of Hollywood studios, Republic Pictures, where they made cheap films about and for hillbillies. Styne, for whom the move meant a drastic cut in his income, went to work as an all-purpose music department, composing the songs, orchestrating the scores, conducting the studio orchestra, and finding himself obliged to create items with names like 'Poppin' the Corn', 'Crackerbarrel County' and 'That Ain't Hay'. Experiencing all the symptoms of artistic constriction, Styne demanded fresh collaborators and, when asked to name one, opted for Loesser, who soon found himself the innocent victim of a transfer deal resulting in his banishment to the wilds of Republic and the promotion of John Wayne, who went off to make pictures for Paramount. Loesser arrived at Republic burning with rage and filled with loathing for the culprit, whom he took to be Styne. The collaboration began with Loesser's announcement to Styne that he hated him:

> Look, I'm here for three weeks. I want to finish everything we have to do in a week. Not turn it in till the third week, but I won't be here the last two weeks. So play me some tunes.'
>
> So I played him the first tune. Loesser said: 'What's that tune? That's a great song. Shhh! We won't write that here. I'll borrow you to Paramount. Don't write that here.' He was that kind of a schemer. 'Quiet. Don't play. Lock that up.'

At the end of three weeks Loesser departed, fixed a Paramount contract for Styne, and put words to the melody that was too good for Republic. It finally appeared in an otherwise nondescript Paramount production called *Sweater Girl*, still remembered today for the Styne-Loesser hit, 'I Don't Want to Walk Without You Baby'. By this time Loesser was in uniform, having advised Styne, 'You've been spoiled. There's no one like me. I'll tell you what. If you want someone like me, don't get a clever rhymer, because there is a thing called a rhyming dictionary. Anybody can rhyme. You can find a rhyme for anything. But get a guy who can say something clever and warm, because you need warm lyrics for your music.' With which Loesser took his leave and began to undergo the most phenomenal transmutation ever experienced by a songwriter. He went into the war as a respected lyricist. He came out of it a rich composer.

It is not clear precisely why he now decided to become his own collaborator, except that being required to write for army shows it seemed the most convenient way of going about things. We have Lane's testimony that long before the war Loesser believed he could write tunes at least as good as 'The Best Things in Life Are Free', and later he confided to an associate that there were some mornings when he awoke feeling like Irving Berlin. Lane recalls that he and Loesser once discussed the question of Loesser's composing talent and that Loesser explained, 'Listen, after I write with you and Arthur Schwartz and Hoagy Carmichael and this one and that one, by God, I have got to learn something if I'm smart. You boys showed me how it goes.' Yet Loesser's first attempts to write melodies were more successful than distinguished. Most of them were silly exercises in jingoism, typified by his best-selling song whose title was borrowed from the impulsive Lieutenant-Commander Forgy, a United States naval officer who, finding his career prospects suddenly amended in the most bloodcurdling way at Pearl Harbor on 7 December 1941, placed himself most incongruously in the books of quotations by telling his men, 'Praise the Lord and pass the ammunition.' Dross of a similar style soon followed, and it was not until 1944 that Loesser served notice that a major new popular composer had arrived when he contributed a ballad for an otherwise misguided attempt to film Somerset Maugham's glum allegory of a disintegrating Europe, *Christmas Holiday*, a novel so bursting with thwarted passion and hopeless love that Frank Swinnerton, shrewdest of literary assessors, thought it 'very nearly a masterpiece' and Evelyn Waugh praised its 'accuracy, economy and control'. Any doubts of the book's quality were dispelled by the disapproval of Graham Greene who, of all people, dismissed it because of Maugham's 'odd ignorance of human feeling'. Loesser's contribution to all this was a sad piece called 'Spring Will Be a Little Late This Year', sung in the screen version of Maugham's story by Deanna Durbin, already approaching the premature end of a career grievously mishandled by her paymasters, and soon to effect her inspired and thoroughly praiseworthy escape from the industry. With 'Spring Will Be a Little Late This Year', Loesser's career as a composer was formally launched. In 1948 he published a song for the popular market called 'Slow Boat to China', a spectacular commercial success which was unusually sophisticated for the mass market, although its piquant harmonic sequence owed more than a little to the old Eubie Blake ballad 'Memories of You'. A year later his ingenious duet, 'Baby, It's Cold Outside', written originally as a party piece with which Loesser and his wife could amuse friends, was awarded an Oscar after being inserted into an otherwise regrettable charade called *Neptune's Daughter*. But by this time, Loesser's Hollywood career was virtually over.

In 1948 the would-be Broadway producer Cy Feuer was attempting to create a musical version of that inedible English chestnut, *Charley's Aunt*. His partner was one Ernest Martin, an aspiring master of disguise who had changed his name from Markowitz. Feuer had first encountered Loesser while occupying one of the more wildly comic sinecures of American cultural life, Head of Music at Republic Studios. Now, faced with the challenge of recruiting a team capable of making the arthritic Charley sing and dance, Feuer later claimed to have been so convinced about Loesser that he said to Martin, 'Look, we've got to go with Frank.' Yet both men were so imperceptive that it never occurred to them to invite Loesser to write the music for their first production, even though by now there was copious evidence of his talent. Instead, they decided to extend an invitation to Harold Arlen. But then, having accepted, Arlen changed his mind, at which Loesser began writing words and music unassisted. Rodgers and Hammerstein then invested in the show, which, after a slow opening in spite of fulsome praise from Cole Porter, suddenly rallied in the wake of Arthur Schwartz's claim, published in the *New York Times*, that Loesser was 'the greatest undiscovered composer in America'. *Where's Charley* went on to run for nearly eight hundred performances and set the seal on Loesser's new career.

By now Feuer and Martin were learning about Loesser's peculiarities of temperament, his outbursts of bad temper, his speed of thought, his cheerful arrogance, his little neuroses. Martin was bewildered by Loesser's refusal to sit in a restaurant unless his back was to the wall, while Feuer was reduced to total entrepreneurial disarray by Loesser's refusal to sign a contract to write *Guys and Dolls* until after the show's Broadway opening. Martin remembered him as a typical New Yorker, 'a street boy':

> In California he had this house with a tennis court. The net was always down. He never went outdoors. One day he said to me, 'Let's go and sit in the sun,' which in itself was a remarkable thing. I said 'Okay,' and he said, 'Wait a minute.' He went upstairs and he came down again in a little pair of swimming pants. And he had left on his garters and his shoes and socks. We went out there and we sat in the sun for about five minutes, and that was enough.

As to *Guys and Dolls*, its genesis was a halting affair which very nearly foundered at the start when a libretto written by Jo Swerling was found to lack the required Runyonesque qualities. Meanwhile, Loesser, who had given no formal indication of being committed to the enterprise, turned up one day with four songs based on Swerling's book. By the time the new librettist Abe Burrows had been called in, Loesser had written a complete score based on the rejected libretto. Burrows took one glance at Loesser's songs and was shrewd enough to realize that all he need do was fill in the spaces between the songs, writing scenes related to the lyrics, to arrive at the perfect Runyon scenario. In this sense Loesser could be said to have been the real librettist of *Guys and Dolls*, something of which he was perfectly well aware, as soon became apparent in his relations with his collaborators.

Years later the witnesses seemed to have become confused as to the details. According to Feuer, Loesser's dazzling rhymed lexicon of horseplaying slang, 'Fugue for Tinhorns', with its overlapping, interlocking racetrack terminology, was composed without being assigned any function in the story. Martin then suggested it be placed at the top of the show, where indeed it stands to this day. This pretty myth ignores the existence of 'Fugue For Tinhorns' in an earlier embryonic form, in which clearly it was tailored to perform functions of characterization worlds removed from Runyon's horseplayers. Decades later this original version of the song, 'Three-Cornered Tune', was excavated by the archaeologists of the musical theatre and recorded by Blossom Dearie, at which point it becomes clear that what Loesser must originally have intended was a repetitive theme suggestive of a hurdy-gurdy or music-box, with words, for the virginal heroine Sarah Browne, which so emphatically reject the whole Broadway ethos as to transform the composition into a childlike lullaby. At some stage between conception and opening night Loesser must have had second thoughts about the efficacy of his pastoral device, and was astute enough to create out of it the most effective musical expression of horseplaying philosophy ever published. The episode may seem insignificant except for the way it shows the questing nature of Loesser's mind and his refusal ever to be satisfied with his own work. The point to note about 'Three-Cornered Tune' is that it was a perfectly adequate, rather charming affair embellished with one or two refinements in the structure of the lyric; nine writers out of ten would have settled for it happily enough, but Loesser, feeling he could do better, transformed it into something remarkable.

It was while *Guys and Dolls* was in rehearsal that Loesser's inability to control himself in a crisis developed into a godsend for annalists and biographers. Burrows claimed that the phrase 'the oldest established permanent floating crap game' had come out of his libretto During the out-of-town try-out in Philadelphia, he and Loesser agreed that the phrase sounded less like dialogue than a lyric. It was then removed from the libretto so that Loesser could construct a song around it. Understandably once it was completed it constituted the sort of item likely to give performers considerable food for thought. According to Burrows, the choreographer was taking the cast through the song for the first time, attempting to resolve the problem of who might make something of which line, when Loesser came thundering down the aisle ranting away about the quality of the singing. When the choreographer attempted to mediate between author and actors, Loesser told him, 'You shut up.' When Burrows then interceded, Loesser turned on him and spat out, 'You're Hitler. And you're working for me. I'm the author. You're working for me.' The cast then began to sing out loud from sheer fright, as Loesser left the premises to buy some ice cream before retiring to his hotel. Worse was to befall an actress called Isobel Quigley, deputed to sing a song called 'I'll Know'. Mr Markowitz always believed that the song was unsingable because of the wide leap which occurs in the first line, 'I'll know when my love comes along'; between the words 'love' and 'comes' there occurs the interval, rarely encountered in popular song, of a seventh. But the leap, though awkward, is by no means as impossible as Mr Markowitz thought it was. A specialist like Sarah Vaughan or Ella Fitzgerald could have navigated it without any trouble and perhaps might even have contrived to make a virtue out of it. But those singers who find their way into stage musicals are usually chosen as much for their physical attractions and acting ability as for any great gifts as singers, which is why the definitive versions of the songs of the Broadway theatre have never been performed by the artists who introduced them. Miss Quigley very soon discovered that, like almost every other professional young lady in the musical theatre, she was obliged to deploy one vocal tone, vaguely soprano-like, for 'love', and quite another, more contralto-ish, for 'comes'. This very common failing began to exasperate Loesser, who, after enduring several unavailing attempts by Miss Quigley to navigate the leap, decided on a new and highly original method of bringing about the required effect. Stepping up on stage, Loesser rushed over to Miss Quigley and charitably bestowed upon her what Rusty Charley gave the iceman's horse. Loesser subsequently mollified the sobbing Miss Quigley with a costly bracelet, but the most revealing aspect of this appalling exhibition of loutishness is that Feuer and Markowitz evidently found it hilarious. Then again, entrepreneurs are almost never punched in the face, which is in itself a sad comment on the ethics of musical comedy. Most alarming of all is the light the incident casts on the temperament of the first Mrs Loesser. Her husband, for all his neuroses and outbursts of anger, was considered the less difficult of the two, a remarkable general opinion explaining the notorious definition of his lady as the evil of two Loessers.

It is the greatest of all the many virtues of *Guys and Dolls* that the closer one examines Runyon's life and works, the better and the truer the musical seems to be. Remembering Ellen's detestation of Saratoga and the foundering of Miss Singleton's marriage plans on the rock of the *Breeder's Guide*, consider 'Adelaide's Lament', in which the ever-loving adenoidal Adelaide bemoans her single state:

> When they get on the train for Niagara she can hear church bells chime,
> The compartment is air-conditioned and the mood's sublime,
> Then they get off at Saratoga for the fourteenth time . . .

Again, 'Fugue for Tinhorns' must be seen in the light of Runyon's pathetic belief in the status of the Form Book as holy writ. And the Burrows line, 'the oldest established permanent floating crap game in New York', converted by Loesser into a song, is a faultless exposition of the spirit which moved Runyon on the night he took a Hollywood greenhorn to one of these games, which 'crossed Manhattan in a winding route of upstairs haunts and secret passwords and ended up in the grey light of dawn in the Bronx'. The one wild incongruity to be found in *Guys and Dolls* occurs in Sky Masterson's invocation to the fates, 'Luck Be a Lady', which is a great deal further from Runyon than it is from one of the lions of late Victorian England, and which casts its shadow across one of the most bizarre episodes in the history of popular music.

At some time in the 1950s Frank Sinatra recorded a version of Kipling's 'The Road to Mandalay', a musical setting of the poem registered in 1907 by the American composer-singer Oley Speaks (1874–1948). The Kipling estate, controlled after his death by his malapert daughter Elsie, took such exception to the Sinatra recording that it was banned in Britain, although the item was released in the United States without noticeable detrimental effect on either Kipling's reputation or the remnants of Empire. In 1977, when the author of the poem had been dead for the requisite fifty years, the Sinatra recording duly appeared on the British market; two years later there followed an innocuous biography, originally commissioned by the wayward Elsie and subsequently banned by her for no reason that she could remember. This comedy of literary manners has some bearing both on the Kipling estate and the roots of *Guys and Dolls*, and if Frank Sinatra had only realized it at the time he recorded Kipling's song, he might well have had the pleasure of putting the wayward Elsie to rout. For it seems that in spite of her vigilance, there had been a most spectacular instance of the works of her father being adapted for a rather more plebeian arena than she approved. For the fourth chapter of Kipling's *Kim* opens with the lines:

> Good luck, she is never a Lady,
> But the cursest queen alive . . .
> Greet her – she's hailing a stranger,
> Meet her – she's busking to leave.
> Let her alone for a shrew to the bone
> And the hussy comes plucking your sleeve.

which is so close in spirit to, and even to the letter of, Sky Masterson's big song in *Guys and Dolls* as to make us wonder to what extent Loesser was conversant with the works of Kipling. Whatever the answer, he was certainly in tune with Runyon, and may even be defined as a perfect Runyon character. After *Guys and Dolls* he advanced further along the road to autonomy by writing the words, music and libretto of a musical version of Sidney Howard's prize-winning play of 1925, *They Knew What They Wanted*. Loesser's version, entitled *The Most Happy Fella*, was so crammed with music as to approach the frontiers of opera, but although he continued to write more musicals and although his *How to Succeed in Business Without Really Trying* was awarded a Pulitzer Drama prize in 1962, never again did he quite achieve the felicity of his Runyon adventure. Among his own works he preferred the love songs to the clever joke-songs. 'I'm in the romance business,' he used to insist, and would ask friends, 'Which song made you cry?' One of those who could have provided a short answer was the unfortunate Miss Quigley. Towards the end, when he was writing words, music, libretto and co-producing, some cynic asked, 'Does he get the girl as well?' In fact he did, marrying his own leading lady Jo Sullivan. He was a bumptious, impossible, freakishly gifted man who never quite reduced himself to absurdity, not even on those sublime mornings when he awoke saying, 'I feel as good as Irving Berlin today.' For there were some days when he was right. He may also have been more of a sentimentalist than he liked to admit. Those who remembered him in his beginnings took due note of the fact that when *Guys and Dolls* opened on Broadway, its musical director was a man called Irving Actman. When Frank Loesser finally smoked himself to death on 26 July 1969, he was sitting cross-legged in bed, plugged into a breathing machine and whiling away the last few hours before death by smoking a last cigarette. Four years later an old man called Benjamin Caplan died in Baltimore under circumstances which both Runyon and Loesser might have relished. Caplan, the real-life model for Harry the Horse, dropped dead in the act of putting fifty dollars on a filly in the third race at Pimlico. She finished fourth.

IRVING BERLIN

CHAPTER EIGHT

Irving Berlin

In the spring of 1881, Alexander Alexandrovitch, Tsar of all the Russias, patron saint of American popular art, ascended the throne and proceeded to solve one of his country's most pressing problems, the lack of any considerable export trade. Within weeks of his ascension he was exporting Russians by the thousand, and the fact that by this policy he was depriving the nation of its most valuable asset, the next generation, did not at all bother Alexander, a brutal noodle incapable of two consecutive thoughts, or possibly even one. Among his many dazzling strokes of policy was the realization that the family Baline, resident in the village of Temun in Siberia, constituted a grave threat to the security of the Empire, a shaft of political insight so brilliant that none of the preceding Romanovs had ever suspected it. In 1892 a troop of Cossacks galloped into Temun, burned it down, slaughtered as many of its inhabitants as they could find, and galloped out again, understandably euphoric at having registered the first military victory any of them could remember. Whether or not Alexander Alexandrovitch would have been rendered penitent had someone informed him that the regime had just done everything it could to exterminate the most successful Russian composer of all time is doubtful. The Romanovs had never been much good at thinking, and Alexander, wasting no time on regrets, proceeded with his grand plan to perform some deed of spectacular goodness for his country, finally succeeding in 1894, when he died – only to be succeeded by an even bigger idiot, his son Nicholas.

Meanwhile the Balines had been among the few survivors of the massacre, and might have taken the affair as a heartening augury for the future. Throughout the century the greatest creative artists had been those who incurred the wrath of the Romanovs. But the Balines, homeless and terrified, were too busy devising ways of staying alive to bother about the future of Russian music. They decided to emigrate, and by the end of 1892 were in New York, where they lived on the East Side in a condition of deprivation so close to starvation that there were days, so the story goes, when the Baline children found it hard to tell the difference. By now there were seven of them, and their father, a lowly religious functionary, found it almost impossible to feed them all. One of the brood, the four-year-old Israel, contradicted the legend by pointing the moral that abject poverty by no means implies abject misery. Revisiting the old homestead in Cherry Street, in what had once been the Italian quarter, at a time in life when a printer's error and his own industry had long since transmuted him into Irving Berlin, he reminisced:

> You know, you never miss luxury until you've had it. I never felt poverty because I'd never known anything else. Our family was enormous. There were nine of us in three rooms, and in the summer some of us slept on the fire escape on the roof. I was a boy with poor parents, but let's be realistic about it, I didn't starve. I wasn't cold or hungry. There was always bread and butter and hot tea. I slept better in that tenement house than I do right now in my nice bed in Beekman Place.

When Berlin was eight his father died, so the boy left school and started to sell newspapers, his first connection with literature. For some years he worked at whatever he could, depositing the proceeds each night in his mother's apron, till at fourteen he finally succumbed to the siren song of popular music as it drifted across from the nearby Bowery. He became a busking bum.

In 1902 all America was singing the big hits of the season, 'Bill Bailey, Won't You Please Come Home?', 'Ragtime Cowboy Joe' and 'In the Good Old Summertime', while still showing deep affection for the great sensation of the previous year, 'The Honeysuckle and the Bee'. On Broadway George M. Cohan was just about to come into his inheritance, although another two years were to go by before his horseracing melodrama *Little Johnny Jones* would overwhelm the nation with 'Yankee Doodle Dandy' and 'Give My Regards to Broadway'. There is a sense in which Cohan and Berlin are complementary figures. Each combined inexhaustible melodic and versifying energy with a keen business acumen, and each expressed the spirit of the urban masses of his generation. Cohan, the brash pride of the Irish, reflects in his songs something of the world of brownstone houses brimming with boarders which is preserved in the tall stories of O. Henry; Berlin maintained the succession by writing songs which were the musical analogue to the even taller ones of Damon Runyon. But, having made that point, it becomes essential to qualify it by noting that Berlin's life spans so vast a period – even his active musicianship accounts for half of the century –

that his best work reflects not one musical generation but several. His earliest work sounds like bad Cohan on an off-day. The prime achievements of the 1930s have become the symbol of Hollywood at its most stylish and self-confident.

At sixteen Berlin became a singing waiter in a saloon called the Pelham Cafe, owned by another Tsarist export, one Mike Salter, who paid the new recruit seven dollars a week and whatever he could find in tips. One of the musclemen hired by Salter to keep what was whimsically referred to as the peace, one Jubal Sweet, later recalled the Berlin operating style:

> Like it was yesterday I remember Oiving Berlin. Looked like a meal or two wouldn't hurt him. Wasn't strong and didn't look like he would get away with a nickel or a dime that one of the other guys claimed . . . This here Kutch sorta took to the kid and seen to it that nobody stuck nothing over on Oiving. Now a singing waiter couldn't be stooping over every time a coin hit the floor. Spoil his song. No, he'd keep moving around easy, singing all the time, and every time a nickel would drop he'd put his toe on it and kick it or nurse it to a certain spot. When he was done he had all the jack in a pile, see? Oiving got to be pretty good at it, only he wasn't so casual, like Kutch. Nervous like, and he had a neat flip of the ankle. Like you'd brush a speck offa the table with your fingers.

After two years at the Pelham, Berlin found that establishment was faced by a grave crisis. A rival establishment was stealing Salter's thunder – featuring not just a singing waiter, but a singing waiter who wrote his own songs. A certain Al Piantadosi, a waiter at Callahan's Saloon, was drawing the town with his sensational song 'My Mariuccia Take a Steamboat'. Something had to be done to salvage the honour of the Pelham Cafe. Already the saga is taking on the shape of an O. Henry fable. Salter, who was a great enthusiast for Berlin's parodies of well-known songs, now instructed him to write something of his own. One of the other waiters supplied the tune and Berlin quickly wrote 'Marie from Sunny Italy', which was published and earned its lyricist the huge sum in royalties of 37 cents. He soon moved on to Jimmy Kelly's where they paid him more money for less hours, and it was here that he was spotted by one of the managers from the Harry Von Tilzer Music Company. Von Tilzer was one of the most successful songwriters of his generation; by the time Berlin was brought to him he was famous for 'A Bird in a Gilded Cage', and had just enjoyed even greater acclaim for 'Wait Till the Sun Shines, Nellie'. His great unwitting Freudian masterpiece, 'I Want a Girl Just Like the Girl that Married Dear Old Dad', still lay in the future, but his list of battle honours helps to underline the homeric nature of Berlin's career, rooted in the old bar-room balladry and extending far into the history of modern Broadway. Piantadosi, who also went on to a successful career as a composer of popular songs, was far closer in style to Von Tilzer than to Berlin; in 1913 he wrote 'The Curse of an Aching Heart', and two years later perpetrated the famous pacifist tract, 'I Didn't Raise My Boy to Be a Soldier', deservedly buried some years later by Groucho Marx, who destroyed it at a stroke by retitling it 'I Didn't Raise My Boy, He Played the Joker'.

Berlin first became a composer in 1908, in the aftermath of the 1908 Olympic Games in London, where an Italian waiter called Dorando Pietri became a celebrity by not winning the Marathon. After leading all the way, Pietri collapsed within a few feet of the tape; soft-hearted Londoners carried him over the line. Amid great uproar, Pietri was disqualified and the winner by default named as the American runner Hayes. But while Hayes collected the gold medal, it was Pietri who won immortality, which included a song. 'Dorando' is a revealing example of how dreadful the emergent Berlin's lyrics could be:

> Just then Dorando, he's a-drop.
> It's not fun to los the mon'
> When the son of a gun run
> Dorando, you're a good-for-not'.

Berlin, who appears to have believed that athletes were paid money to enter the Olympic Games, was certainly paid money for the song, which he took to the publishing house of Watterson and Snyder after the vaudevillean who had commissioned it refused to honour his contract. Watterson, a forbidding man who had made his money from selling diamonds, and whose headstone is the name J. Watterson Watkins in the first Gershwin Brothers musical, *Lady Be Good*, asked Berlin to sing the song, at which the supplicant hastily improvised a melody as execrable as the lyric. Watterson bought the piece and asked Berlin for more. Having found one theme in the newspapers, Berlin scoured the press to find another, and soon came up with the 'Salome' scandal. Richard Strauss's opera had excited a great many non-operagoers who had heard that one of the ladies of the chorus was required at one point in the story to step forward and perform one of the hoariest jokes in vaudeville, the Dance of the Seven Veils. Young Berlin, having squeezed a feeble joke out of mock-Italian, now decided to get some laughs out of his fellow Jewish immigrants, and composed a piece called 'Sadie Salome', to be the story of a distraught fiancé whose young lady, the errant Sadie, has taken to doing a strip on stage. The song sold three thousand copies and led to a regular job at Watterson and Snyder's for its author. Berlin now began collaborating with Snyder on a song a day, sometimes two, until in 1909 he achieved his first genuine hit, a rare fragment of Berlin in that it was a collaboration with another distinguished songwriter:

One night in a barber shop I ran into George Whiting, a vaudeville actor, and asked him if he could go to a show with me. 'Sure,' he said, and added with a laugh, 'My wife's gone to the country.' *Bing!* There I had a commonplace familiar title line. It was singable, capable of humorous upbuilding, simple, and one that did not seriously offend against the 'sexless' rule; for wives and their offspring of both sexes, as well as their husbands, would be amused by singing it or hearing it sung. I persuaded Whiting to forget the theatre and to devote the night to developing the line with me into a song. Now the usual and unsuccessful way of handling a line like that is to dash off a jumble of verses about the henpecked husband, all leading up to the chorus running, we'll say, something like this:

> My wife's gone to the country,
> She went away last night.
> Oh, I'm so glad, I'm so glad,
> I'm crazy with delight.

Just wordy, obvious elaboration. No punch. All night I sweated to find what I knew was there, and finally I speared the lone word, just a single word, that made the song – and a fortune. Listen:

> My wife's gone to the country.
> Hurrah, hurrah.

Hurrah. That lone word gave the whole idea of the song in one quick wallop. It gave the singer a chance to hoot with sheer joy. It invited the roomful to join in the hilarious shout. It everlastingly put the catch line over. And I wasn't content until I had used my good thing to the limit. 'She took her children with her – Hurrah, Hurrah'.

This is Berlin being ingenious retrospectively. The 'hurrah' device was anything but the wonder-device he seemed to think it was, but at any rate the song flashed through the world of vaudeville and became newsworthy to the point where the *Evening Journal* commissioned Irving to write two hundred additional verses, which he did in double-quick time. What really sold the joke was the truth lying behind it. The sowing of wild oats was by now one of America's burgeoning industries, and Berlin was by no means the only writer to cash in on the craze for adultery. His old employer Harry Von Tilzer had just produced a song with the same theme but with a much more attractive title: 'I Love My Wife, But Oh, You Kid!'. What Tilzer lacked, however, was a gift for anecdote. Sensing that his song had touched a nerve somewhere in the corporate body of a cheerfully fornicating republic, Berlin indulged in the sort of whoppers which had always been an intrinsic part of the Tin Pan Alley sales pitch, and which were to become part of the mercantile equipment of later composers, particularly Cole Porter. Encouraged to exuberance by sudden success, Berlin lapsed into romantic melodrama verging on bedroom farce:

> A true happening was the inspiration for this song. In July, a New York woman set out for Ocean Grove and, on arrival, discovered that her watch and a small fur collar were missing. She thought it had dropped on the soft dining room rug, so she wired her maid at home: 'Let me know if you find anything on the dining room rug.' A few days later a letter arrived from the maid saying, 'This is what I found this morning: three cigarette ends, 36 burnt matches and one pink slipper.'

The same nonsense characterizes the incident of Berlin's sudden irruption into global celebrity two years later. In the wake of mass hysteria inspired by his new song, he tended to wax solemn about its cultural, musical and social implications. The facts were less convoluted and much more interesting. In 1910 Berlin composed an instrumental march which followed the structural dictates of the ragtime convention. It was then tried out at a cabaret restaurant and found wanting. It went back into Berlin's bottom drawer and remained there until the spring of 1911, when Berlin received one of the profession's accolades, an invitation to join the Friar's Club, a show-business brotherhood intent on charitable deeds performed with the maximum self-publicity. On 28 May, at the New Amsterdam Theatre, the new recruit was asked to participate in one of the acts at a concert, for which he would be required to provide an original song. Dusting off his march, Berlin added some words and found himself the possessor of 'Alexander's Ragtime Band'. The Friars greeted the song with no more than mild interest, after which the song floated around the vaudeville circuits, where it was sung by Berlin's fellow-Russian Al Jolson. Any faint chance it might have had of being written up after the night at the New Amsterdam had been scotched by one of those far-off events which nobody could have predicted. On 29 May, on the afternoon following the concert, William Schwenck Gilbert, accompanied by the Misses Preece and Emery, decided to bathe in the waters of the ornamental lake at 'Grimsdyke', his lordly estate on the northern fringes of London. While the two young maidens were bathing, one of them, Miss Preece, began to flounder, at which the 74-year-old lyricist jumped in to rescue her. Miss Preece survived the moment, Gilbert did not, and on the day when someone in New York journalism might conceivably have had a good word to say for Berlin's new song, Gilbert stole all the available space, as usual. Berlin's song finally found its way into one of the few Broadway summer productions, *The Merry Whirl*, where it suddenly turned the popular song world on its head. By midsummer the heatwave was becoming a threat to New York life, but the mediocre *Merry Whirl* battled on, sustained by the new song sensation. Meanwhile in Chicago the music-hall star Emma Carus, who was billed as 'The Female Baritone' and looked every inch the part, was bellowing the song twice nightly, much to the delight of the local population. All this was an acute embarrassment to Messrs Watterson and Snyder, who had not bothered to prepare themselves for this overwhelming demand, and were now obliged to ask rival printing companies to take some of the orders. Rumours swept America that Berlin would collect $50,000 before the end of the year; whatever the figure, he was never again to regard himself as a poor man.

Why 'Alexander's Ragtime Band'? In a candid moment years later its author confessed that its runaway success had amazed him. Only tenuously connected with authentic ragtime, the song is a compromise between syncopation, bugle calls and even a snatch borrowed from Stephen Foster. Berlin probably came close to the truth when he said that he had cashed in, not on ragtime but on the word describing it, much as two generations later words like 'rock 'n' roll' became saleable. It was not ragtime but the idea of ragtime was in the air, and Berlin was shrewd enough, or lucky enough, to pluck it down. Yet 'Alexander's Ragtime Band' is by no means remarkable in its sentiments, and could by no stretch of the imagination be regarded as the harbinger of the new age. 'Shine on Harvest Moon', composed by an amateur, the vaudeville star Nora Bayes, is a more original construction which first appeared as early as 1908. And better than either Berlin or Miss Bayes had been the Canadian entertainer Sheldon Brooks, who in 1910 composed the remarkable piece 'Some of These Days', which, for harmonic surprise and originality of construction, leaves all its rivals of the day far behind. Yet it was 'Alexander's Ragtime Band' which was chosen by the fates as the anthem of the new century. By the end of 1911 Berlin was a partner in the publishing house of Watterson and Snyder, and was appearing as a singer on stage in New York and London. He had no singing voice and never pretended otherwise. The sound which seeped out of his puny frame was so weak that, in the words of the friend whom Arthur Schwartz was so fond of quoting, 'To hear him, you have to hug him.'

Ever since his apotheosis at the Pelham Cafe, Berlin had led a charmed life. Until 1912, when he fell in love with Dorothy, sister of Ray Goetz, a well-known songwriter who had added to the stockpot of popular art by writing 'For Me and My Gal', and was later to enjoy some success as a Broadway producer. Irving was twenty-five, Dorothy nineteen, when they were married in Buffalo. To escape the winter weather they honeymooned in Havana, where they wandered straight into a typhoid epidemic. Within months Dorothy was dead of the fever, and her newly-wed husband, half-crazy with grief, was whisked away by his brother-in-law, who brought him to Europe in the hope of easing the pain. The forlorn couple passed through London and Paris, and at some time in their travels Berlin wrote a stark, simple waltz, 'When I Lost You', in which he poured out his despair. All his life Berlin has been adamant to the brink of litigation that his private life is his own affair, that his work is disconnected utterly from that life, and that anybody who suggests otherwise is a charlatan and a scoundrel. So be it, but when a man contorted by the spasms of a tragic bereavement writes a ballad of unbearable sadness called 'When I Lost You', what is the rest of the world to assume? There were to be other instances of autobiography creeping into Berlin's work, at least one of which he not only acknowledged but insisted upon. But as for the rest of his life and experiences, mum has always been the word, except when Berlin himself has chosen to break the silence.

One aspect of his private life Berlin has been happy to blazon across the headlines. He is one of the most rampant jingo patriots of the age, and has never missed an opportunity to wave the flag. This love of country, born of gratitude, dates from the moment he stepped off the boat on to American soil with his parents in 1892. He looked at the benignity all around him and marvelled. In Russia they tried to set you on fire. Here they left you in peace to starve. For the rest of his professional life Berlin repaid the debt many times over. When the United States entered the Great War in 1917, he enlisted, and before long was writing a show whose proceeds would go to military charities. This show, *Yip Yip Yaphank* made vast sums of money for the troops through public performances, but the income from some of the songs must have been considerable too. One of his musical assistants during the genesis of *Yip Yip Yaphank* has shed a revealing light on Berlin's working methods which illuminates the enigma of the born musician without musicianship. The songwriter Harry Ruby, who was himself to advance to the front rank of songwriters, was working at the time as a piano plugger for Watterson, Berlin and Snyder, when he received a call to join Berlin at the army camp:

You see, he always had a piano player to take down his melodies — at one time he had four of them working for him, just to take down his songs. He'd come up to me in the morning while I was out there with him and he'd say 'Take this down,' and sing me a melody — some song that's become a classic now. I'd take it all down and I'd ask him, 'When the hell did you write that?', and he'd say, 'Oh, I was up all night. Do you like it?' And I'd say it was great, and I'd play it back for him to hear what he'd dictated — and he'd listen and he'd say,

'You got one chord wrong in there.' And he'd be right. He couldn't *play* the chord, but he could hear it all right.

The story might not be so pointed were Ruby a mere office hack whose own ear was not sensitive enough to qualify him as a talented musician. But Ruby, composer of 'Who's Sorry Now', 'Three Little Words' and 'Give Me the Simple Life', possessed an innate gift for hearing the aptest harmony. Yet the gift was not acute enough to measure up to Berlin's stringent demands. Years later the orchestrator Robert Russell Bennett was to offer the identical testimony, describing how Berlin would ask him to play a new melody, complete with harmonies. At one point Berlin would stop him, ask him to try a different chord, then a second, then a third, before finally Bennett hit on the combination Berlin was hearing inside his own head but could not formulate in technical terms. Perhaps it was incidents like these which go as far as any to explain the apparent mystery of Berlin's musicality, which was centred inside his ears rather than on diplomas. *Yip Yip Yaphank* raised $150,000 for army charities, Berlin's first public gesture of thanks to his adopted land. It was not to be his last.

When the war ended he began demonstrating a business acumen very nearly on a par with his gifts as a composer. He became sole owner of a powerful new publishing house, Irving Berlin, Inc.; and he became half-owner of a new Broadway theatre, the Music Box, which was to introduce some of his most famous pieces. For the opening production, a revue called *Say It With Music*, he composed a successful quick-step as the title song; the second annual edition produced another hit, 'Lady of the Evening'. It was in 1923 and again the following year that Berlin amended the procedure by which he compiled his 'Music Box' scores, in a way which once again shows how, for all the vehemence of his denials, he did from time to time use music as a way of expressing his deepest emotions. Halfway through the run of the 1923 edition, he added to the existing score an extra item which had become a hit in its own right earlier in the season. Its title was 'What'll I Do?'. In the following year the interpolated hit was 'All Alone'. Both were waltzes, a sure sign that Berlin's private life was in turmoil. In moments of emotional extremity he seems to have turned for solace to three-quarter time, just as he had on the death of his wife, a tragedy indirectly responsible for 'When I Lost You'. This time the source of his passion was a blissfully happy one. He had fallen in love once more, with Ellin Mackay, daughter of Clarence Mackay, one of those incomprehensible tycoons who nurtured the bizarre conviction that buying something for five cents and selling it for six was somehow more moral than writing a song like 'A Pretty Girl is Like a Melody'. Mackay bitterly opposed any suggestion of a marriage, but neither of the lovers cared a fig either for his prejudices or his bankroll. Their defiant courtship and marriage became an ongoing saga in the society columns of the New York press, which happened to be one of the estates of American life with which the bride was intimately familiar. A talented journalist, she was later to contribute to *The New Yorker*, and to publish several novels. The effect of all this publicity was to shove Berlin into the ranks of the fashionable, an elevation from songwriter to socialite which had one ironic effect, the cementing of an improbable relationship with Cole Porter. For it fell out that Mrs Berlin was a good friend of Mrs Porter, and now that Irving was the son-in-law of the president of a conspiracy called Postal Telegraph, he was no longer considered to be beyond Porter's tightly constricted pale. While Porter envied what he thought of as the Jewish strain in his rival's music, Berlin was always effusive in his praise of Porter, sending him congratulatory notes and telegrams on successful opening nights, and even consoling him in moments of trial, as we shall see.

But the most important thing in professional terms about his marriage to Ellin was the astonishing vein of rich romanticism in three-four time which it released. Between 1921 and 1926 he published so many of these songs, and to so great an effect, that had he never written anything else, he would have earned the title of America's Waltz King. The series began with 'All Alone', proceeded with the two 'Music Box' interpolations, continued with 'Always' and then with 'Remember', written during a holiday in London, before ending in 1926 with 'Because I Love You', which revealingly enough was published at the same time as 'How Many Times Must I Tell You I Love You?' and 'At Peace With the World'. It is no wonder that ordinary people all over the planet responded so fulsomely to these trifles. They were able to find in the sentiments of these sweet waltzes a reflection of their own feelings, which were, after all, identical to Berlin's during his courtship and marriage. This is what the virtuoso lyricist Johnny Mercer meant when he defined Berlin as 'a genius who writes for the girl in the Five-and-Ten'. The waltz sequence was not only an example of private emotions spilling over into public places which Berlin could not deny, but it made his romance something celebrated by everyone who ever sang in the bath or whistled while he worked. As one of Berlin's biographers put it, 'All of America, as well as large sections of Great Britain, was serenading Miss Mackay by proxy, along with Berlin.' And the most famous moment of all in this musical spectacular came when Berlin announced that his wedding gift to his beloved would take the form of ownership of one of his songs. This most astute of all songwriters, this man who all his life defended his words and music from encroachment with the ferocity of a tigress protecting her young, was breaking his own golden rule. He was giving away the copyright of 'Always', although admittedly keeping it in the family.

The accident of this gift has provided posterity with a dim clue to the most exotic mystery of all about Berlin, the extent of his wealth. As the years went by and still he never followed his contemporaries into the grave, he became the butt of jokes. He was said to be so rich that the government was paying *him* income tax. Cynics speculated that having been told that you can't take it with you, Berlin had decided not to go. The question of financial reward for songwriters is a vexed one. By the time of Berlin's marriage, the convention had been established that one quarter of the income from a song be paid to the composer, another quarter to the lyricist, and the residue be retained by the publisher. The comic inequity of this arrangement has always riled successful composers and lyricists, but the only effect it had on the pragmatic Berlin was to transform him into his own publisher, making him unique financially as well as artistically. He could collect one hundred per cent of all incomes from all his songs, even those written in the early days from Watterson and Snyder, whose copyrights he bought back from his old employers. but if he was taking all the moneys accruing to the songs, what sort of sums were involved? In 1946, in the twentieth year of Mrs Berlin's ownership of 'Always', the income from the song over the previous twelve months amounted to about $60,000, the bulk of which was raised by allowing the song to be interpolated into three Hollywood productions, all three of which helped to revivify sheet music and recording sales. By multiplying that income by twenty, to account for the intervening years, and then knocking off something to allow for a few lean years, we arrive at a sum in the region of one million dollars. Then allow for the fact that 'Always' has maintained its public appeal for a further forty years, multiply the new total by, say, fifty, to include in the calculations Berlin's other big moneymakers, throw in the commissioning fees from the Hollywood studios, the royalties collected from Broadway shows, plus Berlin's investments as a producer and his additional income from the songs by other writers published by Irving Berlin, Inc.; and we find ourselves drifting out of the world of profit and loss, into the realms of the fantastic.

Berlin has always been perfectly frank about his methods; when asked which kind of song he most enjoyed writing, he replied, 'Hits'. And in the attempt to score these hits, his methods were tireless, ingenious, even devious, and here and there quite ruthless. More than any other great writer of popular music Berlin has embraced the concept of self-plagiarization. What is revealing about these burglarizations of himself is the unfailing knack he had of improving on the original. The one possible exception may be 'Always', whose most memorable feature is the sudden stroke of empirical originality in its second eight-bar section, when, on the words 'When the things you planned', the melody echoes itself in a new key, moving from F major to A major with no harmonic preparation. In 1933 Berlin published a popular song called 'Maybe It's Because I Love You Too Much', in which the identical device turns up again. In the 1933 Broadway revue *As Thousands Cheer*, the past and present mingle to produce one huge moneymaker and one classic exhibition of consummate musicianship. *As Thousands Cheer* was presented as the dramatized version of a daily newspaper, so that each song and sketch represented various features to be found in each day's edition. The weather forecast was covered by 'Heat Wave', news of a race murder by 'Suppertime', the cartoons by 'The Funnies', and so on. The cast members impersonated the celebrities likely to be found in the paper; Clifton Webb suddenly became Douglas Fairbanks Junior and Mahatma Gandhi, Ethel Waters turned into Josephine Baker, and Helen Broderick portrayed Queen Mary and the Statue of Liberty. At one point in the show, it was agreed that Berlin write a song to cover one of New York's most popular annual events. Rummaging around for an idea, he suddenly recalled one of the more embarrassing failures of 1919, a grisly piece entitled 'Smile and Show Your Dimple'. It soon occurred to him that the song was not grisly after all, only half-grisly. The trouble lay in the words. Suppose he were to dump Berlin the lyric writer, retain Berlin the composer, write a new set of words with a new title and relaunch an old melodic idea? The result was 'Easter Parade'. A more subtle example of recycling occurs in the finale of *As Thousands Cheer*, for which Berlin composed a song with a fanciful lyric, 'Not For All the Rice in China'. In the middle section of this song, the melody begins to drift into other tonalities before returning to the home key. Evidently Berlin found the idea promising but the end result no more than a first draft for what it might eventually become. Three years later, working on a Fred-and-Ginger saga, he refined and elaborated the sketch into a full-blown exercise in miniature of the art of modulation, deploying it as the middle section of 'I'm Putting All My Eggs in One Basket'. The passage, which moves from F major to A flat major to G dominant before returning to the home key of C major, stands more than fifty years later as one of Berlin's most inspired and characteristic strokes, a perfect example of how the natural ear, untrammelled by any sense of what may be proper or practical, achieves felicity by the boldest methods.

Examples of this kind, which abound in Berlin's catalogue, help to justify the reputation he earned early in his career of being single-minded about his work. The achievement of a hit was always to him its own justification, a truth which emerges from one of the most outlandish incidents in the history of the Broadway musical. Indeed, were it not for the fact that the story has impeccable bona fides, provided by the aggrieved party as well as Berlin, it might seem too far-fetched to be taken seriously. One of Berlin's oldest friends was his fellow-Russian refugee, Maurice Abrahams, a sometime songwriter-publisher and one of the very few men who could claim to have collaborated with Berlin. In the days when he was working for Von

Tilzer, Irving, eager to write anything with anybody, had worked with Abrahams on a piece called 'Queenie My Own', which was published to no effect. Later, when Berlin was working for Watterson and Snyder, Abrahams came to him with an idea for a song about railways. Legally Berlin was obliged by his agreement with his employers not to write anything for anyone else. But the Abrahams idea appealed to him, and he decided to develop it. The Result was 'Pullman Porters on Parade', which Berlin, torn between pride and prudence, credited to the pseudonymous Ren G. May, an anagrammatic joke linking him with the song without offering legal proof that it was anything to do with him. A few years later the song turned up in the most bizarre of contexts. The P. G. Wodehouse novel *Jill the Reckless* tells the story of a musical comedy *The Rose of America*, from inception to first night, incorporating in the process as much information on the workings of the musical show as even the most zealous student could require.*

The Ren G. May subterfuge must have reassured Berlin that when it came to the legal niceties, Maurice Abrahams was more than ready to improvise. The bonds between them were tightened by the marriage of Abrahams to Belle Baker, a renowned vaudeville performer who was another of Berlin's allies from the days of his beginnings. In 1915 she had enjoyed acclaim for her singing of Berlin's tear-jerker, 'When I Leave the World Behind', after which she retained in him the confidence that he could produce successful songs at the drop of a hat. Belle had begun in the New York Yiddish theatre but had soon moved out into the deeper waters of vaudeville, where her bombastic style and spectacular silhouette quickly made her a star. Belle was a small, dumpy girl who was said by some to measure as much from back to front as she did from head to toe, and it may well have been these vital statistics which first attracted Florenz Ziegfeld, who saw her in action for the first time on board an ocean liner returning from Europe. Ziegfeld's companion on that trip was a millionaire called Leonard Replogle, an ambiguous figure whose one abiding hobby may be deduced from the name he gave to his yacht, 'The Wench'. He and Ziegfeld appear to have been inseparables, and certainly they were both in attendance when Belle did her stuff at the ship's concert. Ziegfeld was overwhelmed; he and Replogle agreed that here was a Broadway star in the making. All she needed was the vehicle. They would provide one. Later, when the enterprise had collapsed in fiasco, Ziegfeld tried to shift the blame on to Replogle, but everything which now happened had the unmistakable aroma of Ziegfeld about it. On returning to New York, he decided that only the best was good enough for Miss Baker, by which, of course, he meant that only the best was good enough for

The powers-that-be make it impossible to give a sample of this lyric but the curious reader will find it preserved in the text of Wodehouse's novel.

Ziegfeld, and decided to approach the songwriting team of Richard Rodgers and Lorenz Hart with a view to persuading them to write a score suitable for Miss Baker to bellow across the footlights of the New Amsterdam Theatre.

He must have known perfectly well that Rodgers and Hart were at that time engaged on the composition of a musical for Lew Fields; he surely suspected also that not even Rodgers and Hart at their most prolific could write two scores at once. Nevertheless, he met the songwriters and was insistent that they accept his offer to write a show for Belle Baker, which would be ready to go into rehearsals, he told them, 'in a few weeks'. Inexplicably Rodgers and Hart agreed, the composer giving as his excuse his extreme youth and the aura that the name of Ziegfeld carried:

> As soon as I heard the name Ziegfeld it was like Moses hearing the voice of God on Mount Sinai. Ever since 1907, with his first 'Follies', Ziegfeld had been the acknowledged master-producer. He was the Great Glorifier, whose shows were the most dazzling and whose stars were the most celestial. His name on a bill was an acknowledged guarantee of quality, glamour and success, and so when Florenz Ziegfeld called, Dick Rodgers went running.

Rodgers's religious dementia in the face of his producer was regrettable but perhaps understandable. Rodgers was only twenty-four years old. Before he had done with the show for Miss Baker, he was to know what it felt like to be one hundred and twenty-four. In a daze he and Hart set to work to complete two shows at once. The Fields production was to open on 27 December, Ziegfeld's on 28 December.

Peggy-Ann, the Fields show, was about a heroine who is so disturbed by the argument she has had with her lover that she goes home and dreams the entire action of the play. This alarming idea, based on an old show called *Tillie's Nightmare*, incorporated talking fish, singing pirates, and a marriage ceremony in which a telephone directory is substituted for the Bible. *Betsy* was more straightforward, owing something to the plot of *The Taming of the Shrew* but not otherwise particularly Shakespearean. Betsy, played by Belle, has three brothers who are not allowed to marry until they find a mate for her. The plot actually made *Peggy-Ann* seem quite sober by comparison, incorporating a balloon number, two intrusions by Borrah Minnevitch and his Harmonica Symphony Orchestra, and a song in which the ladies of the chorus pelt the audience with hot dogs. Considering the intense pressure under which they were working, it is remarkable that Rodgers and Hart did not confuse the two plots. As it was they did reasonably well to turn out a goodish score for *Peggy-Ann* which included 'Where's That Rainbow?'. Meanwhile, the birth-pangs of *Betsy* involved persistent in-fighting between the producer, the songwriters and the librettists. Rodgers later wrote that it was 'an enormous show with dozens of elaborate scenes' which needed to be on the road for months. Instead it had a one-week trial in Washington before coming home to roost at the New Amsterdam. On 27 December, with twenty-four hours to go to the apotheosis of Belle Baker, Rodgers and Hart were naturally present at the first night of *Peggy-Ann*, which went off well enough to please them. Meanwhile, over at the New Amsterdam it was dawning on Belle Baker that Rodgers and Hart had left her holding a large turkey. There was, in her forthright opinion, absolutely nothing for her to sing that was worth singing. Most musical comedy leading ladies, finding themselves in this predicament, would have demanded a few new costumes and hoped for the best. But Belle was a vaudeville performer, raised on panic, chaos and last-minute improvisations. A lady could work miracles in twenty-four hours if only she kept her wits about her. The wits in this case proved to be her husband and her old friend Irving Berlin. This is the version of the conversational exchanges between them on the telephone as reported by Belle's son:

'Irving, I'm opening in this show tomorrow night, and there isn't a Belle Baker song in the score, and I'm so miserable. What can I do?'
'Belle, I'll be honest with you. All I have is a song in my trunk. I've often thought it would be great for you, but I never got around to finishing it.'
'Irving, please come over here. Maury is here. We'll feed you, and he'll help, because even something half finished by you is better than what I've got now, which is nothing.'

Berlin then arrived at Belle's home, where he worked through the night completing his melody and writing a lyric. At seven that morning Belle telephoned Ziegfeld and told him that Irving had written her a great song and that if she couldn't sing it in the show she wouldn't appear. Ziegfeld agreed, telling her, 'For God's sake, don't tell Rodgers or Hart.' At this point, versions begin to diverge. According to Belle's son:

I went to the opening that night. I was up in the balcony. At about eleven my mother came on and she sang 'Blue Skies' for the first time. The audience went crazy. They really had been starved all night for her to do one like that. Would you believe that the audience made her sing that song over and over again, twenty-four times. And that on the twenty-third reprise she forgot the lyrics. Berlin stood up – he was sitting in the front row – and they finished the chorus singing together.

Rodgers interpreted the night's events very differently:

Almost at the last minute, without saying a word to anyone, Ziegfeld bought a song from Irving Berlin and gave it to Belle Baker to sing in the show. Not only did the interpolated number get the biggest hand of the evening at the premiere, but Ziegfeld had also arranged to have a spotlight pick out Berlin, seated in the front row, who rose and took a bow.

Rodgers does have the grace to add that '"Blue Skies" was a great piece of songwriting, easily superior to any Larry and I had written for the production,' and concludes from the episode that 'Ziegfeld was not a nice man'. Belle's son says that Rodgers and Hart refused to speak to his mother for the next twelve years. The two writers at least had the satisfaction of seeing *Peggy-Ann* survive for over three hundred performances. Ziegfeld hastily closed *Betsy* after five weeks. After Maurice Abrahams died in 1931, Belle resumed her vaudeville career, appeared in two movies, made a few dozen recordings, including something called 'Ginsberg from Scotland Yard' but, surprisingly, not 'Blue Skies', and died in 1957 in her sixty-third year. Historical perspective suggests that she may not have been altogether justified in dismissing the songs from *Betsy* out of hand. More than sixty years after the event, one or two superior singers, notably Tony Bennett, took to singing one of Belle's solos in the show, 'This Funny World'; the last few lines may well have appealed to her sense of irony:

> If you are broke you shouldn't mind.
> It's all a joke, for you will find
> This funny world is making fun of you.

The most curious thing of all about this freakish tale is that as the recriminations rose on the air, echoing down the years, causing estrangements between Ziegfeld and Rodgers, Rodgers and Belle, the librettists and everyone, no breath of criticism or reproach ever seems to have attached to Irving Berlin. How long, one wonders, was it before Rodgers and Hart could bring themselves to speak to him? And when finally they did, what did they say? Rodgers remained silent on the point.

The Great Depression in the American economy coincided with a personal decline in prices for Berlin, whose muse, if it did not quite desert him between 1928 and 1932, certainly gave him cause for anxiety. Of course what constituted a barren period for him would have been embraced with rapture by most other songwriters. In 1930, when his spirits were said to be at their lowest, he produced 'Let Me Sing and I'm Happy' and 'Putting on the Ritz'. The latter song was one of several which Berlin wrote describing the lives of the rich from the vantage of the poor. In 1937 he composed 'Slumming on Park Avenue', and in the

1940s the most derisory one of all, 'A Couple of Swells'. There was one
other noteworthy event during this curious twilight period, something
which flung Berlin into the role of an O. Henry hero who comes good in
the last line. Clarence Mackay was experiencing those difficulties
which can assail a man when he finds himself short of ready money.
Magically Mackay's problems helped him overcome his distaste for a
parvenu son-in-law as he accepted a loan of one million dollars in cash.
Any faint anxiety that Irving really required the million to be paid back
was dispersed in 1932, when he suddenly began producing song after
song in the old style. Two individual items swept America, 'Say It Isn't
So' and 'How Deep is the Ocean', and there was a new show, *Face the
Music*, a spoof of the Depression which had the Rockefellers and the
Vanderbilts eating at the Automat, and which included one item, 'Let's
Have Another Cup of Coffee, Let's Have Another Piece of Pie', whose
words show how sharply Berlin could express his derision. It was not a
period when the reputation of President Hoover was at its zenith. All
sorts of vituperation were flung at his head by a wide assortment of
outraged citizenry, but none reduced the old buffoon to greater ridicule
or with a more casual contempt than Berlin's suggestion that the best
way of helping the economy to maintain its equilibrium was to buy more
coffee and pie. Berlin published something else in 1932, one of those
single unattached songs whose genesis was unconnected with any plot.
Its title was 'I'm Playing with Fire', and although Bing Crosby scored a
considerable success with it, the song soon fell back into anonymity. It
has remained unregarded ever since, yet it was to be the key piece in an
extraordinary puzzle a few years later, the vital component of an
extravaganza of self-quotation unsurpassed in the annals of American
song.

There now began the most dazzling passage of Berlin's life, the years
when he accepted at last the offers of the movie moguls. Between 1935
and 1938 he composed the songs for five productions, three at RKO
Radio, two at Twentieth Century Fox, and once again produced work of
such lasting quality that, had he never done anything else, his place
would be assured. Berlin's attitude towards the movie industry was one
of lofty condescension. Like Kern, he held the heads of the studios in
genial contempt and never lost an opportunity to let them know it. He
negotiated his own terms, chose his own projects, and conducted
himself throughout like a man performing a charitable act. In the light
of his relentless financial practicality, his choice of RKO seems
quixotic. The studio was at crisis point by the time Berlin arrived. The
receivers were in, the coffers were bare, and extinction loomed. It
seems likely that what tipped the scales in RKO's favour so far as Berlin
was concerned was Fred Astaire. In 1934 the studios had enjoyed some
success with *The Gay Divorcée*, a loose adaptation of the Broadway show
The Gay Divorce, with music by Cole Porter. Reactions to that film had

suggested to at least one of the executives at RKO that it was the Astaire-Rogers partnership which held out the only hope of financial salvation. The executive was Pandro S. Berman, a small saturnine man literally born into the industry. The 'S' in his name stood for nothing, and neither, said the wags, did Berman. But in any appraisal of America's outstanding songwriters he remains a key figure. It was Berman alone who prevailed upon the studio to use, in quick succession, Cole Porter, Berlin, the Gershwins and Jerome Kern as sources of supply for the Fred-and-Ginger series. Because of this good judgement, Berman has been credited with the invention of a new style of screen musical, and rightly so. His gambling on the naturalism, comparatively speaking, of the Astaire-Rogers pictures at a time when the photographic fantasies of Busby Berkeley at Warners were sweeping the board, was a stroke of great perception. People who watched the Berkeley battalions being made to resemble fantastic exfloriations seen from a point in the ceiling would gawp and gasp at the supernatural. When they saw Fred and Ginger conducting a courtship through choreography, they were inspired to go down to the local palais de danse and try it for themselves. Berman was wise to perceive that there is escapism and there is escapism, and that the Astaire brand encouraged people to identify with it, whereas Berkeley's brilliant trickery could only alienate the audience, trapped in a three-dimensional world.

But Berman was not quite the fount of infallibility his boosters have suggested. Having purchased the rights of *The Gay Divorce*, he indulged in the usual Hollywood exercise of disembowelling the very property whose contours had tempted him to bid for it; he jettisoned the entire score and commissioned new writers to provide fresh songs. Of Porter's outstanding score, only 'Night and Day' was retained; among the casualties was the exquisite 'After You, Who?'. But Berman saw that he would get better results if the raw materials were more subtly integrated. From now on each Astaire-Rogers epic would have original music written by one man or at any rate one team. His first choice was Berlin, who now composed one of the two or three greatest scores of the modern era. With *Top Hat*, the democratic, as distinct from the ennobled musical comedy reaches a point of perfection. Eric Rhodes, who plays the obligatory decadent mittel-European rival for Ginger's hand, and whose punctilio is hopelessly outmanoeuvred by Astaire's banter, is a Count Danilo come to judgement, the Ruritanian popinjay shrunken to the proportions of a supernumary in a drama which thirty years earlier he might have dominated. Sleepy English eccentricity, the Wodehousean balance to Astaire's metropolitan pep, is represented by Eric Blore. Which element contributes most to the thistledown perfection of *Top Hat* it is impossible to say, but certainly the engine driving events along is Berlin's wonderful score. So much of the music has graduated into the pantheon of popular art that it becomes impossible to regard it today with the eyes and ears of innocence: Astaire in top hat, white tie and tails gunning down the chorus boys with his heel-taps; Fred and Ginger caught in a storm in 'Isn't This a Lovely Day'; and 'Cheek to Cheek', the most famous use of the dance-song as a declaration of love. To this day there is an element of breathless delight in the reactions of those working inside the iridescent bubble of Berlin's contrivance. Ginger Rogers has described how the film became the talk of the industry because of Berlin's score. Astaire's recollection was more personal:

> I just loved his music and I was delighted when they got him to do this. And Irving thought the same about getting me to do it because he liked the way I did things.

Berlin's reaction was even more fulsome:

> I never would have written 'Top Hat, White Tie and Tails' or 'Cheek to Cheek' or 'Isn't This a Lovely Day' if I didn't have Astaire and Rogers to write to.

What nobody has remarked is the unfailing originality, resource and, here and there, heretical impudence which characterize the music. 'Cheek to Cheek', for example, is endowed with two middle sections instead of one. Even more remarkable is the structure of 'Top Hat, White Tie and Tails', whose daring is so absorbed into the piece that it has gone unnoticed ever since. The verse begins with one of Berlin's favourite devices, the syncopated figure which cuts across the divisions of the bar-lines: 'I just got an invitation through the mails.' Berlin returns to this pattern when reaching the middle section of the chorus: 'I'm stepping out my dear . . .' But whereas the verse comprises conventional four- and eight-bar blocks, the middle section, which in the American popular song is almost always of eight-bar duration, consists of ten bars, split into two five-bar sections, a device so unthinkable that for two generations singers and dancers have enjoyed it without noticing anything unusual; only when the working jazz musician, approaching his material with a view to improvising in the customary four- and eight-bar patterns, encounters it, does the stupefying heresy of Berlin's device become apparent. This was one of his greatest gifts, the ability to break any rule he chose without making the result sound alarming or ungainly.

The same independence of the conventions of his craft can be heard in what Berlin wrote for the sequel to *Top Hat*. There had to be one, because the picture, praised as the best black-and-white musical ever made, took over $3,000,000 on its initial release. Its production cost was about $650,000, so Berman understandably decided to produce it all over again, except that Fred would exchange his tails for a sailor suit. Berlin would once again provide the songs. There was, however, a problem. In spite of the bonanza of *Top Hat*, the studio was still broke. How was Berman to persuade Astaire and Berlin to work for nothing? Each man was now at the very apex of his fortunes, able to demand whatever he pleased. The solution was simple. In return for involving themselves in *Follow the Fleet*, Astaire and Berlin would each receive ten per cent of the gross in lieu of a fee; Berman would receive ten per cent as a reward for thinking of the idea, and the studio would be permitted to collect the residue. Once again the formula worked like a charm. If *Follow the Fleet* does not quite match the peerless sense of style which may be seen to this day in *Top Hat*, it incorporated several scenes of surpassing brilliance, and one which transcends the normal canons of judgement altogether. The convention had long been established of Astaire in tails, yet the setting of *Follow the Fleet* dictated that he be seen throughout sporting bellbottoms. The writers circumvented this grave crisis by having Fred and Ginger doing a ship's concert at the climax of the story, for which the two dancers could return at last to that never-never world of gold cigarette cases and priceless pearls to which their fans had become conditioned. For this sequence Berlin composed one of the outstanding songs of the decade. With 'Let's Face the Music and Dance' he excelled himself both musically and lyrically. Throughout its length the song moves between the contradictory tonalities of C major and C minor, drifting between the two to create the ambiguity of a charming mystery. Structurally the piece sees Berlin yet again ignoring the conventions of rigid symmetry which governed the popular music of the period, although when we hear the song it sounds perfectly normal. In fact the first section runs for fourteen bars, the second for sixteen, and the final section extends to eighteen. The structure is tightened by the lyric device of rhyming each of the three opening statements: 'trouble ahead . . . fiddlers have fled . . . teardrops to shed'. The most pertinent of all the comments on 'Let's Face the Music and Dance' have been made by the dance historian Arlene Croce:

> The song is like one of those brave ballads of the Depression written by Schwartz and Dietz – 'Dancing in the Dark' or 'Alone Together' – and the mood is awesomely grave. . . . What I find moving in this noble and almost absurdly glamorous dance is the absence of self-enchantment in the performance. Astaire and Rogers yield nothing to Garbo's throat or Pavlova's Swan as icons of the sublime, yet their manner is brisk.

Follow the Fleet repeated the success of *Top Hat*, but by the time the next picture in the sequence was under way, Berman was parleying with Jerome Kern for the production which was released as *Swingtime*, while Berlin moved across to Twentieth Century Fox to provide songs for a Dick Powell feature called *On the Avenue*. Again Berlin produced a score consisting more or less entirely of hits, but it is the biggest song of all which discloses his astonishing guile and dexterity when it came to lightening the workload. It was not easy composing for Powell, who loathed the very act of singing and counted the days till he might play dramatic roles or, better still, become an executive, which he eventually did. But Powell's unwillingness to be a musical star inhibited Berlin not in the slightest. *On the Avenue* is best remembered for 'I've Got My Love to Keep Me Warm', at which point we are able to sit back and enjoy the amazing exhibition of ducking and weaving put on by Berlin as he fashions a new song out of a little of this and a little of that. Everything about this song, from its title to its harmonic sequence, is borrowed, and the one factor which transforms the plagiarism into high comedy is that throughout this ingenious exercise Berlin is plagiarizing nobody but himself. Astaire was fond of recalling how Irving helped him pass the time when the arrival of the first Astaire baby was imminent. The pair of them would sit playing gin rummy, and Irving always won by chatting distractedly and then without warning – snap 'Gin'. Astaire countered this device by learning from the backstage people what song Berlin was currently writing, and would begin to whistle it during the card game in apparent innocence, knowing that the moment Berlin identified it he would panic at the thought that he was composing a new song already published by someone else. Whether or not Astaire realized it, Berlin's anxiety was justified, because too often he really was working on a song already published – by himself.

It will be recalled that five years before starting *On the Avenue*, Berlin had had some success with a piece called 'I'm Playing with Fire'. Here was the idea for the Powell song, of love generating heat. This brought him as far as a title: 'I've Got My Love to Keep Me Warm'. But Berlin remembered something else about that ancient Crosby hit. It had had a verse. It had registered on nobody. Verses never do. Why not use that verse as the new chorus? By doubling the time-value of the notes of the verse of 'I'm Playing with Fire', he had arrived at his new chorus. He now decided to use as his harmony for the first four bars of the middle section the same sequence which had proved so effective in 'How Deep is the Ocean' and, all those years ago, for Belle Baker and 'Blue Skies'. There remained only the question of a new verse for 'I've Got My Love to Keep Me Warm', and a variation on the generation-of-heat idea for the words in the middle section. The challenge of the verse Berlin met simply by ignoring it. On the living stage the verse had always been the causeway across which the performers skipped on the road from speech to song. But in the cinema this sometimes ponderous transition was becoming passé, or at any rate Berlin convinced himself it was. Had not an earlier Astaire movie, *Roberta*, featured a sumptuous ballad called 'Yesterdays' to which Jerome Kern had not bothered to attach a verse? If Kern, why not Berlin? 'I've Got My Love to Keep Me Warm' would go into the world verseless. That left the words for the middle eight, and historians of musical cinema have Pandro S. Berman to thank for the way, all unwittingly, he explained how Berlin fitted the last borrowed brick into the patchwork edifice of 'I've Got My Love to Keep Me Warm'.

Berman is the one indispensable witness for anyone curious about the mechanics of the screen musical, because not only did he produce several of the most successful in the genre, but in the course of doing so he employed four of the greatest songwriting teams of the age. Who better to deliver comparative judgements? Again, he is the ideal interviewee because of his eagerness to impart the details of his achievements. When I went to keep my appointment with him, I found him standing at his own front gate, jingling the small change in the pockets of his denim suit, peering into the bright Pacific sunlight for some sign of the approach of the limey. We sat in his drawing-room and in no time an hour had passed in talk of the dead lions of the industry. He had once had an unhappy experience trying to sell opera to the American cinema-going public, which is a trick marginally more difficult than getting your royalties from a film company. *I Dream Too Much*, starring Lily Pons, had clearly been one of the major disappointments of his career, and in his determination to convince me of its virtues, he thrust a shooting script under my nose. I could not tell him that I required no shooting script to remind me of the joys of *I Dream Too Much*, which had reduced me to a state of narcolepsy when taken to see it in my tenth year. All I wished to hear from Berman was his recollection of the songwriters with whom he had worked. 'What was Kern like?' I asked.

'Oh, Jerry was fine. No trouble.'

'And the Gershwins?'

'Oh, they were a pair of very nice gents. Very educated.'

'What about Porter?'

'Nice man. Lot a dough. No trouble though.'

'What about Berlin?'

Berman became thoughtful, glanced over his shoulder, and then said with a faintly conspiratorial expression on his face, 'Turn the machine off.'

Experience had taught me that whenever a Hollywood or Broadway veteran requests the interviewer to stop the tape machine, something approaching the truth is about to emerge. Berman now began to describe his experiences of Berlin. 'He was fine. Great writer. But

Irving is a difficult man.'

'How was he difficult?'

Berman then recounted the following tale. When *Follow the Fleet* was completed and certain to make money, he decided to hold a celebration for all the principals. 'In this very room where we're sitting.' Just then the shadow of a woman flitted across the french windows. Berman nodded in the direction of the shadow and said, 'That's Evelyn Keyes. You hearda Evelyn Keyes?' I nodded respectfully. He seemed proud to be able to put a genuine star on show for me, rather as though he had produced her in the cinematic sense.

'Anyway, Irving was invited, naturally.' Towards the end of the evening something unusual had happened. Rain had started to fall on Beverly Hills. As Berlin was preparing to go, he asked Berman to lend him a coat. The two men are around the same height and build, so Berlin's request was reasonable enough. It so happened that Berman had recently had a new overcoat made, but in that benign climate he had not so far had any occasion to wear it. He handed over the coat and Berlin left. *Follow the Fleet* went in release, *Swingtime* went into production, and Berlin moved over to Twentieth Century Fox to write the score for *On the Avenue* At which point something unusual happened. Rain began to fall on Beverly Hills. Berman went to fetch his overcoat. It wasn't there. He then remembered lending it to his friend Irving, who must have forgotten to return it. Berman then telephoned Berlin asking for the return of the overcoat. Berlin insisted he had sent it back with his driver the day after the party. Berman denied this, and began to get testy, very nearly accusing the world's richest musician of absconding with his overcoat. Now Berlin began to get testy too, responding with angry remarks like: 'Who needs an overcoat? Listen, Pan, I don't need any overcoat.' The argument had then sputtered out, leaving both parties in a condition which Wodehouse would have defined as not altogether gruntled. After telling me his story, Berman sat there silent for a while before saying, 'So you see, Irving could be difficult.'

I started to laugh. Berman remained comically solemn. 'What did you say to him when you heard the song?' I asked.

'What are you talking about? What song?'

It then dawned on me that for forty years Berman had been grieving for a lost overcoat without realizing that his friend Irving had used the dispute as the inspiration for the lyrics in the middle section of 'I've Got My Love to Keep Me Warm'. I sang him the relevant words as accurately as I could, those which refer specifically to the dispensability of overcoats.

'The sonofabitch,' Berman said.

The rift between them could not have been so very wide after all, because in 1938, placing the welfare of the studio, to say nothing of his ten per cent arrangement, before the purloined overcoat, Berman invited Berlin to come back and write a third Astaire picture. This was *Carefree*, which contains one authentic masterwork, 'Change Partners', and one accident. The plot tells how Fred, the unlikeliest psychiatrist in the world, cures Ginger, its most improbable patient, of her phobia. At the point where light breaks through and she realizes she loves the psychiatrist, the black-and-white screen bursts into glorious technicolor. Naturally the moment of transition calls for a song, and Berlin quickly obliged with 'I Used to Be Colour-Blind', an ingenious and melodious piece whose *raison d'être* never becomes apparent to audiences because of the sad fact that at the last minute the studio discovered that the cupboard was bare and there was no extra money to pay for the technicolor. They used the song anyway, and Astaire was delighted to be able to introduce such outstanding material. Berlin then returned to Twentieth Century Fox, for an Alice Faye saga titled *Alexander's Ragtime Band*, an indifferent production containing yet another sumptuous ballad unjustly forgotten by the millions ready to caterwaul 'White Christmas' at the drop of a cracker. This ballad, 'Now It Can Be Told', has about it a matchless purity of line which Berlin seemed able to produce without effort and to order, yet since the disappearance of the picture into the vaults, the song is never used, and would have died outright but for a retrospective recording by Ella Fitzgerald.

It would have been hard to convince anyone in 1939 that the career of this American phenomenon had yet to achieve its zenith, yet it was not until 1942 that Berlin finally vaulted out of the constraints of his profession into the record books. After the Berman episode he had continued to work for Hollywood, even though to him home always meant New York. In 1942 he was assigned to an Astaire-Crosby feature called *Holiday Inn*. In one sequence we find Crosby, basking under the California sun, singing a maudlin ditty about sleigh bells and trees glistening under snow. It was called 'I'm Dreaming of a White Christmas', and, in the context of masterpieces like 'Cheek to Cheek' and 'Let's Face the Music and Dance', was of little merit. But the entry of the United States into the war, and the subsequent drafting overseas of hundreds of thousands of men to climes never likely to see a single snowflake, led to a khaki run on the song which filtered back to America and became so large an issue that Berlin was obliged to call a press conference, at which he was asked if 'White Christmas' was to become the classic song of the war. The suggestion was inept. 'White Christmas' was to become the classic song of Christmas, which meant that it had a life extending far beyond the end of the war. At the conference Berlin was asked to perform the piece, which he did, much to the confusion of the gathered journalists, who were not expecting the references in the verse to orange groves and sunlight, originally inserted to fit the backdrop for Crosby in *Holiday Inn*. The moment the conference was over Berlin telephoned his office, giving strict instructions that the verse be deleted from all future printings. The Crosby commercial recording has been selling ever since, and at the last count had passed thirty million; recordings by others are said to have passed a hundred million. All comment becomes superfluous.

Berlin might never have returned to Broadway had it not been for the sudden death of Jerome Kern in 1945, when the great modulator was about to embark on the score of a new musical based on the life of the sharpshooter Annie Oakley. Berlin was called in and, much against his will, was persuaded to replace Kern. He had assumed that his wartime activities, reviving the old army show of the first war, updating it as *This is the Army*, appearing in it all over the world and raising just under ten million dollars for charity, would be his last escapade in the live theatre. But the challenge of Annie Oakley proved too seductive to resist. *Annie Get Your Gun* ran over a thousand times in New York, over a thousand in London, and was later made into a movie. As a series of variations on a theme, the score is blinding, containing one example of several types of song, each one executed with undiminished flair and colour, from the obligatory waltz, 'The Girl that I Marry', through a battery of comic songs to the romantic ballad 'They Say That Falling in Love is Wonderful', and a deliberately contrived showstopper which soon became adopted as the anthem of the theatrical profession. The sentiments of 'There's No Business Like Show Business' combine the mawkish and worldly in a most peculiar way, but whatever our reactions may be to the lyric of the song, it has to be accepted that Berlin was in deadly earnest when he wrote them. He really does believe in the message of the song's title, because for him it proved to be absolutely true.

While *Annie Get Your Gun* was running, Berlin celebrated his sixtieth birthday. He was now old enough, and certainly rich enough, to retire. But the acclaim verging on hysteria with which the Oakley musical had been received tempted him to go on for a while. In 1949 he wrote words and music for a show based on the building of the Statue of Liberty; it was called *Miss Liberty* and ran for 308 performances – by Berlin's exalted standards a bit of a flop. The following year he treated another aspect of American public life by writing *Call Me Madam*, a show based so blatantly on reality that in the programme Berlin printed this disclaimer: 'The play is laid in two mythical countries. One is called Lichtenburg, the other is the United States of America.' A socialite called Mrs Perle Mesta had just been appointed by the President as Ambassador to Luxembourg, which was more than enough of an excuse to put the farce to music to be sung by Ethel Merman. *Call Me Madam* ran more than twice as long as *Miss Liberty*, after which Berlin really did seem to have retired. Then in 1962 he was tempted by a satiric idea called *Mr President*, which failed through no fault of his. Gradually Berlin's public activities fell away. Then his public appearances became rare, until, by the time he became the slightly dazed recipient of his own centenary honours, he was little more to most people than a name on a sheet of piano music, and even to his associates a disembodied voice on the telephone.

He remains a phenomenon, a man who started to write songs before there was any radio, who made his first fortune before the war before the last one, who was the first great songwriter of the golden age and who has proved also to be the last. Every other composer and lyricist in the profession has deferred to him, acknowledged him as the most eminent figure among them. Here is Kern in 1925:

> At a dinner in London I was asked what, in my opinion, were the chief characteristics of the American nation. I replied that the average United States citizen was epitomized in Irving Berlin's music. He doesn't attempt to stuff the public's ears with pseudo-original ultra-modernism, but he honestly absorbs the vibrations emanating from the people, manners and life of his time, and in turn gives these impressions back to the world – simplified, clarified, glorified. In short, what I really want to say is that Irving Berlin has no place in American music, he *is* American music.

And there was that piquant moment when Berlin adopted a tone of fatherly solicitude with Cole Porter, of all people. In 1937 Porter had enjoyed a commercial success with a song he loathed, 'Rosalie', written as the title-song for one of Louis B. Mayer's inanities. When sales of the song were at their height, Porter bumped into Berlin, who congratulated him on his latest success. Porter replied, 'Thanks a lot, but I wrote that song in hate, and I still hate it.' To which Berlin replied, 'Listen, kid, take my advice, never hate a song that has sold half a million copies.'

The greatest joke of all was that Berlin had done it all without knowing one musical term from another, without achieving even moderate mastery over any keyboard, without understanding the words in common usage among musicians to describe the things he was writing. Wisely he made a virtue out of his own limitations. Instead of doing what he could to conceal his ineptitude at the piano, he publicized it, making his custom-built piano with the cranking lever to change key so notorious a news item that when he retired it was placed reverently inside the Smithsonian, where to this day incredulous visitors gaze upon it in stark disbelief. Berlin remained cheerful about the badness of his piano playing, but we begin to wonder exactly how bad was bad? Bad enough at any rate to ruin his own songs. Alan Lerner repeats a story told to him by Moss Hart, who had been co-writer with Berlin for *As Thousands Cheer*:

One day Irving came rushing excitedly into his apartment. He had found the finale for Act One. It was called 'Easter Parade'. Irving is a self-taught pianist and musician, but his musical invention is so original and so musical that trained composers like George Gershwin and Jerome Kern used to shake their heads in envious disbelief. 'That son of a gun,' Jerome used to say helplessly, 'How does he do it?' But there is no doubt Irving is no Gershwin at the keyboard. He sat down and played 'Easter Parade' for Moss. It sounded terrible. Moss was in a dilemma. Finally he said, 'Irving, play "Blue Skies" for me.' Irving played 'Blue Skies' and that sounded terrible. Moss then said, 'Irving, the finale is terrific.'

One wonders if Berlin bothered to tell Moss Hart that his terrific finale had been published fourteen years earlier under another name. If he did, he would have been sure to make a joke of it. P. G. Wodehouse recalled being very nearly involved with Berlin in 1924 over a show called *Sitting Pretty*:

The dinner took place at Irving's apartment on West 46th Street. This was a novel duplex penthouse that had taken his fancy. He had had to buy the building in order to get it, but that sort of thing was a trifle to Irving. He believed in doing himself well.

There was a broad corridor that descended in a series of steps, each step an eight-feet-square platform, to the big living-room that faced the street. Moulded glass panels by Lalique lighted this handsome passage. These were fringed with big potted plants, and standing in front of two of them were tall wooden stands on which stood a pair of brilliant-hued toucans. They added the final touch of magnificence, and it occurred to the authors that Fabulous Felix (the songwriter Ivan Caryll) must be kicking himself for never having thought of toucans. Only Felix would have had five.

As they came down from the dining-room, their host put out his hand to one of the birds, which immediately proceeded to strike like an offended rattlesnake, its terrifying bill missing the hand by a fraction of an inch.

'I'd be a bit distant with those fowls, if I were you,' said Plum. 'They're liable to take your finger off.'

'Yes,' laughed Irving, unperturbed, 'And it might be the one I play the piano with.'

The most revealing of all the jokes at his own expense was the one Berlin made when George Gershwin, intimately familiar with Irving's piano method, was about to give the first performance of his *Concerto in F*. Berlin wired George:

I hope your Concerto in F is as good as mine in F sharp. Seriously Georgie I am rooting hard for the success and glory you so richly deserve.

By all reports he has somehow contrived to smuggle across the frontier of extreme old age the same sharpness of response, the same reactions of the hungry fighter towards the songs. Occasionally pressure has been brought to bear on him from unexpected quarters. Norman Granz has described how, having scored such success with Ella Fitzgerald's 'Song Book' recordings of the works of Cole Porter and Rodgers and Hart, he received a telephone call from Berlin, who requested that his own work receive the same accolade. When pressed, he told Granz that he was being given a hard time by his own grandchildren, who, not having too clear an idea of what the old boy had done with his life, kept telling him how wonderful Rodgers and Hart were. Berlin was so anxious to educate his family that he offered Granz a special reduced royalty rate. Granz then recorded 'The Irving Berlin Song Book', and was so excited by the results that he complied with Berlin's request that the moment the acetates were ready, he be allowed to hear them. Granz duly arrived at Berlin's house, to find the old boy sitting up in bed flanked by two executives from the publishing house. As each of the perfect versions of his work came up, Berlin expressed approval, but whenever the song in question happened to be one of the less publicized – 'You're Laughing at Me', perhaps, or 'How About Me' or the priceless 'Lazy' – he would turn on his aides and berate them for not having made the item a hit all those long years before.

A reporter reviewing the life and times when Berlin was in his ninety-ninth year was told by the ever-loving Ellin, herself now eighty-five, that Irving was a man who liked his routines to remain unaltered. 'Every evening we dress for dinner,' she said, 'and I always sit on Irving's right. It saves me doing the right side of my hair.' But Ellin, who died a few weeks after the centenary celebrations, may have been underrating the old boy, who is said to have retained his appreciation of a good-looking dame into the last years. On his eightieth birthday he was offered congratulations by Arthur Schwartz, who, intending no more than a friendly joke, asked Irving how things were going with the ladies these days. To Arthur's surprise, Berlin seemed to take the inquiry quite seriously, and said with talmudic wisdom, 'Arthur, a man of eighty is not like a man of seventy,' leaving Arthur to decide precisely how serious he was. He was certainly in earnest when, at ninety-nine, he was approached by one of the young lions of Hollywood with a view to leasing out 'Always' yet again for exposure in a new production. His refusal to grant permission amazed the executive, who could not resist asking why. Berlin's explanation: 'I'm saving it for a future project.' If such a project were to exist, and if it were graced by one of Berlin's old songs, the audience would surely be astonished at the depth to which its emotions were stirred by the strains of melody. 'What'll I Do?' can be heartbreaking enough if we accept it as its author meant it to be accepted, with perfect sincerity; when deployed as the musical symbol of the pathos of time past in the screen version of *The Great Gatsby*, the song seemed suddenly to be as intrinsic a part of its epoch as the novel itself. Berlin too, it seems, has been a teller of tales. Regarding one of them, he has been adamant about his intentions. In 1927, not long after the Belle Baker fracas, he published a sad minor dirge with slavonic overtones, called 'Russian Lullaby'. People have usually taken it to be a routine sentimental exercise, and have chosen not to bother with the import of the words. Berlin has been known to get vehement over this, because he has always insisted that 'Russian Lullaby' is explicitly anti-Russian.

Its message is perhaps a shade too murmurous to be noticed, but this is certainly not true of the one last strand in the patriotic tapestry woven by Berlin throughout his life. His gestures of gratitude became positively effusive during the Second World War, including 'I Threw a Kiss Into the Ocean' (1942), whose proceeds went to the Navy Relief Fund; and, in the same year, 'Angels of Mercy', which helped fund the American Red Cross. The largest gift of all dates back to 1918, when Berlin was compiling the score of *Yip Yip Yaphank*. He had written a *treble forte* patriotic rouser for the finale, but was so discouraged when Harry Ruby, his transcriber, groaned at the thought of yet another jingo hymn, that he withdrew it from the show and tucked it away in the bottom drawer, where it lay undisturbed for the next twenty years. In 1938 Ruby received a wire from Berlin reading: 'Be sure to listen to Kate Smith tonight on the radio.' Kate Smith was an elephantine soprano whose weekly transmission of popular songs was one of the most successful shows of its day. Berlin had decided that, with another war imminent, the time was ripe at last for jingoism, and so, cannily selecting the most emotive date in the calendar, he had given Miss Smith the twenty-year-old relic. Its title was 'God Bless America', and it was first heard on Armistice Day, 1938. Its profits, now numbered in hundreds of thousands of dollars, are donated to the Boy Scouts and Girl Guides of America. Some people believe it to be the American national anthem. It might just as well be, and is sure to be sung long after Berlin has followed Kern, Porter, the Gershwins and company into the past. One last and long-running smack in the eye for Alexander Alexandrovitch, Tsar of all the Russias.

RICHARD RODGERS and LORENZ HART

CHAPTER NINE

Richard Rodgers

THE ENIGMA OF COLLABORATION has no resolution, a truism which has often prompted those involved in the process to make jokes about it. Sammy Cahn likes to be asked which comes first, the words or the music, because he can reply, 'First comes the phone call.' W. S. Gilbert, on being asked the same question, is said to have answered 'Yes,' even though in his case there was a simple response: so far as he was concerned, the words always came first. With regard to the pains of collaboration there is a third example of facetiousness which, intentionally or not, is something more than a laugh. Richard Rodgers once answered the words-music question with 'First comes the advance' – a response which could, so far as Rodgers was concerned, be defined as a joke concealing deadly mercantile intent. Rodgers, who started as an eager, unworldly teenager overawed and overwhelmed by the urbanity and command of his craft of Lorenz Hart, ended as the shrewd producer of other people's shows, and a man who had mastered the art of deducing what would be popular and then writing it. This might appear to be the only rational way of approaching the irrational craft of songwriting, except that Gershwin cared only for the joy of composition, and only thought of what to do with the song after it was written. When I once asked Ira why, if George was such a dominant figure in the musical theatre of the 1920s, he was obliged to watch a masterwork like 'The Man I Love' discarded from the score of three different shows by three different producers, his response was: 'George and I felt it was less troublesome to write a new number than to defend a number that was in doubt.' Or, to put it another way, the song was the thing. It was written. It existed. Whether others wished to avail themselves of its facilities was their business. The song had served its function, of giving the delight of creation to those who had brought it into being. Even Kern, a stickler for contractual form so ruthless that the most avaricious Hollywood moguls were consistently routed by him, often composed the most involuted structures for the sheer pleasure of the work, and in spite of his fear that the general public would find the end result incomprehensible. If Rodgers extracted any joy from his work, he never conveys as much in his autobiography, which is the sort of detached account we might expect from, say, an actuary or an architect. This may be due either to a misplaced sense of decorum or to authorial ineptitude. On the other hand, Rodgers's father was a doctor who had performed his errands of mercy with no particular ardour, and his son conveys the same impression of someone going about his professional business with some detachment.

What makes Rodgers such a rewarding case for study is the unusual consistency of his working arrangements. In a long and phenomenally successful career, stretching over more than fifty years, he worked with only two collaborators of any consequence. At the very end of his life, deprived by death of a true and tried partner, he turned to new lyric-writers, but all these attempts at remarriage proved as brief as they were barren. There was even one interlude in 1962 when, in a despairing attempt to resolve the problem, Rodgers recruited himself; *No Strings* is a revealing example of what a clever man may do with a set of songs when he possesses long experience, a useful instinct and no flair for versifying. The Rodgers oeuvre is effectively contained within two other careers, those of Lorenz Hart and Oscar Hammerstein, with each of whom he enjoyed long and prosperous partnerships. From 1918 until 1943, the generic term 'Rodgers-and-Hart' came to signify a certain style of composition: witty, original, full of amusing, unpredictable twists and turns both harmonically and lyrically, possessing a lightness of texture and a deftness of touch even in the sad ballads of unrequited love, which conveyed in some oddly appealing way the efflorescence of youth. From 1943 until 1960, the phrase 'Rodgers-and-Hammerstein' was equally redolent, but of qualities so radically changed from Rodgers-and-Hart as to be virtually antipathetic. Of the thousands of working musicians and singers who still approach Rodgers-and-Hart with the eagerness of kindred spirits, there is hardly a one who warms to the popular appeal of Rodgers-and-Hammerstein. As for the vast theatre-going armies who continue to march on the great Rodgers-and-Hammerstein set pieces, their knowledge of or interest in or affection for Rodgers-and-Hart is vague to the brink of indifference. It would be only a slight over-simplification to say that while Rodgers-and-Hart has triumphantly outlived the incident of production to become part of the standard repertoire of modern popular music, Rodgers-and-Hammerstein has failed to move out of the theatre, chained for ever to the context of the theatrical event for which it was conceived. No doubt Rodgers, who all his life pursued the chimera of something called the integrated score, that is, a score which arises directly out of the dramatic process and carries that process forward, would claim that this very failure of the Hammerstein songs to venture out into the nightclubs and on to the bandstands and the recital stages is the ultimate proof of their superiority as dramatic pieces. That may or may not be so, but the world does not arrange its affairs in that way. Affection for a song arises, not out of its dramatic context, but from its intrinsic merit as a performable piece of music. 'Edelweiss' retains the shreds of credibility only in the Biedermeier context of nuns and children. 'The Lady is a Tramp' happens to come from a 1937 musical called *Babes in Arms*, but its viability as a performing piece depends not in the slightest in our awareness of who originally sang it and why, because it possesses a generality which most of the Hammerstein songs do not possess, and perhaps were never meant to possess. This is the most striking thing by far about the career of Rodgers: the drastic extent to which his compositional style altered with the identity of his collaborator.

The glib conclusion has been that when he was young Rodgers benefited inestimably from the liberating vernacular style of Hart; once that advantage was removed, the mannerisms of the melodies regressed into a safe and oddly venerable balladry. Undeniably Rodgers the later master suffers horribly from any comparison with his own young self. Indeed, it is hard to believe that the inspired creator of melodies like 'This Can't Be Love' and 'A Ship Without a Sail' could ever have sunk to the bathos of 'You'll Never Walk Alone' or the Soliloquy from *Carousel*. But to ascribe all the virtues of the first partnership to Hart, simply because those virtues are missing from the second with Hammerstein, is to misapply the instrument of deductive reasoning, and perhaps inflict a grievous injustice on Rodgers in the process. That the rhythmic buoyancy of his writing declined from the day that Hart retired, there can be no shadow of a doubt. What is disconcerting is that the circumstances suggest strongly that Rodgers desired this change, took measures to bring it about, was delighted with the result, and at last aggrieved to discover the sustained interest in the Hart songs. Robert Kimball, editor of Hart's *Collected Lyrics*, has written that Rodgers 'seemed disinclined to say much about his years with Hart':

> On one of his last try-out forays to New Haven, for *Two By Two*, he agreed to speak to interested Yale students about the American musical theater. Near the appointed meeting place, a large poster, advertising a revue of songs 'By Rodgers and Hart' caught his eye. 'I can't believe it,' Rodgers said, looking at the poster. 'Larry's been dead for twenty-seven years. Why are young people born after he died interested in these early songs?'

The fatuousness of Rodgers's rhetorical question is regrettable, but perhaps understandable. Those creative artists plagued by the sneaking suspicion that their finest work was achieved in youth always have a vested interest in avoiding the subject. Rodgers's obtuseness in the face of continuing admiration for his work with Hart calls to mind the petulance of Orson Welles when in later years anyone was tactless enough to invoke the theme of *Citizen Kane*. Nonetheless, the truth behind what might justifiably be termed Rodgers's compositional schizophrenia is rather more complex than detractors of the later Rodgers have perceived. So far from being astonished at the sustained interest in Hart, Rodgers must have understood that it had been brought about by an act of his own, as we shall see. But the answer to this issue of which is the truer Rodgers has much to do with that nebulous process by which two men who may not necessarily be compatible conspire to create one song. Which comes first?

The two men met in the winter of 1918–19. Hart was twenty-three, Rodgers sixteen, and the seven-year difference represented a vast gulf in experience and confidence. When Rodgers was still a child, Hart had been creating a reputation as a brilliant campus versifier; when Rodgers arrived at Columbia, it was to find that although Hart had long since moved on, the easy expertise of his couplets still hung on the air. Every summer from 1908 to 1913 Hart worked as an entertainments organizer at various Boys' Camps. Arthur Schwartz's story of how he pursued Hart to the last of these camps gives some idea of the awe in which Hart was held by his contemporaries, even though he had as yet achieved little professional recognition. By the time he met the teenaged Rodgers, he was a lyricist with ten years' practical experience behind him. It says something for his powers of forbearance that he saw no impediment to a partnership, one which was to endure very nearly unto death. Although he still had his reputation to make, Hart by the time he encountered Rodgers was already one of the most original young writers in America; 'I love to Lie Awake in Bed', written for a mere Boys' Camp romp, is already far beyond the range of most of the Tin Pan Alley hustlers.

The early years of the partnership were taken up with work of a nature so comically parochial in origin as to sound like the invention of a parodist. Between 1919 and 1924 Rodgers and Hart provided scores for shows requested by the Oppenheim Collins Mutual Aid Association of Brooklyn, the Institute of Musical Art, the Free Scholarship Fund of the New York Child Labour Committee, Park Avenue Synagogue, and the Evelyn Goldsmith Home for Crippled Children. There were also a few attempts at professionalism. In 1919 the first Rodgers-and-Hart song was published. It was called 'Any Old Place With You' and incorporates one of the best-known of all Hart couplets:

I'll go to hell for ya
Or Philadelphia.

The song was interpolated in a show called *A Lonely Romeo*, and must at any rate have brought the two young men to the notice of the extraordinary Harry Bache Smith, writer of more than 120 Broadway shows, including nine in one season, the man who had first introduced Jerome Kern to the pleasures of bibliomania, invented the title 'Ziegfeld Follies', and is said to have attended one of Flo's weddings as Best Man and taken the opportunity to present the groom with a writ for non-payment of royalties. Of the thousands of songs for which he must have provided the words, only one has survived, 'The Sheik of Araby', an archaic piece guaranteed a sort of immortality through the happy accident of a reference in *The Great Gatsby*. In the light of the homely naïvety of its words, it would be interesting to know what Smith made of the ingenious contrivances of 'Any Old Place With You'. In 1920 the Rodgers-and-Hart partnership was involved with six songs in a New York production called *Poor Little Ritz Girl*. In 1924 they provided two songs to *The Melody Man*, and in the following year their song, 'Anytime, Anywhere, Anyhow', whose lyric has never been discovered, found its way into a production called *June Days*. It all sounds a rather sorry tale of six years of drudgery, most of it unrewarded. But it would be a mistake to assume that until they won a reputation Rodgers and Hart were frittering away valuable creative energy. Much of what they wrote for the charity shows and the synagogue entertainments was later to appear to much greater effect once their work was in demand. In fact, had they and their contemporaries only realized it, Rodgers and Hart had already arrived as early as 1922. They had embarked on an uncommissioned work called *Winkle Town*, whose score consisted of sixteen songs, more than half of which eventually found a place in other productions. One of them was to make history. But the irony attaching to the team's first hit is upstaged by an even greater. The libretto for *Winkle Town* was co-written by Oscar Hammerstein.

In 1925 some of the players with the Theatre Guild, working at the Garrick Theatre, decided to put together a small revue, to run for two or three performances. The actress Edith Meiser had been tipped off that young Rodgers might be worth interviewing. At their meeting Rodgers played a succession of songs from the amateur shows, which gave Miss Meiser no confidence in him. He then played a song from *Winkle Town* entitled 'Manhattan', and the partnership was under way at last. The revue which followed, *The Garrick Gaieties*, is one of the great symbolic moments in the evolution of the modern musical theatre. Conceived as a weekend squib, it ran over two hundred performances and established Rodgers and Hart as two of the likeliest young songwriters in the profession. From Miss Meiser we get a thumbnail sketch of Hart which shows how little he changed during his short life:

> I remember Larry Hart coming into the theatre. This little bit, almost a dwarf of a man. I always thought he was the American Toulouse-Lautrec. He was that kind of a personality. But an enchanting man. He had what is now called charisma. He had such appeal. He was already balding. He had this enormous head and a very heavy beard that had to be shaved twice a day. And of course that big cigar that always stuck out of his mouth. And he was always rubbing his hands together. This was his great gesture when he was pleased. And we adored him. Dick we were terribly fond of, but Larry was adored.

Once 'Manhattan' had made its impression, Rodgers and Hart were commissioned to write production after production; with each one they confirmed their reputation as the young idea in songwriting. Hart's sister-in-law has given a slightly confused description of their working methods:

> There was never any set rule. If a melody Dick was experimenting with at the piano caught Larry's ear, he grabbed a lead sheet and came up with a lyric. If Larry came up with an idea and Dick nodded, that was it.

But as the years went by and Hart's condition deteriorated, he was rarely present when Rodgers was composing. Even Mrs Hart's description suggests that most of the time the first creative stirrings came from the composer. However, once the song was written, Hart often eclipsed his partner in imaginative quality. He was one of the first of the modern school to refer to his own work, in 1926. The joke was well noted, but was so obvious that the rest of the subtleties contained in the song have never received their just due. In the spring of 1926 *The Girl Friend* opened, and within weeks one of its songs, 'Blue Room', had become one of the great successes of the year. A few weeks after the appearance of *The Girl Friend* came a second edition of *Garrick Gaieties*, with a song defending the rustic life to balance the metropolitan bias of 'Manhattan'. With 'Mountain Greenery' Hart ran riot, using split words to attain unexpected rhymes, like

> Beans could get no keener re-
> Ception in a beanery.

and in the second verse the rhyming of 'planned which is' with 'sandwiches'. Such devices were not original. A hundred years earlier, as Hart well knew, Byron had composed the couplet:

> But – Oh! ye lords of ladies intellectual
> Inform us truly, have they not hen-pecked you all?

What Hart was doing with the popular song lyric was not inventing new forms, but introducing into its province ideas and devices which till now had hardly been considered practical. He played further tricks with his own skills when writing the songs for *Peggy-Ann*, which opened in December 1926 even as the strains of 'Blue Room' were becoming familiar to millions of people. In *Peggy-Ann* the heroine sings to the hero of the hopelessness of life; he responds by agreeing with her. 'Where's that Rainbow' is rich with topical allusion, but not quite as audiences perceived it. The first sixteen bars run as follows:

> Where's that rainbow you hear about?
> Where's that lining they cheer about?
> Where's that love nest
> Where love is king ever after?
>
> Where's that blue room they sing about?
> Where's that sunshine they fling about?
> I know morning will come
> But pardon my laughter.

Ever since 1918, when Chopin had been dug up and obliged to dance to Tin Pan Alley's rhythms with 'I'm Always Chasing Rainbows', the idea of rainbows had been an overworked device, which culminated a few years later with 'There's a Rainbow Round my Shoulder', and again at the end of the 1930s with 'Over the Rainbow'. Hart's allusion to a lining was more specific, a reference to the Jerome Kern hit of 1921, 'Look for the Silver Lining'. The love nest was a playful reference to Louis Hirsch's great hit of 1920, 'The Love Nest'. The allusion to sunshine could have been aimed at any one of a dozen songs, from Irving Berlin's 'Some Sunny Day' to Ira Gershwin's 'Sunny Disposish'. But the point is that by referring to songs written by his professional rivals Hart was again extending the range of the popular song. How true the anecdotes were remains unknown, as usual, but certainly some of the richest stories collapse in the face of a little innocent research. One of the most celebrated of all tales involving the genesis of a song concerns a piece called 'My Heart Stood Still', which appeared in two productions during 1927, *One Dam Thing After Another*, for C. B. Cochran at the London Pavilion, and *A Connecticut Yankee* at the Vanderbilt Theatre in New York. According to Rodgers, this is how the title surfaced:

> Another reason why we went to Paris was to see if we might not have misjudged it the first time we were there. Somehow this time the

French seemed more friendly, or perhaps it was just that we were getting used to the Parisian way of life. What made our stay doubly enjoyable was that we ran into two girls we had known in New York. We made a happy foursome taking in all the expected sights, and a few unexpected ones too.

While we were escorting the girls back to their hotel one night in a taxi, another cab darted out of a side street and missed hitting us by inches. As our cab came to a halt, one of the girls cried, 'Oh, my heart stood still.' No sooner were the words out than Larry casually said, 'Say, that would make a great title for a song.' When the cab stopped I took out a little black address book and scribbled the words 'My Heart Stood Still'.

According to Rodgers, Hart quickly forgot all about the incident, but some time later, striving for ideas to use in the Cochran show, Rodgers came across the note in the address book, refreshed Hart's memory, and soon the song was written, complete with Hart's affecting touch of poetic imagery, 'That unfelt clasp of hands told me so well you knew'. The story has all the elements required for an anecdotal set piece, to be seized upon later by biographers unversed in the art of moving from discord to resolution. There is the cosmopolitan setting, the romance of a foursome, the innuendo of love in a taxi, the threat of danger, and the heavenly ease with which the germ of a famous song is plucked out of the air. The tale incorporated one other ingredient. It is bogus, as Rodgers certainly knew. Were the anecdote to have concerned the genesis of a famous poem, or novel, or play, the academics would have hit the road decades ago, seeking out the two fortunate young ladies in the taxi, and deducing from their researches which of the two blurted out the title. And had the sleuths ever caught up with the ladies, the first question would have been, 'Why did you never subsequently feel the temptation to come forward and claim your fragment of glory?' The hunt would have been rendered virtually impossible by Rodgers's failure to give the names of the two girls, or even to hint at their identity. This is not to say that they never existed, or that the incident in the taxi never occurred, but there is much more persuasive evidence to push us to those conclusions.

In another context Rodgers has paid tribute to the Kern-Wodehouse series of small-scale musicals staged at the Princess Theatre between 1917 and 1919:

They were intimate and uncluttered and tried to deal in a humorous way with modern, everyday characters. They were certainly different – and far more appealing to me – from the overblown operettas, mostly imported, that dominated the Broadway scene in the wake of *The Merry Widow* and *The Chocolate Soldier*.

Rodgers certainly saw all the Princess shows, and even claims to have watched one of them, *Very Good, Eddie*, at least half a dozen times. He also mentions by name *Oh, Lady! Lady!*, which opened on 1 February 1918, ran 219 performances, and inspired Wodehouse's successor as drama critic at *Vanity Fair*, Dorothy Parker, to write:

> If you ask me, I will look you fearlessly in the eye and tell you in low, throbbing tones that it has it over every other musical comedy in town. . . . Bolton and Wodehouse and Kern are my favourite indoor sport. I like the way they go about a musical comedy.

Among the Kern-Wodehouse numbers which reduced Miss Parker to such breathless delight was something called 'You Found Me and I Found You', in which the following exchange occurs between hero and heroine:

> SHE: I got a soaking,
>   Now, wasn't that provoking
>   One day when it began to rain.
> HE: You simply made my heart stand still.
>   Just think, you might have caught a chill.

The fact that Wodehouse had deployed this over-publicized phrase ten years before the notorious non-collision in a Paris taxi detracts not at all from the song in *A Connecticut Yankee*, which is far superior in every way to the Kern-Wodehouse trifle. But the propensity of distinguished songwriters to wax a shade too poetic about their past is a warning to the researcher, who too often stumbles upon contradictory evidence. Did Cole Porter really need to seek out the far exotic corners of the earth in order to compose 'Begin the Beguine' and 'Night and Day'? Did Howard Dietz really find the most apposite and successful title of his life by running an eye along the contents of a bookcase? When Noël Coward composed 'I'll Follow My Secret Heart' under a sort of self-induced hypnosis, did he also conceive the lyric? And what of the most outlandish scenario of all, bequeathed by Jerome Kern? In 1932, working on a musical called *Music in the Air*, with Rodgers's future partner Hammerstein, Kern and his wife went for a break to a house party in Nantucket:

> Kern was awakened one morning by a bird singing just outside his window. The warbling so enchanted him that he awoke Eva and they listened together. When the bird flew away, Jerry sang the melody over and over to himself. Then, since he and Eva had not gone to bed until shortly before dawn, he went to sleep. When he awoke again late in the morning he set about writing down the theme. To his

dismay he could not recall it correctly. Nor could Eva sing it for him. He dressed and went downstairs to the piano, but soon gave up in frustration. The song that had seemed so memorable and simple just a few hours before eluded him completely. The incident spoiled his whole day. But by a stroke of luck the bird obligingly reappeared near his window ledge the next morning. Kern grabbed a pencil and an index card that was nearby and stole downstairs. As quietly as he could in the sleeping house he put the tune on paper, writing below it: '6 a.m. Bird song from the willow tree outside east window. J.K.' As Kern noted, 'It was a complete phrase and a perfectly rounded melodic treatment.'

The fragment was soon identified as the song of the Cape Cod Sparrow, and quickly developed into 'I've Told Ev'ry Little Star', generally conceded to be second-best to the show's memorable ballad, 'The Song Is You'. *Music in the Air* was one of those Fritzi-Mitzi-Rudi-Trudi Bavarian excesses representing a lamentable reversion to the bad old days of the Austro-Hungarian ascendency on Broadway, but 'The Song Is You' stands triumphantly above the wreckage. There is no evidence that the sparrow was ever invited to become a member of the American Society of Composers, Authors and Publishers, or that it ever composed any other useful songs.

As for 'My Heart Stood Still', Wodehouse never referred to its roots but understandably considered it permissible for him to deploy it as freely in his prose as he once had in his lyrics. In 1949 the Christmas book trade was enlivened on both sides of the Atlantic by the publication of *The Mating Season*, in which Bertie Wooster finds himself the house guest of a Mr Haddock, of Haddock's Headache Hokies. At one of the crises in his affairs Bertie says: 'My heart stood still. I clutched at the windscreen for support and what-whated.' When things deteriorate even further, he adds: 'My heart stood stiller,' and when finally panic sets in he remarks: 'My heart, ceasing to stand still, gave a leap and tried to get out through my two front teeth.' There is another tenuous link between Rodgers and Wodehouse: in 1929 the songwriter worked on an unproduced musical called *The Play's the Thing*, which, to judge from the few surviving lyric fragments, was an adaptation of Ferenc Molnar's play. Historians of the theatre song will find among those fragments a Hart rhyme which was to turn up a generation later in *My Fair Lady*, the rhyming of 'Budapest' with 'rude a pest'.

Three years before the aborted musical version of Molnar's play, Wodehouse had collaborated with Guy Bolton to translate it into a straight play, which ran for a year in New York in 1927 and, later, for six months in London. When it was revived, again successfully, in New York in 1948, it was one of Wodehouse's most useful morale-builders after the miseries of the war. *Simple Simon* proved a more profitable venture for Rodgers and Hart. A slapstick vehicle concocted for himself by Ed Wynn, it offers a detailed account of how Rodgers and Hart went about the business of collaboration. One of the songs in *Simple Simon* was dropped for unspecified reasons before the production reached New York. Later that year Rodgers and Hart brought the song to London and slipped it into a Cochran musical featuring a heroine who passes herself off as her own sixty-year-old self so that she can show the effectiveness of some newly marketed cosmetic. Cochran always nominated *Evergreen* as his favourite among all his productions, but almost certainly what endeared the production to him was the music rather than the story, and especially the reject from *Simple Simon*, sung by Jessie Matthews, who was co-starring with her real-life lover Sonnie Hale. Rodgers too must have had a special affection for the piece, because he draws close attention to it in his reminiscences:

> 'Dancing on the Ceiling', rescued from *Simple Simon*, was performed by Jessie and Sonnie all round a huge inverted chandelier that rose from center stage like an incandescent metal tree. The song itself is worthy of some comment because its creation throws further light on the unusually close collaboration between Larry and me. I had composed the music first, and there was something about it that gave Larry the feeling of weightlessness and elevation. This in turn led to the original notion of a girl imagining that her distant lover is dancing above her on the ceiling. Note that in the first two bars, on the words 'He dances overhead', the notes ascend the scale in a straight line, then descend in the third, and then suddenly leap a seventh, from D to C, on the words 'ceiling near'.

It is some indication of the limitations of writing for the live theatre that as late as 1930 Rodgers, Cochran and company could find it daring to build a set of an upside-down room. It was to escape these limitations, as well as for the promise of large royalties, that almost all the successful American songwriters drifted across the continent to Hollywood in the wake of the invention of talking pictures. The fate of Rodgers and Hart at the hands of the film industry is best conveyed by a question Rodgers addresses to readers of his autobiography: 'Two and a half years? What on earth could have compelled me to devote so long a period of time to what was, for the most part, the most unproductive period of my professional life?'

The answer has something to do with Maurice Chevalier, who was making musicals for Paramount. While Broadway languished in the doldrums brought about by the collapse of Wall Street and its aftermath, Hollywood was poised, technologically, to replace New York as the centre of specific levity of musical entertainment. And in the first

Rodgers and Hart production – they had previously been involved in two earlier screen musicals of no particular consequence in 1930 and 1931 – all their hopes of being stimulated by the new freedom of the camera seemed justified. *Love Me Tonight*, Chevalier's 1932 film co-starring Jeanette Macdonald, contains at least two memorable sequences which show the camera liberated from the short-lived convention of anchoring it to a fixed point and shooting the performers as they emoted in front of it. Instead, *Love Me Tonight* did as much as any emergent Hollywood musical to establish new canons of procedure, exemplified by an early sequence of what must in those quaint days have seemed breathtakingly imaginative. Chevalier is a poor tailor who decides to collect the money owing to him from the vicomte who lives in a nearby castle. Before setting out, the tailor sells a coat to a prospective bridegroom and sings a song which the customer whistles as he leaves the shop. He is heard by a passing taxi driver, who starts to whistle this pervasive melody. The cabby's fare, who happens to be a composer, begins to write-down the music, singing each note as he scribbles. Cut to a railway carriage, where the composer is putting words to the tune. The finished article is overheard by a troop of French soldiers in the same compartment. Cut to the open country, where the same soldiers are now marching to the tune. The camera then pans to a gypsy who watches and listens to the soldiers. He dashes to his camp and plays the air on his violin. By now a whole day has passed, and as the music floats up on the evening air from the gypsy encampment, it carries to the ramparts of a nearby castle, where the heroine of our tale stands on a balcony in the appropriate condition of romantic receptivity, and is deeply moved by the song. In this way, with no word of dialogue spoken, hero and heroine are tied in a lovers' knot before they are even aware of each other's existence. It must have given Rodgers and Hart much food for thought that by liberating the action in this way from the trammels of the three-dimensional world, the movie-makers had provided a new and much more sensible way of pounding a new melody into the consciousness of its audience. The old mechanism of wearily reprising a song later in the action of a play was no longer necessary. In *Love Me Tonight*, by the time the heroine has become affected by the song, it has been played more persistently than any producer or librettist would dare to contrive in a conventional work for the stage. The song, 'Isn't it Romantic', has since been acknowledged as one of the outstanding popular compositions of the decade. Something almost as striking occurs in the closing sequence, in which our hero, believing himself to be unloved, departs on an express train, only to be pursued by the boldest of heroines, who takes to her horse in a reckless attempt to win him back. All the while she rides, she sings to her man, who hears her, notwithstanding the roar of the train's engine. The musical theme for this sequence obviously needed to convey rapid movement and deep emotional excitement. This Rodgers cleverly achieves by the very simplest methods, a theme which descends chromatically to a rhythmic accompaniment which doubles up the tempo to create the illusion of pounding hoofbeats. Most ingeniously of all, he and Hart fashioned a song from this outlandish premise which triumphantly sailed away from the constrictions of the plot to become one of the most popular standard songs. To this day, whenever some nightclub chanteuse or concert recital artist sings 'Lover', the remnants of the situation in *Love Me Tonight* can be detected by the vigilant listener, who may well be puzzled by them.

So a brilliant start to their Hollywood career bolstered the hopes of Rodgers and Hart, but never again in their work in the cinema were words, music and action to be so tightly integrated as in *Love Me Tonight*. There was the occasional consolation: 'You Are Too Beautiful' and 'Easy to Remember' rank among the best screen songs of the period. For the rest, it was muddle and confusion best exemplified by the extraordinary fate of the melody written for a 1933 MGM farrago called *Hollywood Party*, a work whose pretensions are symbolized by its cast, which included Laurel and Hardy, the Three Stooges, Jimmy Durante and Mickey Mouse. In one sequence Jean Harlow, who had not up to this point in her career been noted for musical ability, was to be seen and heard addressing a musical request to the Maker of the Universe. This item, to be called 'Prayer', was assigned to Rodgers and Hart, which may have been sheer bad luck, because there were several teams of writers working on the score. The words of 'Prayer' have become notorious as an indication of how the studio bosses misused the talents of the expensive artists for whom they headhunted so zealously:

> Oh, lord, if you ain't busy up there,
> I ask for help with a prayer,
> So please don't give me the air.
>
> Oh, hear me, Lord, I must see Garbo in person,
> With Gable while they're rehearsin',
> While some director is cursin'.
>
> Please let me open up my eyes at seven,
> And find I'm looking through the Golden Gate.
> And walking right into my movie heaven,
> While some executive tells me I'll be great.
>
> Oh, Lord, I know how friendly you are,
> If I'm not going too far,
> Be nice and make me a star.

It would be entertaining to know how serious Hart was when he wrote those bathetic words; both he and his partner must have breathed a sigh of secret relief when neither Miss Harlow nor the song was eventually included in *Hollywood Party*. But the saga of the song had hardly begun. In 1934, still at MGM, Rodgers and Hart were assigned to something named *Manhattan Melodrama*, remembered for two reasons today, each more grisly than the other. When the homicidal madman John Dillinger was shot down outside the Biograph Cinema in Chicago, *Manhattan Melodrama* was the production he had just been watching. One wonders what he could have made of the spectacle in that film of a white actress called Shirley Ross blacked up in a comical attempt to pass herself off as a Negress, singing a piece called 'The Bad in Ev'ry Man', an aria strangely familiar to anyone unfortunate enough to have been exposed to 'Prayer':

> Oh, Lord, what is the matter with me?
> I'm just permitted to see
> The bad in ev'ry man.
>
> Oh, hear me, Lord, I could be good to a lover,
> But then I always discover
> The bad in ev'ry man.
>
> They like to tell you that they love you only,
> And you believe it though you know you're wrong,
> A little hallroom can be awfully lonely,
> And a night can be so very long.
>
> Oh, Lord, perhaps I'll alter my plan,
> And overlook if I can
> The bad in ev'ry man.

Mark Two of the song had little to be said for it, except that it was not as idiotic as Mark One, but an MGM executive called Jack Robbins throught he detected in the contours of the melody a potential commercial appeal. He prevailed upon the writers to attempt what they had never done before and were never to do again: compose a song which had no dramatic context. This they agreed to do, and the result was 'Blue Moon', one of the biggest moneymakers the partnership ever enjoyed.

Their return to Broadway in 1935 now saw them entering their most scintillating period. From this point on, almost every show they wrote was innovatory in one way or another, and contained songs strong enough to outlive the shows by thirty, forty, fifty years. *Jumbo*, for example, required the removal of all the seats from the theatre where it was presented, and their replacement by a circus tent, a device better suited to a Kaufman-and-Hart farce than to the real world of profit and loss. The entrepreneur who masterminded this gamble was the regrettable Billy Rose, whose vaunted sense of showmanship let him down when he placed a radio ban on all the songs from the show on the grounds that once people had heard them there would be no compulsion for them to buy a ticket. This suggests that either Rose thought the songs were so bad that nobody acquainted with them would think the show worth attending, or that the songs so outshone the rest of the action that they were the only element worth attention. The latter likelihood is somewhere near the truth, for in a production in which Durante made his entry riding an elephant, in which Paul Whiteman made his astride a horse, in which animals outnumbered humans, in which a clown played the violin while bananas were being stuffed into his trousers, Rodgers and Hart were responsible for 'Little Girl Blue', 'The Most Beautiful Girl in the World' and 'My Romance', a lyric of wry restraint which denied the need for elaborate romantic trappings:

> My romance doesn't need a castle rising in Spain,
> Nor a dance to a constantly surprising refrain.

Jumbo lost money, inevitably, but Rodgers and Hart gained priceless riches from it because of the identity of its director, a man called George Abbott. A man of deep theatrical sagacity, Abbott was to be instrumental in guiding Rodgers and Hart through a series of projects, all of which advanced the cause of the American musical. In 1936 came *On Your Toes*, the first musical to be presented on Broadway which incorporated a full ballet company. And because ballet companies have to have something to dance to, Rodgers found himself in the unaccustomed position of writing music to which words by Hart were not required. 'Slaughter on Tenth Avenue' was the outcome. The 1937 musical *Babes in Arms* had nothing revolutionary about it, and was a reversion to the over-used theme of why-don't-us-kids-put-on-our-own-show-in-the-barn. What justified the existence of *Babes in Arms* was the astonishing richness of the songs, which included 'My Funny Valentine', 'Where or When', 'The Lady is a Tramp' and 'I Wish I Were in Love Again', the last-named a love-hate duet containing some of the most-quoted lines of Hart's life:

> When love congeals
> It soon reveals
> The faint aroma of performing seals,
> The double-crossing of a pair of heels.

Then came *I'd Rather Be Right*, whose hero was an imaginary President of the United States called Franklin D. Roosevelt. It was the choice of actor to portray Roosevelt which shoved Rodgers and Hart into one of the most embarrassing predicaments of their lives, and which provides posterity with a priceless symbolic passage of arms between opposed generations.

In November 1904, when Rodgers was two years old, a musical opened on Broadway called *Little Johnny Jones*. The leading man was one of the most cantankerous and self-opinionated performers ever to strut the musical stage. The music he sang was composed by the most notorious egocentric in the theatre. The words were written by the most bigoted of all sworn opponents of the formation of any organization protecting the actor's rights. The director was someone not quite unfamiliar with the pleasures of throwing punches at the ladies when under the influence. The story was concocted by the most bombastic, the most bitterly resented, the most arrogant personality of his generation. All these men were George Michael Cohan, who, on one occasion, having been accused of paying himself too lavish a salary, responded by publishing a defence in a periodical called *The Spot Light*:

> I write my own songs because I write better songs than anyone else that I know of. I publish these songs because they bring greater royalties than any other class of music sold in this country. I write my own plays because I have not yet seen or read plays from the pens of other authors that seem as good as the plays I write. I produce my own plays because I think I'm as good a theatrical manager as any other man in this line. I dance because I know I'm the best dancer in the country. I sing because I can sing my own songs better than any other man on the stage. I publish this paper because it reaches people in a position to get my name in other papers. I write these little stories because I think I write them better than other writers of stories. I play the leading parts in most of my plays because I think I'm the best actor available. I pay myself the biggest salary every paid a song-and-dance comedian because I know I deserve it. But believe me, kind reader, when I say, I am not an egotist.

The most remarkable thing of all about Cohan is that he was at least half as gifted as he thought he was. The first performer to advertise himself as a song-and-dance man, the lyricist who did more than anyone to propagate the seedy myth of Broadway as The Great White Way, Cohan was the composer of naïve, unforgettable melodies, a pragmatist who ruthlessly milked the jingo sentiments of his audience with set pieces like 'You're a Grand Old Flag', 'Any Place the Old Flag Flies' and 'Washington, He was a Wonderful Man', who could switch at will to the sentimentality of 'Mary's a Grand Old Name', and who in some indefinable way captured in his best songs something of the essence of the early years of the century, perhaps by fusing the energies of ragtime and the tear-jerking Irish balladry of his childhood. His harmonies are genial, his melodies unsurprising, yet they projected a vigour which, adapted by a resourceful orchestrator, can still stir the blood. The scant recorded evidence suggests that he was a dreadful singer, and his plays are long forgotten. Posterity accepts him as the lovable scamp of James Cagney's portrayal in *Yankee Doodle Dandy*, or as the brash hero projected by Joel Gray in the musical *George M.* But Cohan was nothing remotely like either of these idealizations. His daughter said of the Cagney version: 'That's the kind of life daddy would like to have lived.'

The 1904 show was *Little Johnny Jones*, still remembered for two songs which became American classics, 'Yankee Doodle Dandy' and 'Give My Regards to Broadway'. Later came 'Forty Five Minutes from Broadway', and, in 1917, an indifferent recruiting song called 'Over There', for which Congress awarded him a gold medal. But once the war was over, Cohan the composer-performer was seen to be a relic. He was still capable of the occasional rousing piece, for example 'Ring to the Name of Rosie', dated 1923, and, in the last musical of his career in 1928, the title song of *Billie*. But by now he belonged to the annals of songwriting. His last real success, 'Little Nellie Kelly', published in 1923, was a period piece even as it was being written, and long before Rodgers and Hart were unfortunate enough to encounter him, Cohan was an antique, a salty survivor from the days when men sported billycocks and their ladies carried dead birds on their heads.

Cohan's reaction to the new school of songwriting veered between indifference and derision. He once published a song purporting to extol the work of Irving Berlin, and once said that he greatly admired the multiplicity of talents of Noël Coward. But his reaction to the sophistications of men like Kern, Gershwin and Porter was one of envious contempt. It is not difficult to imagine his mixed emotions on being invited to star on Broadway in a new musical written by other men. There had already been a painful skirmish in 1932, when Cohan appeared in a movie called *The Phantom President*, for which Rodgers and Hart wrote six songs, evidently unaware that Cohan had accepted the role on the understanding that the songs would be his own. Cohan's conduct during the making of *The Phantom President* had appalled Rodgers, who wrote: 'I don't recall that he ever deigned to speak a civil word to anyone.' Against their better judgement, Rodgers and Hart were prevailed upon to work with Cohan on *I'd Rather Be Right*, and it was in September 1937, as Rodgers later recalled, that the famous clash between the generations took place, in an East Side apartment specially chosen with deference to Cohan's taste for elegance:

I played one piano and Margot Hopkins, my rehearsal pianist, was at the other. Moss Hart did the singing. He didn't have a trained voice, of course, but he had excellent enunciation and an oddly charming way of putting over a song. All during the performance Cohan sat with his arms folded, his eyes half closed, his mouth drooping. No matter what the number, neither his expression nor his position changed. He never moved his head, smiled, frowned or said a word during the hour it took. This didn't bother me much, since I'm a quiet listener myself, but once we were finished, Cohan rose from his chair, walked over to me, patted me on the shoulder, mumbled, 'Don't take any wooden nickels,' and then walked out the door. That was that.

I'd Rather Be Right was well received, but Cohan made life as difficult as he could for everyone else, especially Rodgers and Hart, who had committed the unforgivable sin of imposing on the great song-and-dance man ideas about songwriting which were not his own. At one point Cohan even rewrote some of Hart's lyrics, and was severely reprimanded for it. After that he referred to the songwriting team as Gilbert and Sullivan, letting it be known that in his opinion they should write some new tunes. But the most impressive fact of all regarding Cohan's intransigence is that, although the show ran 290 times, it has been written that after the memorable first encounter at the playing of the score, there were no others. Throughout the rehearsal, out-of-town try-out and Broadway run, the rival generations never exchanged greetings again.

In 1938 came a supernatural comedy, *I Married an Angel*, whose only attraction was the song 'Spring is Here'; also a bold attempt by Abbott to turn Shakespeare into a musical. *The Boys from Syracuse* is based on *A Comedy of Errors*, but only loosely. By the time Abbott had completed his adaptation, all that remained of the original text was one line: 'The venom clamours of a jealous woman/Poisons more deadly than a mad dog's tooth.' The score included two songs which soon graduated to standard status, 'Falling in Love with Love' and 'This Can't Be Love'. After two or three unremarkable shows, the partnership became involved in one of the classics of the American musical theatre, by which time the team had further enhanced its reputation by publishing 'I Didn't Know What Time It Was' and 'It Never Entered My Mind', a ballad so bleak that in later years Frank Sinatra took to presenting it as a cameo of a lonely man in the last extremity of romantic despair.

Early in 1940 Rodgers received the following letter:

Dear Dick,

I don't know whether you happened to see any of a series of pieces I've been doing for *The New Yorker* in the past year or so.

They're about a guy who is master of ceremonies in cheap night clubs, and the pieces are in the form of letters from him to a successful bandleader. Anyway, I got the idea that the pieces, or at least the character and the life in general could be made into a book show, and I wonder if you and Larry would be interested in working on it with me.

John O'Hara's series, called 'Pal Joey', reflected all O'Hara's fascination for the world of the professional musician and singer. All his life O'Hara approached popular music and musicians as sounds and people worthy of serious consideration. His texts are sprinkled with musical allusions, and in more than one short story the title derives from a line in a well-known song. One of his biographers has implied that by becoming a frequenter of the Onyx Club in the late 1930s O'Hara became acquainted with Johnny Mercer. We know also that among the suggestions he submitted to *The New Yorker* for profiles were the bandleader Fletcher Henderson and Cole Porter, whom he defines as 'a pretty able guy'. But O'Hara's gods were George Gershwin and his brother Ira. O'Hara's notorious mawkish reaction to the news of George's death, 'George Gershwin is dead but I don't have to believe it if I don't want to,' hardly does justice to his perceptions about popular music, which were limited but often very shrewd. In a letter to a friend written in 1959 he writes of *Of Thee I Sing* that 'Kaufman and Ryskind got a free ride on Ira Gershwin's satire.' In a late novella, *Imagine Kissing Pete*, he writes a deeply moving paragraph about the way in which a popular song, in this case the Gershwin-De Sylva ballad 'Do It Again', can stand as a symbol of a fondly remembered youth when all the rest of the cultural trappings have fallen away. His letters reveal that Rodgers was at best his second or even third choice as the composer for *Pal Joey*. In 1963 he writes to Bennett Cerf about the problems of a writer able to publish both short stories and longer works, making his point by using a musical analogy:

George Gershwin had an assured reputation with his songs, but he also had to write the *Rhapsody in Blue* and the other longer pieces, and would have gone on to bigger and better ones if he had lived. You take a tune like 'Mine', for instance. That's like one of my short stories; it could easily (with a lot of hard work, but easily) become a long piece, but instead of a fugue we have a rich little tune that is only one of many. That is not right. When you have the mastery of your medium that George had (and that I have, let's not kid about that), you simply must not let easy popularity keep you from the big things. There is one of the basic differences between George Gershwin, the composer, and Richard Rodgers, the song writer. Rodgers has to be content with songs, and he now has a song, 'The

Sweetest Sound', that is almost straight Cole Porter – except that Cole Porter would have known how to hold the melodic line.

But George Gershwin was dead by the time *Pat Joey* became a musical possibility, and for reasons he never specified, O'Hara never approached Porter. Rodgers accepted the suggestion, but it would be interesting to know whether, all those years later, he saw the contents of the letter to Bennett Cerf. What followed was inexplicable, although the failure of commentators to notice suggests that none of them had a very clear idea of what O'Hara's stories were about. Joey is a small-time drummer in the mid-1930s who is gradually made to feel inadequate in the evolving musical environment of the times. A great revolution had taken place in 1935 with the accidental discovery by the clarinettist Benny Goodman that a huge dancing public was there to be captured by anyone leading a dance orchestra incorporating a jazz element. Goodman was soon followed by Artie Shaw, the Dorsey Brothers and dozens of lesser claimants. Overnight these leaders became film stars, brand images, international celebrities, simply because young America enjoyed dancing to them. But this new amendment to the form of jazz-cum-popular music cancelled out the slapdash Pal Joeys at a stroke. Joey could never have graduated into the ranks of the new big bands, because neither his drumming technique nor his ability to read music was good enough. His old friend, to whom he sends the letters, has made the leap, has become a bandleader, and is steadily becoming famous and rich, until finally Joey, realizing that he has been left far behind by his old pal, loses his head and closes the last letter:

> Will bet you put yr dough into an insurance innuity and send the rest home to yr mother. I never saw you even pick up a tab for 4 mocha java coffees you cheap larceny jerk if ever there was one. I know you gave me the X X or otherwise I wd be making those so called wise cracks with Robins Burns every Thurs, and wd have my own stable of horses. It is a good thing I only write you letters instead of getting a hinge at yr holy kisser so I could hang a blooper on it. Friend Ted I am speaking to you and will tear this up but always was
> Yr
> EX PAL JOEY
> (Hate yr guts).

Joey speaks with the bitterness of frustration. He has become a victim of a revolution of which he is still hardly aware. His plight was analogous to that of hundreds of other small-time musicians well able to get by in the clubs and dives of Prohibition America but who were rendered ineligible by their own incapacity for inclusion in the new age of the big bands. His plight is dramatic and pathetic, and it is what makes him something more than a comic figure. No remote hint of all this appears in the musical version. *Pal Joey*, the first musical to present an anti-hero, remains a brilliant affair, but it lacks the depths of frustration which O'Hara put into the original letters. Who was the guilty party? O'Hara himself, who adapted his own book for the musical stage, and seemed to become so disenchanted with the whole business that Rodgers confesses to hardly having seen him during the period when the musical was taking shape. The show was a triumph, notwithstanding the Mrs Grundyism of some of the New York critics, and went on to play nearly four hundred times. In 1952 it was successfully revived. It was subsequently made into a musical film bearing even less resemblance to O'Hara's stories than the show, since which time it has become one of the very few pre-war American musicals adult enough to pass muster in the more critical if less melodious forum of the modern era.

It was during the run of *Pal Joey* that Hart's behaviour began to decline to the point where Rodgers had no choice but to consider the possibility of finding a new partner. The disappearances, the drunken bouts, the failure to keep appointments, helped destroy an arrangement which had endured throughout the adult lives of both men. Rodgers insists that he never did find out where it was that Hart kept disappearing to, or with whom. As he grew older, Hart was able to work in concentrated spells whose duration grew shorter and shorter. By the summer of 1941 Rodgers had come to a decision:

> The thought of leaving Larry was the most painful aspect of the whole situation. For the first time since the days when I was struggling unsuccessfully to get a start in the theatre, I was plagued by insomnia. I just couldn't see any way to avoid hurting someone.

The theatrical profession had been aware for some time that the partnership was under increasing strain. The last of all the Rodgers-and-Hart shows, *By Jupiter*, was only completed at all because Hart was drying out in a hospital where Rodgers took a guest room complete with Steinway. Hart was discharged once the score was finished, but on the day the company arrived in Boston for the try-out, he vanished for three days. The tantalizing thing was that although he was racing towards a complete collapse, Hart's gift was unimpaired once he settled down to work. The new show included 'Wait Till You See Her' and 'Everything I've Got', the ultra-romantic and misanthropic, each executed with charm and originality. *By Jupiter* was to run for over four hundred performances, and throughout its run people asked themselves and each other who the fortunate lyric writer would be who received the call from Rodgers. What actually happened took almost everyone by surprise. It was assumed that once Hart fell out, Rodgers would seek the replacement most like him in style. There was, of course, nobody like Hart, but there was one very brilliant lyric writer with a poet's command of language and the ability to fashion the most whimsical rhymes. Had Rodgers desired a new partner to remind him of the old, the experts felt that he would invite Johnny Mercer. Mercer himself half-expected to be approached, and was thought by some to have been disappointed when the call never came. In the light of Mercer's subsequent career, his passing over by Rodgers proved to be a blessing in disguise. In any case, the choice had been made long before people began speculating. In the summer of 1941, while *Pal Joey* was in mid-run, Rodgers invited Oscar Hammerstein to become his partner. The looming possibility of working with Hart on a projected musical version of Ludwig Bemelmans' *Hotel Splendide* had finally brought him to the pitch of resolution. The partnership with Hart was over and done with. All that remained uncertain now was the precise date of the dissolution. In his autobiography Rodgers gives so many reasons to justify his actions that the reader wonders whether he does not protest too much. The 1941 proposition could be seen either as proof of Rodgers's eagerness to escape from the toils of a partnership no longer congenial, or the desperate measure of a man broken-hearted at being obliged to carry on without his oldest friend.

Whatever his feelings about dumping someone who was 'totally dependent on me', Rodgers seems to have taken the tragedy of Hart's decline as a golden chance to alter the direction of his own career. The very fact that he should have selected Hammerstein is a strong hint that Rodgers was bored artistically as much as anything. In justifying his choice of a new partner who had not had a commercial success for several years, he writes:

> I had absolute faith in Oscar's talent. I had seen show after show in which his lyrics were of high quality but whose productions were so stale, flat and obviously unprofitable that nothing could have helped them. I was convinced that any man who could write 'Show Boat' and 'Sweet Adeline' and the lyrics to Kern's 'All the Things You Are' was far from being through. Oscar's kind of theatre was rapidly becoming passé and mine was all too often in a rut. If we both were flexible and dedicated enough, perhaps something fresh and worthwhile could emerge.

Here is disingenuousness rich even for Rodgers. It is true that some Hammerstein productions had been stale and flat. The reason had usually had much to do with Hammerstein's libretto. The fact that Hammerstein could have written so moving a lyric as 'All the Things You Are' and then buried it in a libretto as vacuous as *Very Warm for May*, suggests that while Hammerstein the lyricist was still a formidable proposition, Hammerstein the librettist had really not progressed very far from the wonderful imbecilities of *The Desert Song*. But most revealing of all is Rodgers's contention that his own kind of theatre was 'in a rut'. This from the composer of the score of *Pal Joey*. That Hammerstein's florid poetasting was becoming passé was the understatement of the season. It was already obsolescent when the Austro-Hungarian armies were being flung back with the advent of Kern and Berlin and Gershwin. What Rodgers appears to have desired was certainly something new, but something regressive, something without the acerbity of the modern musical theatre.

Ironically the last Rodgers-and-Hart show, *By Jupiter*, gave the dissolving partnership its greatest commercial success, with a run of 427 performances. But by now Rodgers was preparing to make a musical version of Lynn Riggs's *Green Grow the Lilacs*, a rustic period piece utterly remote from Hart's style. Rodgers went through the formality of inviting Hart to collaborate with him, but says that Hart declined on grounds of ill-health. Hammerstein was then called in. The result was *Oklahoma!*, a show whose commercial success was so astounding as to place the economics of the American theatre on quite a new plane. With Hart, Rodgers had enjoyed great success with runs of three or four hundred. The first collaboration with Hammerstein scored over two thousand, the second just under nine hundred, the fourth just under two thousand, the fifth more than one thousand two hundred, their last nearly fifteen hundred. But in the long view, far more important than the box-office appeal of works like *South Pacific* and *The King and I*, is the stylistic change they effected. Richard Rodgers, who since his teens had been composing songs resilient enough to enjoy a life of their own long after the shows for which they had been written were stone dead, was now writing elegant bromides chained for ever to the characters and situations they illuminated. Rodgers had achieved his ideal at last, the perfectly integrated score. But the cost, as far as the performer-at-large was concerned, has been too vast to compute. Once or twice with Hammerstein the spark was struck, in 'People Will Say We're in Love' and, in *Allegro*, a 1947 production which, by the new criterion, qualified as a disaster with a run of only 315 performances, a song called 'The Gentleman is a Dope'. But the rest of the Rodgers-and-Hammerstein output, vast as it was, staggeringly lucrative though it will continue to be, offers almost nothing in the way of what the professional musician defines as the standard song.

The contrast is a curious one. The Rodgers-and-Hammerstein musicals have about them a faint whiff of something uncongenial to those who are looking for the sort of songs which Rodgers-and-Hart had produced. That something is solemnity. The shows appear to believe in themselves as vehicles for the expression of desirable values. This self-righteousness has occasionally invited the custard pies of the lampooners, as in Groucho Marx's derisory impersonation of the leading man in *South Pacific* singing 'Some Enchanted Evening', or the numberless demolitions of the nuns in *The Sound of Music*. Rodgers would have claimed that what was wrong with the old musicals was their books, in which verdict he was certainly justified. He evidently believed that the libretto of the Hammerstein period was an advance. But as musicals they were certainly a retrogressive step in the evolution of the American musical, which, by the time that Rodgers and Hammerstein were churning it out, had already arrived at the revelations of *Guys and Dolls*, *Kiss Me Kate* and, at last, *My Fair Lady*. It was not that Rodgers's music with Hammerstein was shoddy or hackneyed. On the contrary, his melodies were as elegantly turned as ever. But something had gone out of them, and the knowing ones will usually say that that something was the fizz and sparkle of Hart's wit. The theory is especially inviting to those who feel, possibly quite wrongly, that Rodgers showed an indecent eagerness to grasp the nettle of Hart's collapse. The theory may well be wrong, and the most telling evidence will be found in accounts of how the collaboration with Hammerstein worked.

It will be remembered that with Hart it was usually Rodgers who found the first germ of the song, and who completed his half of the work before Hart had arrived at a lyric. Here is Rodgers describing how he worked with his new partner:

> Working with Oscar was a brand-new experience. For twenty-five years, the only way I could get Larry to do anything was virtually to lock him in a room and stay with him until the job was finished. Oscar's working habits were entirely the opposite. I remember that when I first started talking to him about our method of collaborating, he seemed surprised at my question.
>
> 'I'll write the words and you'll write the music' was all he said.
>
> 'In that order?' I asked.
>
> 'If that's all right with you. I prefer it that way. You won't hear from me until I have a finished lyric.'

which suggests that it may not after all have been Hart who put the animation into Rodgers's music, but Hammerstein who took it out. Whatever the truth, Rodgers in later life was irritated whenever the enduring popularity of the songs with Hart was flung at him. The incident at Yale, when, confronted by a poster advertising Rodgers-and-Hart, he affected astonishment that such ancient material should still appeal, was one example among several of his discomfiture at the spectacle of his own past. But whether or not Rodgers really was envious of his own record, he certainly must have known why the old songs remained so durable. In 1948, after the comparative failure of *Allegro* and the first moves in the adaptation of James Michener's *Tales of the South Pacific*, MGM released a Rodgers-and-Hart biopic called *Words and Music*, in which many of the great Rodgers-and-Hart classics were shot as though being performed on stage. The younger generation, which had little or no knowledge of the songs of the 1920s, but which attended MGM musicals as a matter of course, found itself exposed in one production to the wiles of no fewer than thirty pieces, ranging from 'Mountain Greenery' and 'Manhattan', through 'Where's That Rainbow' and 'Thou Swell', to the exchanges in 'I Wish I Were in Love Again' and the subtle expression of *déjà vu* in 'Where or When'. *Words and Music* was a runaway success, costing less than three million dollars and grossing four and a half million on its initial release, since which time it has become an evergreen and the best by far of the musical biopics. The story was of course feeble, and the facts were bowdlerized in the usual Hollywood hamfisted way. But what was vitally important to the continuing health of Rodgers-and-Hart was the impression it created of the act of songwriting, with Mickey Rooney's portrayal of Hart the central factor. Utterly bogus though the songwriting sequences were, they had been simplified exactly to the point where they might impress a generation of young people eager to be told that the world was a romantic place. If any single production, either on stage or screen, ever rendered the act of writing songs a viable and desirable profession, then it was *Words and Music*, which sent thousands of young people away half-toying with the idea of finding a partner for themselves and searching for the outré rhyme. After *Words and Music*, the catalogue of Rodgers-and-Hart was rendered permanent.

The attitude of Rodgers himself to all this changed over the years. In 1948 Hart had been dead only five years, and Rodgers appears to have been enthusiastic over the biopic, writing to the executive producer Arthur Freed that it was difficult for him to express his pleasure with the vocal performances. He closed: 'I cannot thank you enough.' Thirty years later when the film historian Hugh Fordin was compiling his book on Arthur Freed's years at MGM, he asked Rodgers for an interview about *Words and Music*. Rodgers refused in an abrupt note, 'denying any close links with either Freed or the production'. In mitigation of this churlishness, it should be remembered that by the 1970s, while the songs with Hammerstein for the most part confined themselves to theatrical performance, those with Hart had spilled out all over the place, into the acts of cabaret singers, on to the dance hall bandstand, into the concert halls, on radio and television. And it seemed that just when interest might be dying down, some new event occurred to intensify the admiration the world seemed to feel for Hart. In 1957 Frank Sinatra starred in a screen version of *Pal Joey*. Although it bore only vestigial resemblances to the play, and featured 'Lady is a Tramp' in quite the wrong way – as a reproach addressed to an authentic tramp – the performances of the songs were stunning, and made Rodgers-and-

Hart world-famous all over again, at a point where the partnership with Hammerstein was about to embark on *Flower Drum Song*, in defiance of Wodehouse's strictures on east-is-west. Kenneth Tynan composed the epitaph on this production by sub-titling it 'The World of Woozy Song', and, in truth, only 'I Enjoy Being a Girl' is remembered from the score. Then, at the end of the 1950s, another generation of listeners was introduced to the Hart songs with Ella Fitzgerald's 'The Rodgers and Hart Songbook'. (There was no Rodgers-and-Hammerstein Songbook, by Ella Fitzgerald or by anyone else.) Buyers of the double album were able to discover pearls of musical wisdom which had been rusticating for too long, like 'Ship Without A Sail', with its unique structure of a twelve-bar theme followed by a conventional middle, followed by a closing twelve bars; or the waspish satire of 'Give It Back to the Indians', written in 1939 for a show called *Too Many Girls*, but identical in rhythmic pattern and rhyme-scheme to 'A College on Broadway', a fragment of juvenilia composed for a varsity show of 1920 called *Fly with Me*. Miss Fitzgerald resuscitated 'Wait Till You See Her', 'Here In My Arms', 'Ten Cents a Dance' and 'Dancing on the Ceiling', each one a revelation to those who had never seen a Rodgers-and-Hart stage production. Yet Rodgers in old age could affect surprise that there was any interest in Hart among those born after Hart's death. The struggle between the generations is inevitable in songwriting as in all the arts, and Rodgers himself had had first-hand experience of how rough the fighting can be in his non-encounters with George M. Cohan. But the Hart-Hammerstein dichotomy represents the only instance in the songwriting annals of a popular composer besieged by himself.

Ira Gershwin

To REACH IRA'S ROOM YOU ASCEND a flight of narrow stairs and pass through a spacious bay whose three walls are lined with books from floor to ceiling. Ira is lying on the bed, above the coverlet, attending to the television; he looks frailer than I expected, and yet in some odd way very much larger than life, almost as though he has become the repository of all the social and cultural history he represents. Norman Granz, who has brought me here, takes his cue from Ira and sits in a chair by the bedside watching the screen, on which a faceless pundit is droning on about the cosmic frivolities of the United Nations. While we wait I glance round the room, trying to muster my sensibilities to remember as much of it as I can. I have been granted just this one visit into the distant past, and mean to preserve as much of it as any writer can reasonably hope to. On a table by the window lie two new books, *The Gershwin Years*, by Kimbell and Simon, and *Gershwin, His Life and Music*, by Charles Schwartz; now that the world is beginning to get the achievement of the Gershwin brothers in perspective, the bibliography is growing steadily.

The Schwartz book in particular strikes me as being a peculiar business. Tinged with a kind of crazed Pinkertonian scopophilia, it might almost have been written by someone who believed that the secret of George Gershwin's creative fecundity might conceivably be located in his underpants. The truth is that millions of men of George's generation were identical to him in matters of sexual morality; none of them wrote 'The Man I Love'. Schwartz, described on the fly-leaf as a former jazz musician, should have known better. Nodding towards the book, Ira later referred to Schwartz's disingenuous account of a legal wrangle involving members of the Gershwin family, saying that its inaccuracies were so blatant as to seem almost wilful. In fact, he said, he had found the book so painful

Left: GEORGE GERSHWIN.   *Right:* IRA GERSHWIN.

that he could not bring himself to finish it. [B.G.]

I notice that on the outbreast pocket of the Cambridge blue top Ira is wearing, there are embroidered the initials 'IG'; their presence instantly calls to mind that wistful line from the verse of 'Someone to Watch Over Me', where the girl confides, 'I'd like to add his initial to my monogram'. Gertrude Lawrence had sung it to a rag doll in *Oh, Kay!* in 1926 while masquerading as a housemaid even though she was a duke's sister, which was, as Ira once mischievously observed, 'a not unusual involvement in the Jazz Age'. A vision begins to form of all the madcap stereotypes who populated the musical comedies of the period, the identical twins and the poor little rich girls, the earls posing as butlers and the butlers posing as earls, the gridiron galumphers and the six-day bicycle riders, the comic cops and the ex-cons, the high-born bootleggers – 'Never criticize a man's English if his Scotch is all right' – and the low-down dowager duchesses squired by chortling senators as crooked as old country lanes. I try once again to muster my resolve to keep my head and ask some of the questions I have longed to ask for so many years, in particular the issue of the Gershwin involvement with Max Beerbohm regarding a musical version of *Zuleika Dobson*. None of the Gershwin biographers mentions the episode, which is extraordinary in the light of the passing reference in S. N. Behrman's *Conversations with Max* and the letter quoted by David Cecil sent to George by the eponymous hero of the biography *Max*. I must not forget Zuleika.

The initials on that blue topcoat remind me that 'Someone to Watch Over Me' provides a vivid example of two home truths about the mechanics of songwriting which tend to be overlooked by the world at large; the nebulosity of the process by which a composition finally arrives at its own apotheosis, and the tangled web woven by the songwriters themselves. As to the status of 'Someone to Watch Over Me' as a ballad, Ira has recorded the fact that in its earlier incarnation 'it was fast and jazzy, and undoubtedly I would have written it up as another dance-and-ensemble number. One day, for no particular reason and hardly aware of what he was doing, George started and continued it in a comparatively slow tempo; and half of it hadn't been sounded when both of us had the same reaction; this was really no rhythm tune but rather a wistful and warm one, to be held out until the proper stage occasion arose for it.' So far as the song's lyric is concerned, Ira recalls that in mid-composition he was rushed to a hospital for an emergency appendectomy. A fellow-lyricist, Howard Dietz, offered to help contend with deadlines; among his unofficial contributions to the score of *Oh, Kay!* was the title 'Someone to Watch Over Me'. One wonders how common this division of labour in the musical comedy world might have been, but by a coincidence, on the very day after my meeting with Ira, another lyricist, Paul Francis Webster, told me a more bizarre story of an identical nature. He said that in 1939 E. Y. Harburg, in the throes of putting words to Harold Arlen's ballad for *The Wizard of Oz*, had arrived at the impasse of 'Blank, blank, over the rainbow' and had been unable for the life of him to fill in the missing syllables. Webster had then offered him 'Somewhere' and Harburg had dashed away in gratitude, later repaying the debt by buying war bonds for Webster's then infant daughter. Confusions of this kind were about to crop up at the very start of my conversation with Ira. [B.G.]

The speech at the United Nations ends. Ira clicks off the set by remote control and the conversation begins a shade uneasily. I suggest to him that sometimes a lyricist might safely follow the Wonderland precept of taking care of the sounds and letting the sense take care of itself; my three-year-old son has become so used to hearing me move about the house singing a random couplet of Ira's:

> I just adore what you do,
> More and more and more what you do . . .

that he has taken to echoing my performance, being pleased in his infant soul with the doggerel rhythm of 'morenmorenmorenmore' without understanding its meaning. Ira's response astonishes me. The phrase comes from an early Gershwin song, 'Do What You Do', from a 1929 backstage turkey called *Show Girl*; its lyric is punctuated with verbal cartwheels and aural ingenuities, and it seems doubtful to me if more than a dozen lyricists this century could have written it. Yet Ira has forgotten that it belongs to him. At first he credits it to a contemporary of his youth, Gus Kahn. When reminded of the true authorship he seems genuinely pleased at the thought that the song may indeed be his own work.

Later, when I came home to England and plunged into the warm bath of the archives, the source of the confusion soon became apparent. Ira may have been right after all. Even though the songs from *Show Girl* are almost always credited to the Gershwins, and even though 'Do What You Do' is included in George Bassman's meticulously researched recording series 'The Gershwin Years', Gus Kahn had indeed collaborated with the brothers on the score, an unusual situation brought about by the lunatic convolutions of Florenz Ziegfeld's business methods. In 1928 Ziegfeld signed up the brothers to compose an operetta with the ominous title of *East is West*. Ira takes up the story: [B.G.]

'We were most enthusiastic about this project, and about half the score had been written when, alas, Ziegfeld asked us to do another show for the summer and give up the operetta for the time being. Of course *East is West* never happened because Ziegfeld went broke and no wonder. I remember he gave a man five thousand dollars and sent him to China to buy silk for the show. One of the songs we had written for it was "Embraceable You".'

Ira is being almost excessively charitable to Ziegfeld here. The impresario, having hired the brothers to write *East is West*, happened to read a new libretto whose heroine most flatteringly turns out to be a Ziegfeld Girl. Overcome by the amazing coincidence, and unable to resist the blandishments of its implied flattery, Ziegfeld then persuaded the brothers, with what Ira has somewhere defined as 'his hypnotically persuasive manner, until a contract was signed', to drop the *East is West* project and start on the new libretto, to be called *Show Girl*. Ziegfeld now found himself saddled with two lyricists, for having signed up the Gershwins, he also 'owed Gus Kahn a commitment'. Ira snatched at the arrangement because of the acute shortage of time available before the scheduled Boston opening. The situation was further exacerbated by the fact that there was no libretto for either Kahn or Gershwin to work from, a lack explained by the fact that the librettist in question was the notorious Bill McGuire, by this stage of his career already well on the way to realizing his ambition to decant himself into barrels. McGuire was heard to say in the early stages, with no trace of conscious irony, that he enjoyed hearing the new Gershwin-Kahn songs because 'you can never tell. Maybe I'll get a good idea for a scene from one of the songs.' Sadly, none of the dialogue McGuire wrote for the show was half as funny. In the end *Show Girl*, which in Ira's words 'cost much and lost much', became famous for the inclusion of *American in Paris* themes and for the fact that on opening night the leading lady, Ruby Keeler, apparently lost her nerve while poised at the top of a long high staircase and was inspired to prance to the bottom of it by the inspiriting sound of the words of 'Liza' coming from the stalls, where her husband, Al Jolson, happened to be sitting. The incident has been taken as the very apogee of conjugal devotion and support, but some time later, when discussing the affair with Miss Keeler, I was told that contrary to being an act of reckless devotion, Jolson's interpolation was symptomatic of a man nursing a septic ego. According to Miss Keeler, she was at no time in difficulty, either on the staircase or anywhere else, and was convinced that Jolson had started to sing because he simply could not endure the thought of being present at any first night without monopolizing it. 'It wasn't a very nice thing to do, was it?' said Miss Keeler, mustering the rhetorical question nearly half a century after the event. It is only fair to add that according to one of Ziegfeld's biographers, Charles Higham, Jolson's improvised intercession into his wife's professional affairs had most thoughtfully been included in rehearsals. As for the Gershwins, they did manage, with a little help from their friends, to complete the score in the allotted time. Ziegfeld expressed gratitude in characteristic style by withholding their royalties; an inconclusive law suit followed. In spite of all this, it seems likely that in being taken off the *East is West* project, the Gershwins were fortunate men, for an interesting reason.

At the same time that plans were being laid for *East is West*, that great friend of the Gershwins, P. G. Wodehouse, had been working on a similar epic of cardboard orientalism called *The Rose of China*. Wodehouse claimed for this show the distinction of being the worst ever seen, notwithstanding the received wisdom of these affairs, which was, to quote Wodehouse, 'that with the possible exception of *Abie's Irish Rose* and *Grandma's Diary*, *East is West* is the ghastliest mess ever put on the American stage'. Wodehouse is here referring to the original, non-musical version, and goes on by offering the following advice to aspiring musical librettists: 'Have nothing to do with anything with a title like "The Rose of China" or "The Willow Pattern Plate" or "The Siren of Shanghai" or "Me Velly Solly", in fact, avoid Chinese plays altogether. Much misery may thus be averted.' To hammer his point home, Wodehouse quotes from the original version of *East is West* the heroine's remark, 'Me Plum Blossom. Me good girl. Me love Chlistian god velly much.' Claiming to have forgotten the grisly details, Wodehouse writes that he cannot say after so long a passage of time whether or not the heroine of *The Rose of China* turned out in the end to be the daughter of American missionaries 'kidnapped by Chinese bandits in her infancy, but it would seem virtually certain that she did. All heroines of Chinese plays turn out in the end to be the daughters of American missionaries kidnapped by bandits in their infancy. This is known as Shipman's Law' – Sammy Shipman being the original author of *East Meets West*. As for the truth of the origins of 'Do What You Do', it is buried, probably for ever now, under half a century of backstage chaos. Ira may well be right that 'Do What You Do' is Gus Kahn's, but the bewildered student, rummaging around in the ruins of a lost culture, cannot help wondering if Byron and Shelley ever had the same trouble. [B.G.]

A further demonstration follows of Ira's innate humility, and how little he appears to be aware of the fame of his own versifying. On the previous evening I had been talking to Gene Kelly, who had first sung an Ira Gershwin lyric to a Jerome Kern melody in *Cover Girl*, and who had later persuaded Ira to give his blessing to the compilation of the movie *An American in Paris*, for which George received the ultimate in absurdity, a posthumous Oscar for the best film music of the year. Ira reacts instantly with a critical judgement:

'Kelly was a better singer than he pretended.'

'He told me yesterday that when he recorded "Long Ago and Far Away" he was terrified because Kern came into the control booth to listen. And that when he was preparing for the "Make Way for Tomorrow" sequence he was so in awe of you that he couldn't think of a way to tell you he couldn't use all four of the choruses you'd written. He said he could tell Harry Cohn easily enough, but somehow he couldn't think of a way to tell you.'

Ira smiles at the thought of being more forbidding than Harry Cohn.

Kelly's actual words were: 'Great men like Kern and Gershwin? They needed no more than five minutes to create. I was amazed how quick they were. They were the kind of guys, if the song didn't work at the Boston tryout, you'd have a new song the next morning. They could go up to the hotel room and fix it. They were geniuses in their way, and they're really not given enough credit. Sometimes you hear one of their popular ballads and you start to weep and you find yourself saying, "Wait a minute, this isn't Brahms or Mozart".' [B.G.]

'Incidentally, when I told Kelly I was coming to see you today, he told me to put a question to you. He said to ask you about the fifty unpublished Gershwin songs you have in your trunk.'

Ira performs a philosophic gesture and shrugs: 'What can you do with them?' The question is meant rhetorically, being the expression of a fatalism which is the bitter fruit of a lifetime coping with the vagaries of performers and producers who think they know better. But this time the rhetorical question gets an answer, from Granz, who says, 'Chappells' would publish them and Oscar Peterson would play them', and then adds as a happy afterthought a rhetorical question of his own: 'Who could ask for anything more?' I am astonished when for a moment Ira fails to identify the quotation from his own lyric to 'I Got Rhythm', especially as he himself had quoted it seven years after the publication of 'I Got Rhythm', in the lyric of 'Nice Work If You Can Get It'.

The conversation turns to lyrics in general, and I am struck by how very English the frame of reference has become. One of Ira's oldest friends was ·his professional contemporary and sometime collaborator (on *Oh, Kay!*), P. G. Wodehouse. I describe how, when a friend of mine had recently told Wodehouse that Ira was no longer quite as robust as he used to be, Wodehouse had expressed concern and asked how old Ira was. My friend had then reminded him that Ira was approaching eighty, at which Wodehouse, genuinely shocked, exclaimed 'Good

Lord, is Ira really as old as all that?' At the time this exchange took place, Wodehouse was ninety-two years and six months old.

Ira grins. He is becoming more animated by the moment. He tells us that Wodehouse had often regretted not composing a lyric incorporating all his own Drones Club–Blandings slang like 'old fluff' and 'tinkerty-tonk', but derived a sense of vicarious fulfilment when he heard the Gershwin song 'Stiff Upper Lip' which performs that very function. A few people have noted Ira's elliptical but calculated indication that 'Stiff Upper Lip' is indeed intended to be the salute of one lyricist to another; in the scenario of *A Damsel in Distress*, for which 'Stiff Upper Lip' was composed, Ira had written at the head of the music: 'To be sung by Fred Astaire to Joan Fontaine on the downs of Upper Pelham-Grenville, near Wodehouse, England.' When Ira was a youth, labouring as doorman-cum-receptionist in the barren vineyard of his father's Turkish Baths on Lenox Avenue, Wodehouse had been his lyric-writing idol. He wrote to me in the 1960s, 'I am with you one hundred per cent that Wodehouse's talent in this field has never been fully recognized. No one wrote more charming lyrics than he in the period from just before the First World War to the early Twenties.'

A Damsel in Distress is an interesting example of the interaction between Wodehouse and the Gershwins to which nobody apart from the protagonists has ever paid much attention. It is also a remarkable proof of the proposition that life occasionally has the good sense to imitate art. In the novel *A Damsel in Distress*, published by Wodehouse in 1919, a musical comedy composer called George, who was born in Brooklyn, comes to London to supervise the English production of one of his successes. Ira's brother, who happened to be a musical comedy composer called George who had been born in Brooklyn and had come to London to supervise the English production of more than one of his successes, was much taken by the coincidence. 'I think,' says Wodehouse, 'that that was what attracted him. At any rate, he used his considerable influence in Hollywood to have it done on the screen.' The movie version, almost the last piece of work which George completed before his death, was most spectacularly botched by the higher executives, to whom Wodehouse applies the generic term 'The Manglers'. The end result, insists Wodehouse, was 'suitable for retarded adults and children with water on the brain', but the film is well remembered for its inclusion of 'A Foggy Day', also for the candour of its non-singing, non-dancing and, on that occasion at least, non-acting heroine Joan Fontaine, who later confided to Astaire that the picture had put back her career four years. [B.G.]

Ira warms to the theme of Wodehouse, and while bemoaning the wild inflationary spiral which has put paid to the American stage musical as an economically viable form, quotes his old friend. 'I remember,' says Ira, 'that *Oh, Kay!*, which featured Gertie Lawrence in 1926, cost a hundred thousand dollars and it earned its money back in ten weeks. Today shows can take a year and a half before they get their investment back. In the old days I had a small interest, for instance, in *Of Thee I Sing*, a couple of thousand dollars invested in a show that cost eighty-eight thousand. That show earned about four hundred per cent. Things are very different today. I had a letter from Wodehouse a few years ago, a Christmas card. He always writes letters to me on Christmas cards. He was talking about two shows that had flopped the week before, and he said "Can you imagine, one show cost four hundred thousand, and the other one six hundred thousand, and they only lasted a week. Very different from the days of the Princess Theatre shows when we did a whole new production for twenty-five thousand or so." And then he added the words, "Ira, we are well out of it".'

But of course it is a romantic fiction that in the old days the world was always in a suitably receptive mood for songs of quality. Nobody knows this better than Ira, who had been on the wrong end of the most notorious case in theatre history of creative art being frustrated by the imperceptions of producers and performers. Once again, in recounting what he would no doubt have defined, had he been versifying, as his tale of woe, Ira is more than charitable towards those who botched his work.

'Well, "The Man I Love" is a good example. It was written in 1924 for *Lady Be Good* for Adele Astaire to sing, but after the first week of the try-out in Philadelphia it was taken out, because it seemed to slow up the show, which was really a dancing show. Adele did it most acceptably, but the management felt they didn't need it. In 1927 we were doing a show for Edgar Selwyn called *Strike Up the Band*. Selwyn was crazy about the song and he said he wanted it. But it didn't do well in *Strike Up the Band* either. As a matter of fact the show only played two weeks, although it did better later when we rewrote it. And then Ziegfeld wanted it for *Rosalie*, which starred Jack Donahue, and I had to rewrite the lyric of "The Man I Love" to suit Marilyn Miller. I don't even remember her rehearsing it, and it certainly wasn't in the show on opening night. But the publisher, Max Dreyfus, had faith in the song and he said, "Look, I'm going to spend a little money on this", and I remember that Lady Mountbatten, a great admirer of my brother's, took a copy of the song back to England, and it was played there and in some night clubs in Paris, and lo and behold it became a hit.'

Rosalie, a story based very loosely on the visit to America by Queen Marie of Rumania, remains one of the most spectacular examples of administrative farce in the history of musical comedy, being the only production of its kind to have two librettists, two composers, and two lyricists. Of the harassed sextet responsible for it, Sigmund Romberg was hired by Ziegfeld because of the latter's belief that he knew about Rumania – 'He's been there' – and Bill McGuire was recruited to share the libretto with Guy Bolton despite his gift for defaulting on deadlines. The Gershwins and Wodehouse completed the team, and there was one habit of Wodehouse's which Ira never forgot . . . [B.G.]

'I must tell you about this wonderful, charming man Wodehouse. We collaborated on the lyrics to *Rosalie* for Ziegfeld. We opened in Boston in the big theatre there, I can't think of its name. Anyway, the place was very crowded with Harvard boys and a lot of standees and we were over-long in the first act. I'm five feet six or seven and Wodehouse is very tall, and he was watching the show with me while we were standing at the back, but I couldn't see anything. As I say, we were over-long, and the first act ended at twenty minutes to eleven and the second act was due to start about ten or fifteen minutes later. And I felt a tap on my shoulder from Wodehouse. I said, "What is it?" And he reached in his pocket for his Ingersoll watch and he said, "Ira, it's eleven o'clock. I must toddle off to bed." And he left. This is the opening night of his show. Plum was an avid reader, and naturally he wanted to get up early to go to the bookstalls along the Charles River. But I've never heard of anybody leaving his own show on opening night at the start of the second act because he wanted to go to bed.'

Ira's reference to his own height constitutes a sly quotation from his own works. In a 1925 show called *Tip Toes*, the heroine sings of looking for 'a boy 'bout five feet six or seven'. So far as the extraordinary misfortunes of 'The Man I Love' are concerned, I once asked Ira if George had not been powerful enough to have insisted on the song's inclusion in one or another of the three productions in which it had been tried. His reply comprises one of the most impressive tributes ever paid to the sheer fecundity of an artist like George Gershwin: 'There's no rule about what stays in a score. If some numbers, when the show is out of town, don't receive as much applause and/or comment as hoped for, they are usually out, and new numbers have to be written and substituted. In one show, *Funny Face*, practically half the score was thrown out, almost most of the book, and it was almost completely rewritten by the time, six weeks later, it opened in New York. Some writers might have fought for a to-be-ousted song, but George and I felt it was less troublesome to write a new number than to defend one that was in doubt.' [B.G.]

One of Ira's favourite English eccentrics is Captain Harry Graham

(1874–1936), who perfected the curious art of rhyming truncated words:

> If playwrights would but thus dimin
> The length of time each drama takes,
> 'The Second Mrs Tanq' by Pin,
> Or even 'Hamlet' by Shakes,
> We could attain a watchful att
> When at a Mat on Wed or Sat.
>
> If Mr Caine rewrote 'The Scape'
> And Miss Correl condensed 'Barabb',
> What could they save in foolscap pape,
> Did they but cultivate the hab
> Which teaches people to suppress
> All syllables that are unnec.

Graham was a pure Wodehousean original who had somehow contrived to reconcile a commission in the Coldstream Guards with part-authorship of those two gaseous operatic follies, *Land of Smiles* and *White Horse Inn*; his art of truncating rhymed words finds a celebrated echo in Ira's verse for 'S'Wonderful':

> Don't mind telling you
> In my humble fash,
> That you thrill me through
> With a tender pash.

But Ira had written those lines first, discovered Graham later. I ask him if he has ever heard of an English Edwardian music hall performer called Phil Ray. He shakes his head. A few weeks earlier I had been discussing Captain Graham's bizarre versifying habits with Stanley Holloway, who said that the Captain was not after all quite the first in the field. He remembered being taken one night to the Tivoli Music Hall in the Strand and watching an act billed as 'Phil Ray, the Abbreviating Comedian'. Against a canvas backdrop of bathing machines, rampant crabs, hourglass figures, jolly fishermen and the rest of the music hall seaside gallimaufry, Ray had leaned against a conspicuously two-dimensional fishing smack and proceeded as follows:

> I weren't feeling right
> So I went down to Bright
> To spend a few mins by the sea.
> On Victoria plat
> I patiently sat

With my little portmant on my knee.
Then in from the junc
Came the 3.30 punc,
As they shunted it in from the stat.
Said the guard: 'Make a start,
Room for one, this compart.'
I said, 'Thanks for the kind informash.'
So I journed to Ostend
With a pash lady friend,
And we posed as Watt nymphs on the rocks.
She'd a rather swag rig
And a very fine fig,
And her hair was no stranger to perox.

On hearing that Ray had anticipated him by some thirty-five years, Ira says, 'You never can tell. Somebody told me not so long ago that my line in "A Foggy Day" about the British Museum losing its charm had been anticipated in a letter written to a friend by Isadora Duncan, but I didn't know about it. So I deserve some of the credit too. And I've never found the Duncan reference.' I mention that the phrase 'On the sunny side of the street' turns up in a short story in James Joyce's *Dubliners*, that H. M. Tomlinson's scandalously underrated Fleet Street novel *The Day Before*, first published in the United States at the precise moment when Rodgers and Hart were writing the songs for *Pal Joey*, contains the phrase 'burghered, bewildered and bewitched', which is close enough to 'bewitched, bothered and bewildered' to be interesting, and that Wodehouse in one of his later novels quotes a line of Ira's when one of the young men suggests to his betrothed, 'Let's call the whole thing off.' Ira is still thinking about 'S'Wonderful', and says, 'I must tell you that when we opened with *Funny Face* in Philadelphia, one of the town's top critics saw me one afternoon in the lobby of the Shubert Theatre. We were in the process of changing some things, and I happened to be outside the theatre while the rehearsal was going on. He stopped and asked me how the changes were coming along. He then wondered if I'd done anything about "S'wonderful, marvellous that you should care for me" and so forth, especially the middle part, "You've made my life so glamorous, you can't blame me for feeling amorous, oh, s'wonderful" and so on. He said, "What have you done about that song?" And I said, "What should I have done about that song?" He said, "Well, it contains an obscene phrase." So I said, "What's obscene about it?" He said, "You can't use the word 'amorous'." I don't know what he would think of the licence in the language these days, but at that time he must have thought that a word like "amorous" was better scrawled on a wall than sung from the stage.'

Ira is disarmingly frank about the business of plucking useful phrases out of the air. He had already acknowledged in print, for example, that his title 'Nice Work If You Can Get It' (1937) came from the caption to an old George Belcher cartoon in *Punch*, notwithstanding the fact that the supposedly infallible Eric Partridge in his *Dictionary of Catch Phrases* located the birth of the phrase at 1942. On the subject of originality and plagiarism, Ira recalls another incident in his career with George.

'We were writing a musical called *My Fair Lady*, but at the last minute we changed it to *Tell Me More*. Years later I showed Alan Lerner the original sheet music and he was so intrigued that he went away and looked it up. When he came back he told me that there had been at least three shows called "My Fair Lady" before ours . . .'

In Jablonski and Stewart's reliable *The Gershwin Years*, it says that Lerner almost called his Higgins-Doolittle musical 'The Talk of London' until he was reminded of the old Gershwin show. Among other claimants to the 'My Fair Lady' title was an operetta which opened on its out-of-town try-out in Wilmington, Delaware. One night a blown fuse plunged the entire theatre in stygian darkness, thus placing the audience in the same predicament that the librettists had been in ever since starting the project. Subsequently part of the ceiling collapsed, sadly destroying only part of the scenery. The plot of this bowl of goulash, probably the most inept and ridiculous story-line to appear in any theatre since *The Count of Luxembourg*, is familiar today as *The Desert Song*. [B.G.]

I ask Ira why he and George decided to change their original 'My Fair Lady' title. 'Because we felt it wasn't commercial.'

At this point a white-pinafored nurse enters the room, clearly by appointment. She hands Ira two pills and a tumbler of water. The scholar tosses the pills into his mouth, and before drowning them in the water, ponders the classical allusions of his predicament.

'I feel like Demosthenes with the pebbles in his mouth.'

'Or like Eliza Doolittle with the marbles.'

The nurse departs, and Granz reminds Ira of how Flo Ziegfeld once attempted to prise apart the inseparable brothers Willie and Eugene Howard, famous for their Yiddish dialect routines.

'The two Howards,' explains Ira, 'always refused to work apart. The trouble was that one of them was good and the other one was not so good. Ziegfeld wanted the good one for the *Follies*, and he finally figured out a way to do it: a contract for two thousand dollars a week, but three thousand if only one of them showed up at the theatre. I think sometimes the not-so-good one turned up.'

One occasion when Willie Howard was prevailed upon to work away from his brother was the 1930 Gershwin musical *Girl Crazy*, in which Willie portrayed a Jewish Malaprop whose eponymous song is graced by the most absurd title throughout the range of the American musical, 'Goldfarb, That's I'm'. But then, Ira had been well schooled in immigrant solecisms from a tender age. Although the name of Goldfarb appears in the family annals with reference to a musician with 'a barrel of gestures' who once gave George piano lessons, the character who goes by that name in *Girl Crazy* is clearly the repository of much family lore. The father of George and Ira was the legendary Morris Gershwin, a Russian immigrant at once bursting with pride for his two wonderful sons and not quite equipped to grasp the principles of the highly demanding work at which they were wonderful. To the end of his days the old man persisted in referring to 'Fascinating Rhythm' as 'Fashion on the River', remained convinced that the line in 'Embraceable You' which goes 'come to poppa, come to poppa do' was a direct reference to himself, and once intruded on an elevated discussion on the stature of *Rhapsody in Blue* by introducing the ethics of piecework: 'Of course it's important. It lasts fifteen minutes, don't it?' So far as the Howard Brothers are concerned, and the outcome of their chess game with Ziegfeld, the record suggests that the only edition of the *Follies* in which the family was represented was in 1934; the programme lists both Willie and Eugene. For once in his life it appears that Ziegfeld was outsmarted. [B.G.]

By now the suppliant visitor gets the impression, which is perfectly accurate, that Ira has an anecdote, or a cautionary tale, or a word of wisdom, for virtually every contingency of musical comedy history. And there are two dominant features of his conversation: immense scholarship lightly worn, and a deep respect for other writers in the same line of business as himself. He reminds me that the American writer Harry Smith holds the record for the number of librettos in a career, and that both Arthur Schwartz ('Dancing in the Dark') and Harry Warren ('Lullaby of Broadway') are examples of gifted composers whose art deserved better luck in the way of librettos.

I had talked to both men in the previous few days, and Warren in particular tended to be ribald about the brainpower of producers who were inclined to stop commissioning work from a fellow simply because he had reached pensionable age. To a visitor like myself, from the dark side of the moon cinematically speaking, this was one of the most striking things about Beverly Hills, that all along the capacious drives and avenues, old men dropsical with battle honours sat dozing by pools in the sun, bemoaning the passing of that golden age of songwriting to which they themselves had contributed so fulsomely. And yet this contiguity was apparently merely geographical. Old partners who had once triumphed together and who lived within two streets of each other, might go years without meeting, or even communicating, and, when they learned that I was about to visit some old friend of theirs, would ludicrously entrust me with the duty of conveying kindest regards. When someone in my presence asked Warren what he thought of one of the big song hits of the 1970s, he answered, 'My dog could write a better tune.' Ever since, that remark has taken root in my brain, serving as an instrument of value judgement to be used in threading a path through the dunghills of the New Barbarism in popular music: 'Could Warren's dog write a better tune?' All too often the answer turns out to be 'Yes'. It should be understood that this indignation, which is common enough among the Grand Masters of Warren's generation, is much more than merely personal, and is mounted on behalf of a profession whose standards have become hopelessly corrupted by the advent of a new infantile consumer market. Any creative artist like Warren or Ira is able readily enough to appreciate the nature of the issues at stake, but the archetypal impresario, applying the ethics of accountancy to one of the subtlest of all artistic challenges, is inclined to be less perceptive, as revealed in my conversation with Pandro S. Berman. When I quoted Warren's strictures to him, Berman, who had once reprieved the old RKO studios from bankruptcy by producing the Fred-and-Ginger pictures, had replied, 'Don't feel too sorry for those guys. They're all multi-millionaires', visibly irritated by the thought that there might be any survivors from his own generation who still aspired to a day's work. But he had then added that Warren and Ira Gershwin were great and lovable men, a verdict which appeared to be received truth around Beverly Hills; just as I could find nobody with a good word for Louis B. Mayer or Al Jolson, so there was nothing but lavish praise and affection for Warren and Gershwin, who must surely have been the best-loved celebrities in the whole of Hollywood at that time.

Subsequently I followed up Ira's remark about the record number of librettos in a single career. Harry Bache Smith (1860–1936) enjoyed one of the most amazing careers in the history of popular art, and appears to have been yet another of those close contemporaries of Ziegfeld destined to experience the same faintly ludicrous events which enliven the biographies of the impresario himself. Among the more bizarre episodes in Smith's life was a show called *The Parisian Model*, the only successful musical to have had a deaf director (as distinct from a merely tone-deaf one). It was Smith who first suggested to Ziegfeld that the word 'Follies' might make a good title for a series of annual revues, Smith again who could claim the honour of presenting the most eccentric wedding gift to an old friend, the writ which he served on Ziegfeld on the day of the latter's marriage to Billie Burke, for the sum of four thousand dollars of unpaid royalties. Smith eventually got his money, but it was the end of a beautiful friendship. In one year alone, 1911, he wrote nine shows, and became the first musical comedy librettist of the modern era to score a century with *Love O' Mike* in 1917. He also wrote a show called *The Rich Mr Hoggenheimer*, whose eponymous hero has a wife referred to years later in Cole Porter's 'The Tale of an Oyster'. Smith collaborated with, among others, Victor Herbert, John Philip Sousa, Gus Edwards, Franz Lehar, Oscar Straus, Jerome Kern, Sigmund Romberg and Jacques Offenbach; wrote in all 123 Broadway shows; published an autobiography, *First Nights and First Editions*; and is remembered today, after all those prodigious labours, for the few lines of verse which make up the lyric of 'The Sheik of Araby'. His younger brother Robert Bache Smith (1875–1951) was in the same line of business, but appears to have been the victim of a regrettable tendency to idleness, writing a niggardly 27 shows. The student of Smith family affairs is likely to find himself half-believing that Harry and Robert were one and the same hack, for while Harry is credited with *The Tar and the Tartar*, Robert wrote *The Babes and the Baron*; Harry did *Helter Skelter* while Robert contributed *Twirly Whirly*; Harry wrote *The Wild Rose*, Robert *The Red Rose*; Harry *The Girl from Dixie*, Robert *The Girl from Montmartre*. So far as the style of all these dramatic works is concerned, it is revealing that the case of the unpaid Ziegfeld royalties concerned a libretto called *Moulin Rouge*, in which a sculptor falls for a model called Suzette, who refuses to let him kiss her till he proposes marriage; a demonic presence with the Faustian label of J. Lucifer Mephisto musters several vamps, including Cleopatra and Carmen, to tempt the sculptor who, for reasons unspecified in the libretto, resists them. Ziegfeld's biographer describes *Moulin Rouge* as 'a characteristic Harry Smith concoction'. Of all the items in the Smith oeuvre, however, none has a more promising title than an 1898 item called *Cyranose de Bric-a-Brac*. [B.G.]

I quote Berman's multi-millionaire remark to Ira, who smiles wisely, glances at Granz and says, 'Yes, before taxes.' My mention of Berman has reminded Ira of Astaire, which reminds him in turn of the attempts people used to make to put words to *Rhapsody in Blue*, among them a youthful and totally unknown Arthur Schwartz. 'The only lyric my brother ever approved of was Astaire's. It went: "This is the rhap-so-dy in blue by George Gersh-win, this is the rhap-so-dy", and so on and so forth. People gave my brother no credit for the orchestration of the *Rhapsody* because it was known that Ferde Grofe from Whiteman's band wrote it down. But George told Grofe exactly what he wanted all the way.'

The name of Johnny Mercer arises. Ira praises his cleverness and suggests that the use of the word 'huckleberry' in the lyric of 'Moon River' is what is meant by a flash of inspiration. Two years before, I had asked Mercer if he thought that the great song lyrics would ever receive the scholastic and cultural attention their skill and subtlety demanded. Mercer had thought carefully before giving his answer, which I now quoted to Ira: 'One day, in fifty, a hundred years time, the words of Porter, Hart, Wodehouse, Ira Gershwin, Coward, maybe a few of my own, will be published, recited, analysed, codified. And then forgotten. Like everything.'

Ira observes that Mercer shares the same birthday as W. S. Gilbert, at which point the conversation arrives at last at the destination of all conversations about the art of fitting light verse to music. Gilbert remains the father-figure of all the professional lyricists, the catalyst which brings together the apparently antipathetic English and American musical comedy schools. And of all the American masters, none has studied Gilbert's craft more thoroughly than Ira, or become more intensely aware of the sheer romance of the process by which time and again Gilbert and Sullivan, those two strange bedfellows, kept pulling off the impossible. Jablonski and Stewart have written that 'the ghosts of D'Oyly Carte hovered in the wings of Ira's imagination', and it is said that one night in Philadelphia in 1927, when *Strike Up the Band* was in deep waters, the two brothers were standing glumly outside the theatre one night when 'a cab drew up and two elegant Edwardian clubmen, dressed to the nines, got out, bought tickets, and entered the theatre. "That must be Gilbert and Sullivan," said Ira, "coming to fix the show".' After a lifetime of pondering the enigma of Gilbert's curious insistence on his own musical ignorance – 'I know only two tunes. One is "God Save the Queen" and the other one isn't' – Ira has come to the conclusion that Gilbert must have been bluffing.

'In his Gilbert and Sullivan book, Goldberg describes how Gilbert used to go around fixing words to the translated comic operas from the French, in the days before the Sullivan partnership. The way Goldberg describes it, Gilbert must have been able to hold a tune in his head. He couldn't have got through that much work any other way.' And for the first time Ira rises from the bed, grasps the aluminium frame without which he might tumble forward, and makes his way over to the booklined bay, searching for the talisman, Goldberg's definitive work on the Savoy operas. He scrutinizes the shelves, looking for chapter and verse to substantiate his theory. The ghost of Gilbert has animated him to the point where for the moment he forgets his years and becomes the keen young student of a demanding but intensely pleasurable craft. He cannot find Goldberg, and flutterings in the background from the lady of the house tell me it is time to go. I am unutterably saddened by the thought. What ought I have said to him that I have not said? That of all the men alive, he has always been the one above all others I hoped one day to talk to? That the sweet sapience of his life's work has coloured the thinking and shaped the reveries of my generation? That if, throughout this meeting, I have been inclined to look, in Wodehouse's immortal phrase, 'like an ostrich goggling at a brass doorknob', it is because the air has seemed to me to be full of the shades of identical twins and poor little rich girls, earls posing as butlers and butlers posing as earls, gridiron galumphers and six-day bicycle riders, comic cops and ex-cons, high-born bootleggers and low-down dowager duchesses squired by all those chortling senators? Hardly. The best I can manage is a feeble thank-you. Even as I say it, the paradox of the last ninety minutes suddenly strikes me. It is that in some odd and indefinable way, Ira's conversation, his attitude, his whole demeanour, are shaped by something unspoken and yet dominant, his abiding love for George, the kid brother who died young, and his deep reverence for George's music. He offers his hand, and I suddenly remember the story of how Wodehouse was once taken to lunch to meet Gilbert. Now I can say I have shaken the hand that shook the hand that shook the hand of Gilbert. Nice work if you can get it. It is not until some days later, with my plane in mid-Atlantic, that it suddenly hits me that I forgot to mention Zuleika after all.

Acknowledgements

Extracts from the lyrics of Howard Dietz, Ira Gershwin, Lorenz Hart, Alan Lerner and Cole Porter, including the following, are reproduced by permission of Chappell Music Ltd:

Howard Dietz: 'I Guess I'll Have To Change My Plan' © 1920 Harms Inc., 'Dancing In the Dark' © 1931 Harms Inc., 'Triplets' © 1937 Chappell & Co., Inc.

Ira Gershwin: 'Do What You Do' © 1929 New World Music Corp.

Lorenz Hart: 'Mountain Greenery' © 1926 Harms Inc., 'Where's That Rainbow' © 1926 Harms Inc., 'My Romance' © T. B. Harms Co., 'I Wish I Were in Love Again' © 1937 Chappell & Co., Inc.

Alan Lerner: 'On A Clear Day' © 1965 Chappell Co., Inc., 'What Did I Have That I Don't Have' © 1965 Chappell Co., Inc.

Cole Porter: 'Anything Goes' © 1934 Harms Inc., 'Night and Day' © 1932 Harms Inc., 'Don't Fence Me In' © 1934 Harms Inc., 'Brush Up Your Shakespeare' © 1948 Buxton Hill Music Corp., 'Always True to You In My Fashion' © 1948 Buxton Hill Music Corp.

Extracts from the lyrics by Irving Berlin: 'Durando' © 1909 Irving Berlin Inc., USA, 'My Wife's Gone To The Country Hurrah Hurrah' © 1909 Irving Berlin Inc., USA are reproduced by permission of B. Feldman & Co. Ltd., courtesy of EMI Music Publishing.

All extracts from lyrics by Noël Coward are reproduced by permission of Methuen London.

Every effort has been made to trace copyright holders and we apologise for any omissions.

The publishers wish to thank the following copyright holders for their permission to reproduce the illustrations supplied:

Billy Rose Theatre Collection pp. 94, 112; Cecil Beaton photographs courtesy of Sotheby's, London pp. 50, 74, 152; Popperfoto p. 136; The Hulton-Deutsche Collection Ltd pp. 10, 26, 182; The Kobal Collection p. 210.

Cover montage courtesy of The Kobal Collection with permission from R.K.O.